Towards a Post-Fordist Welfare State?

Can post-Fordist thinking help us to explain and understand the current restructuring of the British welfare state? Post-Fordism – with its emphasis on differentiation, flexibility and choice – has played an important part in debates in the fields of economic sociology, human geography and cultural studies, but it has been largely ignored in the area of social policy. *Towards a Post-Fordist Welfare State?* is the first book to explore the important implications of post-Fordist theorising for social policy and the future of welfare. An invaluable introduction to post-Fordism, it also provides a full critique and an extensive bibliography.

The book brings together leading authors, all of them well known for their contribution to the debates around post-Fordism, to discuss whether these debates can help to explain the emerging patterns of change in the provision of welfare in the UK. They evaluate the argument that we are moving towards a post-Fordist welfare state, and speculate on what sort of welfare system is emerging to regulate the flexible production, differentiated consumption and postmodern culture supposedly characteristic of the contemporary age. They provide concrete examples of how post-Fordist theories can be applied in social policy contexts, covering such topics as processes of state modernisation, local economic development, the restructuring of higher education, public-sector labour flexibility and changes in consumption patterns.

The book will appeal to a wide readership, and especially to students and teachers in social policy and administration, policy studies, sociology, urban and regional studies, politics and public-sector economics.

Roger Burrows is a sociologist working in the School of Human Studies at the University of Teesside, where **Brian Loader** is a Senior Lecturer in Policy Studies.

The State of Welfare
Edited by Mary Langan

Nearly half a century after its post-war consolidation, the British welfare state is once again at the centre of political controversy. After a decade in which the role of the state in the provision of welfare was steadily reduced in favour of the private, voluntary and informal sectors, with relatively little public debate or resistance, the further extension of the new mixed economy of welfare in the spheres of health and education became a major political issue in the early 1990s. At the same time the impact of deepening recession has begun to expose some of the deficiencies of market forces in areas, such as housing and income maintenance, where their role had expanded dramatically during the 1980s. *The State of Welfare* provides a forum for continuing the debate about the services we need in the 1990s.

Titles of related interest also in *The State of Welfare Series*

The Dynamics of British Health Policy
Stephen Harrison, David Hunter and Christopher Pollitt

Radical Social Work Today
Edited by Mary Langan and Phil Lee

Taking Child Abuse Seriously
The Violence Against Children Study Group

Ideologies of Welfare: From Dreams to Disillusion
John Clarke, Allan Cochrane and Carol Smart

Women, Oppression and Social Work
Edited by Mary Langan and Lesley Day

Managing Poverty: The Limits of Social Assistance
Carol Walker

The Eclipse of Council Housing
Ian Cole and Robert Furbey

Towards a Post-Fordist Welfare State?

Edited by
Roger Burrows
and Brian Loader

London and New York

First published 1994
by Routledge
11 New Fetter Lane, London EC4P 4EE

Simultaneously published in the USA and Canada
by Routledge
29 West 35th Street, New York, NY 10001

Typeset in Times by LaserScript, Mitcham, Surrey
Printed and bound in Great Britain by
Mackays of Chatham PLC, Chatham, Kent

British Library Cataloguing in Publication Data
A catalogue record for this book is available from the British Library.

Library of Congress Cataloging in Publication Data
Towards a post-fordist welfare state? / edited by Roger Burrows and Brian
  Loader.
    p.   cm. – (The state of welfare)
  Includes bibliographical references and index.
    1. Great Britain–Social policy.   2. Public welfare–Great Britain.
  3. Welfare state.   I. Burrows, Roger, 1962–   .
  II. Loader, Brian, 1958–   .   III. Series.
  HN390.T66   1994
  361.6′1′0941–dc20   93–42527
                                                             CIP

ISBN 0–415–09968–4 (hbk)
ISBN 0–415–09967–6 (pbk)

Contents

Illustrations

Contributors

Paul Bagguley is a Lecturer in Sociology in the Department of Social Policy and Sociology at the University of Leeds.

Roger Burrows works in the School Human Studies at the University of Teesside.

David Byrne is a Senior Lecturer in the Department of Sociology and Social Policy at the University of Durham.

Allan Cochrane is Dean and Director of Studies at the Open University.

Mike Geddes is Principal Research Fellow in the Local Government Centre at the University of Warwick.

Paul Hoggett is Associate Director for the Centre for Social and Economic Research, University of the West of England.

Bob Jessop is Professor of Sociology in the Department of Sociology at the University of Lancaster.

Brian Loader is a Senior Lecturer in Policy Studies in the School of Human Studies at the University of Teesside.

Christopher Pierson is a Senior Lecturer in the Department of Political Studies at the University of Stirling.

Steven Pinch is a Senior Lecturer in Geography in the Department of Geography at the University of Southampton.

Michael Rustin is Dean of Social Science at the University of East London.

Alan Warde is a Senior Lecturer in Sociology in the Department of Sociology at the University of Lancaster.

Fiona Williams is a Senior Lecturer in Social Policy in the School of Health, Welfare and Community Education at the Open University.

Series editor's preface

In the early 1990s the perception of a crisis of welfare systems has become universal across the Western world. In the USA the problem of funding a fragmenting health care system has become one of the main domestic issues confronting the presidency of Bill Clinton. In Germany, sickness and other benefits are to be restricted. In France insurance contributions are being raised and direct payments extended. In Britain, virtually the entire welfare state has become enveloped by a sense of permanent crisis.

The coincidence of global economic slump and the ending of the Cold War has intensified pressures to reduce welfare expenditure at the same time that Western governments and established political parties face unprecedented problems of legitimacy. Given the importance of welfare policies in securing popular consent for existing regimes and in maintaining social stability, welfare budgets have proved remarkably resilient even in face of governments proclaiming strict monetarist principles. Thus in Britain, despite the often stridently anti-welfare tone of the Thatcher years, the proportion of GDP spent on welfare has remained more or less constant for the past twenty years.

Yet, the crisis of welfare has led to measures of reform and retrenchment which have provoked often bitter controversy in virtually every sphere, from hospitals and schools to social security benefits and personal social services. What is striking is the crumbling of the old structures and policies before any clear alternative has emerged. The general impression is one of exhaustion and pessimism: the sense that everything has been tried and failed and that nobody is very clear about how to advance into an increasingly bleak future.

The forces of the new right have held the initiative for the past decade and more, particularly in the Reagan/Thatcher years on both sides of the Atlantic. The agenda of free market anti-statism has provided the ideological cutting edge for measures of privatisation and a substantial shift in the 'mixed economy' of welfare towards a more market-oriented approach. But it has not taken long for the defects of the market as a mechanism for social regulation to become apparent. In the health service, for example, whole authorities face bankruptcy and in London several prestigious teaching hospitals face closure. As charitable donations and private fees assume growing importance, distorting the pattern of health care provision, older consultants suddenly recall why the health service was nationalised in the first place.

The government response to the impasse reached by free-market reforms has been to retreat into diatribes against the continuing influence of 1960s 'permissiveness' and 'liberalism' in social policy. The project of 'getting back to basics', featuring a return to traditional family values, personal responsibility and conventional morality, has become a recurring theme in the discourse of Conservative Party politicians. Yet the explicitly backward-looking character of this project reflects a lack of confidence about how to move forward towards the new century. Success is by no means guaranteed as moral crusades have a tendency to rebound on their instigators. Government attempts to scapegoat single mothers and errant fathers have provoked a decidedly ambivalent response.

The new right offensive of the 1970s and 1980s proved highly effective in destroying the social democratic consensus that supported the comprehensive state welfare system throughout the post-war period. The fact that early statements emerging from the Labour Party's National Commission on Social Justice appear sympathetic to the move towards the abandonment of the principles of universalism and state welfare in favour of selectivity and market forces confirms the impact of the Thatcher decade. But now that the inadequacy of the market in providing equitable or even efficient welfare services is in doubt, where else is there to turn?

The welfare state emerged in Western societies at the end of the nineteenth century in response to the perception of economic decline and social instability. Today the forms of state intervention in welfare that emerged in the first half of the century are widely held up to blame for fostering the dependency culture which has led to the loss of national economic strength and prestige as well as the process of internal decay manifested in growing poverty, homelessness, crime and drug abuse. Attempts to foster market forces to compensate for the deficiencies of state welfare have increased inequalities without improving efficiency or indeed reducing costs. The result is not only a sense of policy fatigue but a pervasive pessimism about the future of welfare.

The contributors to *Towards a Post-Fordist Welfare State?* have set out to theorise some of the complex and contradictory trends that are currently manifest in the sphere of welfare. They examine the concepts of Fordism, post-Fordism and flexibility, applying and in turn criticising the use of such concepts in the analysis of contemporary welfare. In the process they offer many valuable insights into the restructuring of welfare and provide a significant contribution to the wider theoretical debate on social policy.

Mary Langan
November 1993

Acknowledgements

This volume presents chapters which are substantially revised versions of papers which were first presented at a conference held at the University of Teesside in September 1992. It is with regret that the excellent conference paper contributions by Sylvia Walby, Aidan Kelly, Joe Painter, Gerry Stoker and Karen Mossberger could not, for various reasons, be included here.

Thanks are due to all participants at the conference for making it such a stimulating affair and to colleagues from Teesside, especially those from social policy, public administration and sociology, for their support, good humour and hard work. Despite the chaos, Teesside remains a good place to be.

Special thanks should go to: Mary Rayner and John Carter, who provided the initial stimulus for this volume via their innovative course in *Social Policy and the Restructuring of Britain*; Angela Newton, who, if truth be told, organised the whole thing; and Christa Delaney, Elaine Hodgkinson and Andrea McLeod for excellent administrative support.

The volume is dedicated to the memory of Catherine Marsh.

Roger Burrows and Brian Loader
School of Human Studies
University of Teesside
Middlesbrough

1   Towards a post-Fordist welfare state?

The restructuring of Britain, social policy and the future of welfare

Brian Loader and Roger Burrows

INTRODUCTION

That significant socio-economic changes have occurred in the UK and other advanced capitalist societies over the last twenty years or so is not in any doubt. However, how best to interpret these changes has become a source of much controversy. The literature on processes of 'restructuring' has been marked by a plethora of attempts to make some sort of sense out of recent economic, political and social change. For a while it appeared as if this babble of voices would remain disparate. However, of late three related concepts have emerged around which there has been a crystallisation: *Fordism*, *post-Fordism*, and supposedly linking the two, various manifestations of *socio-economic flexibility*. Dominant interpretations of the contemporary profusion of division and change in the economy and wider society are increasingly being discussed in terms of this conceptual triumvirate (Gilbert *et al.*, 1992).

This new orthodoxy is slowly finding its way into the literature on contemporary social policy and the future of welfare. Models derived from *regulation theory*, the idea of *flexible specialisation* and the notion of the *flexible firm* are now becoming apparent within the literature on the restructuring of welfare.[1] Crudely, it has been suggested that if Fordism is represented by a homology between mass production, mass consumption, modernist cultural forms and the mass public provision of welfare then post-Fordism is characterised by an emerging coalition between flexible production, differentiated and segmented consumption patterns, post-modernist cultural forms and a restructured welfare state.

Is this framework a viable one? Are we indeed moving towards the development of a post-Fordist welfare state? If not how best are we to theorise emerging patterns of division and change in the organisation of the provision of welfare in the UK? It is to questions such as these that the present book attempts to provide some answers.

The volume is organised into three parts. The early chapters examine various macro-theoretical claims and their empirical applications. Part II focuses upon the local welfare state and has more middle-range theoretical concerns. The final part concentrates upon two particularly important dimensions of the post-Fordist hypothesis: notions of flexibility and the analysis of consumption. This introductory chapter very briefly sketches out the contents of each part.

POST-FORDIST ANALYSES OF WELFARE: APPLICABILITY AND CRITIQUE

The most explicit attempt at theorising the post-Fordist (welfare) state is found in the work of Bob Jessop. In his chapter he attempts to clarify the concepts of Fordism and post-Fordism and postulates the state forms which correspond to each. Adopting a 'regulationist' theoretical framework the continuities and discontinuities of the supposed Fordist/post-Fordist divide are ascertained by reference to differences in four areas: the labour process; the 'accumulation regime'; the 'social mode of economic regulation'; and the mode of 'societalisation'.

For Jessop, the ideal typical state form under Fordism is the Keynesian welfare state (KWS). Its key regulatory functions, which complement the Fordist regime of accumulation, are, first, its economic objective to secure full employment in relatively closed national economies by the use of demand management and, second, its regulation of collective bargaining to generalize norms of mass consumption beyond Fordist sectors so that all citizens share in economic growth. However, Jessop's most valuable contribution is his attempt to construct a model of an emerging post-Fordist state which can, perhaps, be used to analyse current developments. This he describes as a 'hollowed-out Schumpeterian workfare state'. Consistent with his view of the post-Fordist regime, the economic and social objectives of the Schumpeterian Workfare State (SWS) are 'to promote product, process, organisational and market innovation in open economies in order to strengthen . . . structural competitiveness of the national economy by intervening on the supply-side'. Thus, social policy is subordinated to the needs of labour flexibility and/or the constraints of international competition.

The chapter by Jessop represents a major statement on the applicability of post-Fordist analyses by one of the leading theorists in the field, and as such it provides a focus – both supportive and critical – for many of the other chapters in the volume.

Paul Hoggett, in the next chapter, offers a second variant of post-Fordist analysis as it applies to the restructuring of welfare. This is usefully identified by Fiona Williams, in her contribution to the volume, as a 'radical technological' model. Together with Robin Murray (1987) Hoggett was one of the first analysts to make an explicit link between restructuring debates and developments in the public sector. In a number of articles (Hoggett, 1987; 1990; 1991b) he has compared the emergence of the 'flexible firm' in the private sector with its attendant decentralised forms, teamworking, franchising and technological basis with decentralisation and quasi-market strategies in the welfare state. A major criticism of this approach has been its implicit technological determinism (Cochrane, 1991; Painter, 1991b). Here Hoggett seeks to refute these allegations by suggesting that it is not only necessary to consider social relations of production but also the contradictions between the forces and relations of production in any explanation of social change. Following Marx he asserts that the driving force of capitalism is growth through 'technique' which usually (although not always) outstrips aesthetic and moral development. But technique does not determine future structure and social relations. Rather, within the general template of the new productive forces – organisational decentralisation, flexibility and centralised strategic control – a range of trajectories are possible. What needs to be established is whether recent Conservative social policies represent a distinctive post-Fordist trajectory. Here attention is focused upon the methodological difficulties of using a post-Fordist schema for interpretive analysis. How do we distinguish between the underlying conditions and neo-liberal predilections? Nevertheless, the assumption, as with Jessop, is that Thatcherism's demonstrable failure is based upon a 'flawed post-Fordist' trajectory as interpreted against some ideal form.

Hoggett's key postulation is that the new forces of production make possible emerging forms of control – from bureaucratic control towards 'remote' control.[2] These new technologies of control are applicable to wider social relations, not merely institutional ones. As Hoggett states, could 'it be that the basic paradigm of social control in the coming period will . . . draw upon models of self-regulating systems, and of remote rather than proximate monitoring and intervention?' The 'incorporational' social control strategies of the 1960s and 1970s could be replaced by 'exclusion'. In particular, Hoggett follows those who suggest that a two-tier welfare system may develop with the concomitant development of an 'underclass' excluded from primary labour markets.

Whilst acknowledging the potential advantages of post-Fordist analyses as a means of understanding welfare state restructuring, Fiona Williams maintains that it is seriously flawed in its present formulations by its dependency upon an 'unreconstructed political economy'. In particular, by concentrating almost exclusively upon social class its exponents fail to give appropriate consideration to social relations based upon gender, 'race', age, disability, sexuality and so on. She claims that this bias manifests itself in two important and related ways. First, dominant interpretations of the Fordist KWS tend not to take on board the centrality of the historical embeddedness of racism and patriarchy in the institutional development of the welfare state, and likewise these social dimensions are not taken as fundamental in models of post-Fordist forms of welfare. Second, and relatedly, post-Fordist analyses fail to recognise the significance of non-class-based collectivities as agents of change and as foci of struggle systematically challenging the social relations of welfare – struggles which cannot simply be regarded as responses to a crisis in Fordism. This is related to the more general criticism of post-Fordism as overly economically deterministic allowing little space for the power of human agency and political struggle in patterns of social change.

Finally, Williams addresses the contention that post-Fordism, through its gloss on social change, fails to identify the complex and often contradictory nature of the neo-liberal trajectory. Although notions of diversity, difference and differentiation form consistent aspects of the post-Fordist template no clear specification has hitherto been available on the interpretation of such issues within analyses of social policy and welfare. Williams identifies three competing notions of diversity and difference as they apply to the restructuring of welfare. The first arises from the market-orientated conception of the consumer with individual preferences being met by a differentiated 'mixed economy' of welfare provision. The second is derived from the requirement in recent health and social care reorganisation that the 'purchasers' of services should assess the individual needs of welfare recipients. Although this is related to the previous quasi-market conception it is complicated by the related necessity of local authorities to produce community care plans in consultation with health authorities and users to identify their population's needs. Unlike the first two considerations, which may be seen as 'diversity from above', the third conception is characterised as coming 'from below'. Equal opportunities policies within welfare state organisations have had a significant influence in recognising the social basis of difference. This has been complimented by other service user movements outside the state who have emphasised the political dimension of difference as a means of challenging social relations of power and inequality. Thus it is possible to identify three distinct and competing discourses around diversity and difference. What is necessary, for Williams, is to ground these discourses in the socially constructed conditions of people's existence.

The power of agency and political struggle is also explored by Paul Bagguley in his chapter. Dissatisfied with the determinism of many post-Fordist accounts of social change, Bagguley wishes to reassert the power of the 'poor' to effect transformations 'from below'. An essential aspect of such an analysis requires us to consider how the opportunities for the collective mobilisation of the poor are facilitated or restricted by welfare institutions. The notion of the welfare state, in either its Fordist or post-Fordist guises, is however too narrowly conceived to be of use. Rather the concept of *welfare regime* is utilised to foreground both the diverse nature of welfare institutions and the differentiated character of social movements which act to shape them. Bagguley modifies the interpretation offered by Esping-Andersen (1990) in order to identify a restructured welfare regime which comprises a variety of layers of welfare forms: past, present and in the process of formation. Furthermore (and following Williams), the concept needs to move beyond the emphasis upon organised working-class determinants of struggle to include other social groups involved in conflict and struggle over emerging welfare regimes.

The complex relationship between welfare regimes and wider social relations is explored through two case studies. The first considers the form of relationship between the state and the unemployed. Here control tends to be based upon a Fordist dependency relationship involving a transition from 'local' forms of provision to centralised forms where there 'was no effective way for political organisations of the unemployed to have clear access to the institutions with which the unemployed were in a day-to-day relationship'. In contrast the second case-study illustrates more recent attempts to use alternative control strategies of the 'poor' at the local state level by means of the poll tax. Here Bagguley suggests we can identify a move away from Foucauldian 'disciplinary' power based largely upon surveillance, normalisation and examination to what he terms 'market power'. In this case however the resistance was sufficiently effective to produce a reversal in state policy. Thus the successful mobilisation of the poor represents a counter claim to the post-Fordist analysis with its emphasis upon the development of a 'dual society' driven by technology and processes of recommodification.

The call for a more cautious interpretation of restructuring is further discussed by Chris Pierson who argues that an analysis of Conservative social policy during the 1980s reveals continuity of provision as much as any discontinuity with the KWS. A consideration of housing policy reveals the limitations of a post-Fordist schema for understanding Thatcherism. Although significantly reducing the amount of public housing and success-fully stimulating an increase in owner-occupation, the Conservatives failed to reduce overall public expenditure upon housing due to the rise in Housing Benefits and mortgage tax relief. Furthermore, the ideological commitment to private property rights produced a perverse investment in domestic property at the expense of industry. A more general look at Conservative social policy leads Pierson to echo Jessop's contention that in the case of Britain at least the most that can be claimed is the possible emergence of a flawed post-Fordism. Many post-Fordist elements were present in the Fordist welfare state: few reforms are directly linked to facilitating 'flexibility'; the welfare state is still required to support the efficiency of the market; and politically driven explanations of social policy are as evident as their economic and functionalist counterparts.

POST-FORDISM AND THE LOCAL WELFARE STATE

In the second part of the book the contrast between advocates of the post-Fordist paradigm and their protagonists is well illustrated by their respective treatments of changes in the local state. Clearly the crisis of the central KWS must also be a crisis for the local (welfare) state. For Cochrane, following the broad conclusions of Part I the post-Fordist thesis is too vague to provide useful methodological tools with which to examine the specificity of the myriad of changes taking place. Whenever the empirical evidence runs counter to post-Fordist formulations its advocates simply fall back on the assertion that it is an ideal type or that they are only constructing abstract models which cannot fit every situation.

Cochrane suggests that it may be more useful to develop 'middle level' concepts on the basis of evidence of actual processes of restructuring before formulating macro-theoretical analyses of the sort introduced in the first part of the volume. He also points to the need to move beyond a narrow concern with local government in understanding changes in the local welfare provision by, for example, utilising the idea of a mixed (domestic, voluntary, private and public) economy of welfare. The adoption of the concept of an 'urban regime' further helps to describe the development of informal networks between business agencies, quangos, local authorities and other statutory agencies. In this context it is possible to understand the attempts by local authorities to seek partnerships with local business interests, in part as a result of their dependency upon business income, but also in consequence of increasing global competition between localities for business investment. Business interests in turn have been keen to influence the welfare agendas of the local state as a means of attracting industry and commerce. Here, welfare is no longer treated as an end in itself but rather as incidental to other ends.

The chapter by Byrne also deals with local manifestations of processes of restructuring and the role of the relationship between the public and the private sectors but with a rather higher level 'of scepticism about the general tenor of identifications of a division between "Fordist" and "post-Fordist" social forms' than demonstrated by Cochrane.

Byrne analyses urban planning processes in Tyneside, Wearside and Teesside in the north east of England in terms of the categories of 'pre-Keynesian, Keynesian and post-Keynesian planning strategies', 'modernisation' and 'postmodernisation' whilst at the same time pouring scorn on what he terms the 'post-Fordist game-show'. His analysis concentrates upon 'old, clapped out, industrial cities' within which nearly 'half of the population of the UK actually lives'. It proceeds by outlining the transition from pre-Keynesian development to Keynesian planning, and then goes on to review the content of the period of Keynesian planning, the second half of which he describes as a 'modernisation' phase. This phase, he argues, was central to facilitating the development of 'flexible accumulation' strategies. The chapter then gives an account of the emergence of 'postmodernisation' in relation to the socio-spatial residue of modernisation. The chapter concludes by considering the most appropriate political strategies 'for planning on the wreckage of modernisation, as subsequently vandalised by postmodernisation'.

Unlike Byrne, Mike Geddes is happy to work within a post-Fordist framework when analysing the role of the local state. Thus, for him, local public services performed a major aspect of the regulation of the post-war regime of accumulation. Following Jessop he argues that the neo-liberal strategy for economic restructuring represents a 'flawed post-Fordism' in the context of the UK. Nonetheless, he maintains that the local state still represents an important forum for the development and creation of alternative post-Fordist regulatory forms. In particular he points to the 'left post-Fordist' strategies of the early 1980s as examples of the possibility for different trajectories.

FLEXIBILITY, CONSUMPTION AND THE FUTURE OF WELFARE

The remaining three chapters of the volume consider notions of flexibility and consumption in post-Fordist theorisations of the restructuring of welfare.

A major feature of the supposedly emerging 'flexible' forms of production is their transformation of time and space (Dunford, 1990; Esser and Hirsch, 1989; Harvey, 1987; 1989a). Thus Fordist welfare services were regarded as being structured around fairly rigid working times and were often provided in and from immovable 'institutions' such as hospitals, benefit offices, schools, council offices and so on. It is, of course, precisely such constraints, which fuelled accusations about the 'unresponsiveness' of public welfare agencies, that have led to 'marketisation' strategies in the public sector in an attempt to break down such barriers to 'consumer choice'.

This theme is taken up by Mike Rustin in his telling consideration of the development of 'flexibility' in higher education – modularity, semesterisation, distance learning, credit accumulation and transfer, international student exchanges and so on. He concludes that institutions of higher education are faced with contradictory pressures. On the one hand, they have to defend the 'innate values of education and scholarship' which can only reliably function in the context of 'relations of "co-presencing", time-boundedness (intellectual tradition) and spatial containment'. On the other hand, the demands of a truly mass system of higher education require innovative responses based upon 'a new model of "flexible specialisation" . . . of freely chosen, customised, but nevertheless craft-produced, educational programmes'. The problem for Rustin is how to avoid a system based upon 'common curricula and routinised delivery (the national secondary school curriculum translated to higher education)' and/or the development of a superficial higher educational supermarket 'in which no meaningful quality of intellectual interaction survives'.

Steven Pinch offers an empirical examination of 'flexibility' in welfare state organisations. It is perhaps the 'core and periphery' schema with its emphasis upon a small highly skilled core of functionally flexible managers responsible for corporate strategy loosely coupled (through sub-contracting, contracts, decentralised offices and computer networking) to peripheral units staffed by 'non-standard' employees which has become the dominant model of the 'flexible firm'. Yet as Pinch reminds us there is little evidence to support the widespread emergence of this model in the private sector, let alone in the welfare state (Penn, 1992; Pollert, 1989). His own analysis suggests that changing work practices are typified more by 'job enlargement' than the development of a functionally flexible workforce; the increase in part-time workers – most usually women – is more often about cost-cutting than flexibility; and contracting-out has been limited in scope and more often than not awarded in-house. The driving force behind organisational changes has been cost-cutting rather than the creation of a responsive public service motivated by improvements in 'quality'. Nonetheless, despite these reservations Pinch still believes that the flexible firm model provides some, albeit limited, analytic handle on the new quasi-market structures of welfare services.

Finally an increasingly important aspect of the post-Fordist debate which has been little considered in relation to welfare restructuring is changes in the mode of consumption in advanced capitalist societies

(Burrows and Marsh, 1992). The general thrust of the argument is that the consumption of Fordist 'universal' standardised welfare services is increasingly undermined by flexible marketised systems and the development of supposedly post-Fordist patterns of consumption. In his chapter Alan Warde examines the theoretical and empirical evidence for some of these claims.

Warde deals with two bodies of literature, both of which claim that an irreversible transformation is occurring in the character of consumption. The first, most closely associated with the recent work of Zygmunt Bauman, predicts the continued decline of state-provided welfare, because it 'presupposes a type of consumer who cannot possibly derive satisfaction from universally provided, collectively financed and state-allocated services'. The second, deriving from regulation theory, argues that 'any resolution of the current crisis of capital accumulation will necessarily affect the nature of consumption practice'. Warde critically considers various contemporary models of the consumer and the supposedly concomitant developments in post-Fordist consumption practices. He concludes that constructing models of 'the consumer' is unhelpful but that an examination of consumption practices in general might be a more promising approach. However, existing empirical sociological research that might demonstrate the case for the emergence of post-Fordist patterns of consumption is lacking. Many of the assertions found in the theoretical literature are 'informed more by the language and strategies of market research and advertising than by knowledge of households and their everyday practices of consumption'.

CONCLUDING COMMENT

Between them the contributors to this volume provide a thorough discussion of the applicability of a range of conceptualisations of Fordism, post-Fordism and flexibility to the analysis of contemporary social policy. To a degree most accept the usefulness of some variant of post-Fordism as a 'sensitising concept' at a fairly high level of abstraction, however most have doubts concerning its more concrete applicability to an analysis of contemporary patterns of divisions and change in welfare provision. It may well be that we are not moving towards the development of a post-Fordist welfare state, but nevertheless we still urgently require more adequate theorisations of the myriad developments occurring within contemporary social and public policy. We hope that this volume will make some small contribution to such a task and inform wider sociological and political debate about socio-economic restructuring and the future of welfare in the UK.

NOTES

1 For readers with little or no prior knowledge of the existing literature on Fordism, post-Fordism and flexibility the opening sections of Chapter 4 by Fiona Williams in the current volume is highly recommended. In addition relatively short and accessible summaries are provided by Bagguley (1991a), Burrows *et al.* (1992), Elam (1990) and Pollert (1988). For more extensive and detailed accounts readers are referred to Aglietta (1979), Atkinson and Meager (1986), Boyer (1990), Clarke (1992), Harvey (1989a), Hirst and Zeitlin (1991), Jessop (1990a; 1992a), Nielsen (1991), Penn (1992), Piore and Sabel (1984), Pollert (1991) and Sayer (1989). The most explicit attempt to apply post-Fordist theorising to social policy and welfare can be found in Gould (1993).

2 A conceptualisation also recently discussed by Cooper (1992).

Part I
Post-Fordist analyses of welfare

Applicability and critique

2 The transition to post-Fordism and the Schumpeterian workfare state

Bob Jessop

INTRODUCTION

Drawing on the French regulation approach and neo-Marxist state theory, this chapter addresses three closely related sets of issues.[1] First, what exactly is involved in theorising the post-Fordist welfare state? Second, approaching the latter as a theoretical object, what might its core features comprise? And, third, is the British state acquiring these features? Arguments about these issues are often vague and, when taken together, frequently prove inconsistent. There is little agreement about the nature of Fordism and post-Fordism in general or the trajectories which might link them – let alone about the post-Fordist state in particular or the transitional regimes which might connect it to its putative Fordist precursor. Unless these problems are resolved, however, it would be premature to anticipate the core features of a post-Fordist welfare regime. Moreover, until these features are spelt out, if only in a preliminary manner, there can be no referent for assessing whether Britain has been moving towards some form of post-Fordist welfare state. It is these three issues in their interconnection that define my agenda here.

Accordingly the first section reviews different understandings of Fordism and post-Fordism, assesses their various implications for analyzing the state, and suggests ways of defining a post-Fordist state and transitional regimes. The next section describes two key transformations in advanced capitalist states during the current global economic restructuring which bear directly on the nature of economic and social policy regimes. These are a tendential shift from a Keynesian welfare state to a Schumpeterian workfare state; and a tendential 'hollowing out' of the national state. Some of the economic and political mechanisms generating these changes are also briefly discussed. The third section then considers the partial, uneven, and still 'flawed' development of post-Fordism in Britain and examines the British state's role in this, with special reference to Thatcherism. The chapter ends with some general remarks on the problems of theorising post-Fordism.

FORDISM AND POST-FORDISM

Even a cursory review of accounts of Fordism and post-Fordism reveals massive disparities in the use of these concepts. I will first deal with the problems regarding Fordism and the Fordist state. This will clarify what is at stake in analysing post-Fordism and the post-Fordist state and thereby provide firmer foundations for my discussion of the British case. In particular, if it could be shown that Britain never experienced an effective Fordist mode of growth, this would cast doubt on whether it could move towards a British post-Fordism.

The nature of Fordism

Drawing on the regulation approach, some order can be introduced into work on Fordism and post-Fordism by distinguishing four alternative referents for these terms:

1 the labour process considered as a particular configuration of the technical and social division of labour;
2 an accumulation regime, i.e., a macro-economic regime sustaining growth in capitalist production and consumption;
3 a social mode of economic regulation, i.e., an ensemble of norms, institutions, organisational forms, social networks, and patterns of conduct which sustain and 'guide' a given accumulation regime;[2] and
4 a mode of societalisation, i.e., a pattern of institutional integration and social cohesion which complements the dominant accumulation regime and its social mode of economic regulation and thereby secures the conditions for its dominance within the wider society (cf. Jessop 1992a; 1992b).

It should be noted here that there is no consensus in regulationist literature as to whether these are simply so many different sites on which Fordism or post-Fordism might arise (without regard to their presence elsewhere), successively emergent levels of organisation (originating in the labour process), or potentially complementary forms of (post-)Fordism whose contingent co-presence helps stabilise the corresponding social relations on any given site. This is not the place to answer this set of questions. For present purposes I will simply assume that a given labour process can exist independently of a corresponding accumulation regime; and that the stability of the latter depends on the contingent co-presence of an appropriate social mode of regulation.[3]

In these terms, Fordism can be defined in terms of its dominant labour process (the mass production of complex consumer durables); its nature as a feasible macro-economic system (a virtuous, balanced circle of mass production and mass consumption in a largely autocentric national economy); its profile as a social mode of economic regulation (notably the role of institutionalised collective bargaining and a Keynesian welfare state); its general implications for social organisation and cohesion (an urban-industrial, 'middle mass', wage-earning society); or even, finally, the co-presence and co-evolution of all four possible Fordist phenomena. Even when these four referents can be separated for analytical purposes, real difficulties remain in operationalising the concept of Fordism. For there is considerable scope for discongruence between its structural forms and its expression in strategic paradigms on each dimension as well as for significant local and national variations. In general, it seems to make most sense to ground the distinctiveness of Fordism as a phase of capital accumulation in its key features as a social mode of economic regulation (Jessop, 1992b).

Focusing on Fordist regulation is not sufficient in itself to identify the Fordist state. We should also decide whether to treat it as a state in a Fordist society, as an inherently Fordist state, or as a strategically selective Fordist state.[4] In the first case, the state would be seen as *contingently* Fordist (if at all) due to Fordism's dominance in the economy and/or wider society. This would lead the state to acquire secondary Fordist features or, at least, make it likely that it is controlled by pro-Fordist forces. Hence, if it were situated within an economic or societal system with different properties, the same generic state form would acquire different secondary features or, at least, be controlled by different forces. This suggests, in turn, that it would perform different functions. Second, in treating it as a Fordist state, the state system would be *necessarily* Fordist. Thus, it would, by virtue of its structural forms, themselves essentially Fordist in character, sustain Fordism as an accumulation regime, social mode of economic regulation, or mode of societalisation. Once installed, such a Fordist state would help ensure the reproduction of Fordism until such time as economic crisis-tendencies and/or the social antagonisms inscribed in Fordism overwhelm its regulatory capacities. The third approach, which avoids the state-theoretical pitfalls of either alternative, namely, instrumentalism and structuralism respectively, focuses on the *contingently necessary* character of the Fordist state. This would have basic structural features congruent with Fordism and thereby tend to sustain Fordism. But the extent to which this occurs would depend on the prevailing balance of forces and their respective strategies. For the moment I will concentrate on the more ambitious agenda of characterising the structural forms and functions of the strategically selective Fordist state. For, even if these ultimately prove elusive, one can still revert to the more limited agenda entailed in discussing the state in a Fordist society.

In this context the Fordist state (as opposed to state in Fordist society) can be defined in at least four ways. These correspond to the different possible referents of Fordism more generally. It could be characterised in terms of:

1 the nature of the labour process within the state sector itself (e.g. Hoggett, 1987);
2 the state sector's direct economic role in a Fordist accumulation regime (e.g. Overbeek, 1990: 114–19);
3 the state's wider role in the social mode of economic regulation linked to such a regime (e.g. Moulaert *et al.*, 1988; Painter, 1991b); or
4 its role in securing the institutional integration and social cohesion of a social formation within which Fordism in one or more of its possible guises is dominant (Hirsch and Roth, 1986).

Although it may be interesting to investigate how far the labour process in the state is Fordist (or quasi-Fordist) in character, this would tend, in the absence of other criteria, to reduce the state to one among several sites of economic activity. It would thereby lose its distinctiveness as a state. Nor, indeed, is there any *prima facie* reason to expect the labour process within the state to have much direct bearing on its functions for the wider economy or society. Focusing on the direct economic characteristics of the public sector could also lead to neglect of the distinctive features of the state as a whole. Conversely, looking at a state's role in securing Fordist soci-etalisation might make it hard to distinguish a Fordist state proper from a state which maintains the social cohesion of a society which happens to be Fordist. This suggests that the most promising approach to the 'Fordistic' character of the state is the distinctive contribution of its form and functions *qua* state in securing a distinctively Fordist mode of economic regulation. This corresponds to the general state-theoretical argument that a state is capitalist (in this context, 'Fordist') to the extent that it creates, maintains, or restores the conditions for the expanded reproduction of capitalism (here, Fordism) (Jessop, 1982: 221-7). However, in applying this general argument to the particular case in hand, and given the current high level of theoretical abstraction on which the argument is being conducted, one should focus on the ideal typical (or 'normal') form of the Fordist state. This would comprise a state system whose structural forms and strategic capacities complement the key structural forms and dynamic of a Fordist accumulation regime and thereby facilitate the routinisation of that state's contributions to (regularising) Fordist growth.[5]

In this context I suggest that the typical form of the Fordist state is that of the 'Keynesian welfare state' (KWS). In abstract terms and from a regulationist perspective,[6] we can treat the KWS as performing two distinctive functions in addition to the generic functions of a capitalist state. First, economically, it aims to secure full employment in relatively closed national economies and to do so primarily through demand-side management. In this way it tries to adjust demand to the supply-driven needs of Fordist mass production with its dependence on economies of scale and full utilisation of relatively inflexible means of production. And, second, it tries to regulate collective bargaining within limits consistent with full employment levels of growth, to generalize norms of mass consumption beyond those employed in Fordist sectors so that all citizens might share the fruits of economic growth (and thereby reinforce effective domestic demand), and to promote forms of collective consumption favourable to the Fordist mode of growth. The concrete forms of the KWS and the specific modalities through which it has attempted to realize these functions have naturally varied from case to case. Thus one can distinguish among KWS regimes in terms of their typical forms of economic and social intervention (liberal, corporatist, statist), their internal articulation, social bases, their distinctive political projects, and the hegemonic projects with which they are associated. But these mainly constitute secondary variations on the key features of the Keynesian welfare state.

The meaning of post-Fordism

A satisfactory account of post-Fordism would treat it like Fordism – distinguishing its various levels as well as their structural and strategic moments. Before attempting this, however, we should justify 'posting' Fordism in this way. A minimum condition for referring to post-Fordism is to establish the nature of the continuity in discontinuity which justifies the claim that it is not just a variant form of Fordism but does actually succeed Fordism. Without significant discontinuity, it would not be *post*-Fordism; without significant continuity, it would not be post-*Fordism*. This double condition is satisfied where: post-Fordism has demonstrably emerged from tendencies originating within Fordism but still marks a decisive break with it; or the ensemble of old and new elements in post-Fordism demonstrably displaces or resolves basic contradictions and crises in Fordism – even if it is also associated with its own contradictions and crisis-tendencies in turn (Jessop, 1992b). In this context post-Fordism could be related to the continuity in discontinuity found in one or more of the dimensions of Fordism, namely, the labour process, accumulation regimes, social modes of economic regulation, or modes of societalisation. And this in turn would give a basis for defining a typical post-Fordist state analogous to the Fordist state discussed above.

Even if this broad approach is accepted, one further issue remains to be agreed. So far we have indicated how one might go beyond mere temporal succession as the criterion for defining post-Fordism; but this leaves unresolved the reference point for defining the 'post-ness' of the post-Fordist state. This could be related to the latter's discontinuity relative to Fordism in general or the distinctive features of its political precursor in particular. In the former case the transition to a post-Fordist state could be linked to tendencies originating in Fordism and/or to the displacement or resolution of its basic contradictions and crises. This transition may occur independently of any crisis in the state itself. Conversely, in the latter case, the morphogenesis of the post-Fordist state would be grounded in tendencies emerging initially within the Fordist state itself and/or in the search for solutions to the latter's own contradictions and crises. Thus a state crisis could play a key role in the emergence of the post-Fordist state. This issue could perhaps be resolved by definitional fiat but there may also be different routes to a post-Fordist state or state in post-Fordism (some of which are illustrated in Figure 2.1 below).

Whichever definitional solution is adopted (or specific historical transformation process discovered), one should not offer a simple functionalist account of the post-Fordist state, such that its new form follows from its new functions. In either case one ought to show how the state manages (or is managed) to achieve this. And one should also be wary about conflating mere rhetoric or declared aims and the actual achievement of a transition

1	Crisis of Fordist economy	→ Post-Fordist economy	→ Post-Fordist state	
2	Crisis of Fordist state	→ Post-Fordist state		
3	Crisis of Fordist economy	→ Fordist state crisis	→ Post-Fordist state	
4	Fordist economy structurally coupled to Fordist state	→ Economic crisis → State crisis	→ Post-Fordist economy structurally coupled to post-Fordist state	
5	Crisis of Fordism	→ Post-Fordism	→ State in post-Fordism	

Figure 2.1 Post-Fordism and the transformation of the state

Note: These trajectories by no means exhaust all theoretical possibilities.

from Fordism to post-Fordism. This is especially problematic because, whereas Fordism is nowadays discussed mainly in terms of its structural properties, its successor is more often related to strategic perspectives, discourses, and continuing experimentation to find a stable accumulation regime and mode of regulation.

Key features of post-Fordism

Let us now briefly review possible features of post-Fordism. These can be considered in terms of the same four dimensions as were earlier specified for Fordism. Thus, as a *labour process*, post-Fordism can be defined as a flexible production process based on flexible machines or systems and an appropriately flexible workforce. Its crucial hardware is micro-electronics-based information and communications technologies. This pattern could properly be labelled post-Fordist in so far as it emerges from the Fordist labour process itself and/or helps resolve the crisis of Fordism. Indeed, by looking at how post-Fordism operates from the latter viewpoint, we can include process and product innovations which emerged outside any immediate Fordist context. Flexible specialisation complexes which have long co-existed with Fordist mass production and now seem to have won a new lease of life both materially and ideologically could be included here; so could the new technologies (such as micro-electronics, biotechnology, and new materials) which have a key role in overcoming some of the problems of Fordist control or materials-intensive production (Altvater, 1991; Roobeek, 1987). In seizing on these new or recharged sources of flexibility, capitalists hope to overcome the alienation and resistance of the mass worker, the relative stagnation of Taylorism and mass production, competitive threats from low-cost exporters in the Third World, and the relative saturation of markets for standardised mass-produced goods; and/or to meet the growing demand for more differentiated products, for action to brake the rising costs of non-Fordist service sectors (especially in the public sector), and for measures to boost productivity in manufacturing.

As a stable *mode of macro-economic growth*, post-Fordism would be based on the dominance of a flexible and *permanently innovative* pattern of accumulation.[7] As such its virtuous circle would be based on flexible production, growing productivity based on economies of scope and/or process innovations, rising incomes for polyvalent skilled workers and the service class, increased demand for new differentiated goods and services favoured by the growing discretionary element in these incomes, increased profits based on technological and other innovation rents and the full utilisation of flexible capacity, reinvestment in more flexible production equipment and processes and/or new sets of products and/or new organisational forms, and a further boost to productivity due to economies of scope and constant innovation. Post-Fordist growth need not involve generalizing core workers' rising incomes to other workers and/or the economically inactive. Indeed, as post-Fordist accumulation will be more oriented to worldwide demand, global competition could further limit the scope for general prosperity and encourage market-led polarisation of incomes. Besides its emergence from and organisation around genuinely post-Fordist labour processes, this new accumulation regime could also be treated as post-Fordist in so far as it resolves (or is held to do so) crisis-tendencies in its Fordist predecessor. These were the relative exhaustion of the growth potential which came from extending mass production, the relative saturation of markets for mass consumer durables, and the disruption of the virtuous circle of Fordist accumulation due to inter-nationalisation and the problems this created for national regulation. In these respects post-Fordism transforms mass production and goes beyond it, segments old markets and opens new ones, and is less constrained by national demand conditions.

As a *social mode of economic regulation*, post-Fordism would involve supply-side innovation and flexibility in each of the main areas of regulation. Thus the wage relation would be recomposed with a polarisation between skilled and unskilled workers; there would be greater emphasis on flexibility in internal and external labour markets; a shift would occur towards enterprise- or plant-level collective bargaining; and new forms of social wage would develop. The enterprise system could see a shift from the primacy of the hierarchical, well-staffed, bureaucratic 'Sloanist' form of corporate structure towards flatter, leaner, more flexible forms of organisation. Forms of organisation between hierarchy and market will become more important in managing strategic inter-dependencies both within and among firms and in responding quickly to changing demands. Profits of enterprise will depend on the capacity to engineer flexible production systems (or to design flexible service delivery systems) and to accelerate process and product innovation; the search for technological rents based on continuous innovation in products and processes; and economies of scope. In turn competition will turn on non-price factors such as improved quality and performance for individual products, responsiveness to customers and customisation, and rapid response to changing market conditions. The money form will probably be dominated by private, rootless bank credit which circulates internationally; and state credit will be subject to limits set by the logic of international money and currency markets. Moreover, with the growing emphasis on differentiated forms of consumption, commercial capital will be reorganised to create and serve increasingly segmented markets. Finally, state intervention will shift in the ways noted above and described more fully below.

Together these forms seem to comprise a distinctive social mode of economic regulation. They also appear to emerge from tendencies inherent in Fordism and to resolve at least some of its crisis-tendencies. Thus some of the new structural forms and regulatory practices arose from attempts to manage the crisis of Fordism, others from attempts to escape it; some are primarily defensive, others offensive. Among the problems they help solve are: the collapse of Fordist incomes policies and the crisis of Fordist labour market institutions, the contradiction between Fordist wage forms and the post-Fordist need to promote responsible autonomy, rising R&D costs, rapidly changing and shortening product life cycles, greater risks of market failure, the availability of technologies permitting greater task integration and easier communication between divisions, and so on. Politically, the new forms of state intervention respond to Keynesian stagflation, the fiscal crisis of the state, slower productivity growth in the welfare state compared to the private sector, the rigidities and dysfunctions of bureaucratic administration and planning, the growing resistance shown by class forces and new social movements toward the forms and effects of the Fordist state, and so forth.

It is too soon to anticipate what a post-Fordist *mode of societalisation* would be like. As yet there is no obvious predominant post-Fordist mode of 'societalisation' comparable to Americanisation in the Fordist era. Instead we find an unresolved competition between the Japanese, West German and American models – each of which is, in any case, encountering mounting problems on its home ground. At best we could describe the societalisation effects of the uneven transition toward post-Fordism from case to case. This will be one of our tasks in discussing Thatcherism (see below).

Implications for the post-Fordist state

We can now give some flesh to the skeletal notion of a post-Fordist state. For present purposes it is useful to distinguish between possible transitional and consolidated forms of this state. A transitional regime would be one that: facilitates a transition to post-Fordism in one or more of the labour process, accumulation regime, or mode of regulation; and/or copes with the societal repercussions of such a transition, thereby securing the social cohesion without which post-Fordism could not be consolidated. Given the potential variety of its functions in such a transition and its own presumptively transitional character, the specific forms of a transitional regime are somewhat indeterminate at this level of abstraction. Indeed, these will largely depend on the institutional legacies and struggles of the Fordist era from case to case and on the specific forms of crisis and struggle associated with the transition.[8] It would clearly be worth exploring whether effective transitional regimes are as well-suited to preserving the fruits of a transition once it has occurred as they are to promoting its rise. To the extent that this role is performed, the state could also become a consolidated post-Fordist regime.

The shift from Fordism to post-Fordism would seem to involve any transitional post-Fordist regime in a complex array of tasks besides those typical of any capitalist type of state. These tasks derive from its location at the intersection between a previously consolidated Fordism in decline and a putative post-Fordism in the ascendant. In this sense the transitional regime is Janus-faced and must engage in creatively destructive interventions. It must both 'roll back the frontiers' of Fordist state intervention and 'roll forward' those for post-Fordist intervention. The first set of activities not only involves ending the exceptional, crisis-oriented state forms and functions associated with Fordism in decline but also weakening the normal, routinised forms of intervention associated with the KWS as a whole. The second set is just as complex, albeit for different reasons. For a transitional regime must also pursue various measures to establish the conditions for a post-Fordist 'take-off' as well as begin to consolidate the 'normal' state forms and functions associated with post-Fordism. Neither the first nor the second set of tasks is ever structurally inscribed in the form of a transitional regime or strategically pre-scripted by the transitional conjuncture. They both involve chance discoveries, search processes, and diverse struggles. This makes the whole question of transitional regimes complex and uncertain. Time alone is the test of whether a putative transitional regime will prove adequate to its alleged task. This indicates the need for *ex 'post'* analyses of how post-Fordist states emerge rather than *ex ante* (and therefore teleological) accounts of the necessary forms of a transition to post-Fordism.

Now, whereas a transitional post-Fordist regime could well play an active role in regard to all dimensions of the transition, a normal consolidated post-Fordist state is largely defined in terms of its role within a specific social mode of economic regulation in 'regularising' a post-Fordist mode of growth. Thus, given our earlier remarks on normal states or regimes, it can be defined as a state whose structural forms and functions complement the key structural forms and dynamic of a post-Fordist accumulation regime and so promote the routinisation of that state's contributions to (regularising) post-Fordist growth. Such a state can only develop to the extent that the strategic selectivity of the Fordist state is transformed to suit the emergent features of a post-Fordist accumulation regime and to complement the other core structural forms of the post-Fordist social mode of economic regulation. From both regulationist and state-theoretical perspectives, moreover, one would expect the new state form to be sustainable in its core features within a stable post-Fordist context.

For the moment I will focus on the problems involved in defining the consolidated post-Fordist state and only then turn to transitional post-Fordist regimes. This may seem to be putting the cart before the horse but is necessary to provide some criteria for assessing the direction of change in the transition. As regards the normal, consolidated post-Fordist state, we must proceed in two steps. We must first detail the key features of a post-Fordist accumulation regime, and then establish what structural forms and strategic capacities correspond to this. Although it could well be argued that it is too soon to specify this state form, some initial clues can be gleaned from a careful description of apparently fundamental tendencies in the current restructuring and their implications for state forms and functions. Further clues can be inferred from the nature of states in national and regional economies which are proving more or less effective in the current restructuring (Jessop, 1993a). But even here there are problems in assessing now the longer term effectiveness and significance of these allegedly post-Fordist states. It is the complexities and consequences of the former approach which concern us below in dealing with Thatcherism as a possible transitional post-Fordist political regime.

THE NATURE OF THE CONSOLIDATED POST-FORDIST STATE

The initial response to the crisis of Fordism and its state did not produce a post-Fordist state. Instead it typically involved intensifying the features of the Fordist state, reinforcing and complementing them. This was reflected in some circumstances in efforts to promote full employment despite stagflationary tendencies and to maintain welfare commitments despite tendencies towards a fiscal crisis; and in others, in an increasing emphasis on economic austerity and social retrenchment to squeeze out inflation and reduce public spending. Which of these tendencies predominated depended on state capacities and the prevailing balance of forces from case to case (Keman *et al.*, 1987; Scharpf, 1987). In all cases we could refer to a *conjunctural transformation* of the Fordist state rooted in its attempts to manage Fordist crises and limit their repercussions on its own organisation and unity. When such measures failed to restore conditions for Fordist accumulation and precipitated a crisis *of* (and not merely *in*) the Fordist

KWS, economic and political forces alike stepped up the search for a new state form hopefully able to solve the contradictions and crises of Fordist accumulation and re-stabilise the state system. I argue that what is gradually emerging from this search process is a *structural transformation* and *fundamental strategic reorientation* of the capitalist state. The tendential product of this search process can be described as a 'hollowed-out Schumpeterian workfare state'.

The Schumpeterian workfare state

In so far as this restructuring and reorientation of the economic and social functions of the KWS system succeed, they tend to produce a new state form which could be termed a 'Schumpeterian workfare state' (SWS). In abstract terms, its distinctive objectives in economic and social reproduction are: to promote product, process, organisational, and market innovation in open economies in order to strengthen as far as possible the structural competitiveness of the national economy by intervening on the supply-side; and to subordinate social policy to the needs of labour market flexibility and/or to the constraints of international competition. In this sense it marks a clear break with the KWS as domestic full employment is de-prioritised in favour of international competitiveness and redistributive welfare rights take second place to a productivist re-ordering of social policy (see above). In this sense its new functions would also seem to correspond to the emerging dynamic of global capitalism (see below). Equally, just as there were different forms of KWS, we can expect differences across societies in this new form of state.

The 'hollowing out' of the nation-state

The national state is now subject to a series of changes which result in its 'hollowing out'. This involves two contradictory trends. For, whilst the nation-state still remains politically significant and even retains much of its national sovereignty (albeit as an ever more ineffective, primarily juridical fiction reproduced through mutual recognition in the international community of nations), its capacities to project its power even within its own national borders are decisively weakened both by the shift towards internationalised, flexible (but also regionalised) production systems and by the growing challenge posed by risks emanating from the global environment. This loss of autonomy creates in turn both the need for supra-national coordination and the space for subnational resurgence. Thus we find that the powers of nation-states are being limited through a complex displacement of powers upward, downward, and outward. Some state capacities are transferred to an increasing number of pan-regional, pluri-national, or international bodies with a widening range of powers; others are devolved to restructured local or regional levels of governance within the nation-state; and yet others are being usurped by emerging horizontal networks of power – local and regional – which by-pass central states and connect localities or regions in several nations. In many cases these changes are closely linked to the reorientation of these capacities to Schumpeterian workfare measures.

The origins of the 'hollowed out' Schumpeterian workfare state

Four changes have undermined the congruence between Fordism and the KWS in the current phase of capitalist development and thereby created pressures for the development of this new state form. These changes are:

1 the rise of new technologies;
2 growing internationalisation;
3 the paradigm shift from Fordism to post-Fordism; and
4 the regionalisation of global and national economies.

Although Fordism only figures here as a paradigm deployed to make sense of economic changes, its crisis and transformation is intimately related to the other shifts. I will briefly comment on the implications of all four for state reorganisation.

First, given the growing competitive pressures from Newly Indus-trialised Countries (NICs) on low-cost, low-tech production and, indeed, in simple high-tech products, the advanced capitalist economies must move up the technological hierarchy and specialise in the new core technologies if they are to maintain employment and growth. States have a key role here in technological intelligence gathering, creating independent technological capacities, promoting innovative capacities, transferring technology and technical competence so that as many firms and sectors as possible benefit from the new technological opportunities created by R&D activities under-taken in specific parts of the economy (Chesnais, 1986: 86). Moreover, given that the budgetary and fiscal pressures on states as national economies become more open, states must shift industrial support away from efforts to maintain declining sectors and towards promoting new sectors. Alternatively, given that the new core technologies are generic and applicable to many different fields of production, states should at least intervene to restructure declining sectors so that they can apply new processes, upgrade existing products, and launch new ones. In all cases the crucial point is that state action is required to encourage the development of new core technologies and their application to as wide a range of activities as possible to promote competitiveness.

Second, as internationalisation proceeds apace, states can no longer act as if national economies were effectively closed and their growth dynamic were autocentric. Small open economies had already faced this problem during the post-war boom, of course; now even large, relatively closed economies have been integrated into the global circuits of capital. Thus key macro-economic policy instruments associated with the KWS lose their efficacy with growing internationalisation and must be replaced or buttressed by other measures if post-war policy objectives such as full employment, economic growth, stable prices, and sound balance of payments are still to be secured. Moreover, as the national character of money is subordinated to the flows of international currencies, and as internationalisation emphasises the character of wages as costs of pro-duction, the basic domestic premises of Keynesian welfarism are called into question. Consequently almost all states have become more involved in managing the process of internationalisation itself in the hope of minimising its harmful domestic repercussions and/or of securing maximum benefit to its own home-based transnational firms and banks. They must get involved in managing the process of internationalisation and creating the most appropriate frameworks for it to proceed. Among the many activities included here are: introducing new legal forms for cross-national cooperation and strategic alliances; reforming international currency and credit systems; promoting technology transfer; managing trade disputes; developing a new international intellectual property regime; or developing new forms of regulation for labour migration. This leads to the paradox that, as states lose control over the national economy, they are forced to enter the fray on behalf of their own multinationals.

Third, as the dominant techno-economic paradigm shifts from Fordism to post-Fordism, the primary economic functions of states are redefined. Fordism was typically associated with a primary concern with demand management within national economies and with the generalisation of mass-consumption norms. This reflected the belief that Fordist mass production was supply-driven and could only be profitable when high levels of demand were maintained and markets for mass-consumer durables expanded. The class compromise supporting the Fordist Keynesian welfare state also encouraged this pattern of economic intervention. But the transition to a post-Fordist paradigm is prompting a reorientation of the state's primary economic functions. For the combination of the late Fordist trend towards internationalisation and the post-Fordist stress on flexible production has encouraged states to focus on the supply-side problem of international competitiveness and to attempt to subordinate welfare policy to the demands of flexibility.

Fourth, alongside the trends towards internationalisation and globalisation, we can see the formation of supra-regional triad economies and the re-emergence of regional and local economies within the nation-state. This complex articulation of global–regional–national–local economies is related to the 'hollowing out' of the nation-state as its powers are delegated upwards to supra-regional or international bodies, downwards to regional or local states, or outwards to relatively autonomous cross-national alliances among local states with complementary interests. But a key role still remains for the nation-state as the most significant site of struggle among competing global, triadic, supra-national, national, regional, and local forces. Moreover, given these conflicts, it also has a key role in the development and strengthening of national innovation systems; and the maintenance of social cohesion still depends on the state's capacities to manage these conflicts.

Given these complex and intersecting changes, a new state form would seem to be appropriate to the re-regulation of an emerging accumulation regime. A SWS seems well-suited to this task. For its strategic orientation to innovation takes account of the enormous ramifications of new technologies; its concern with structural competitiveness recognises the changing terms and conditions of international competition as well as its increased significance; its restructuring and reorientation of social reproduction towards flexibility and retrenchment signifies its awareness of the post-Fordist paradigm shift as well as the impact of internationalisation on the primary functions of money and wages; and its complex 'hollowing out' reflects the complex dialectic between globalisation and regionalisation. Thus it seems that the 'hollowed out SWS' could prove structurally congruent and functionally adequate to post-Fordist accumulation regimes.

The SWS could also be seen as having a post-Fordist nature to the extent that its emerging functions resolve (or are held so to do) the crisis-tendencies in the KWS and help to secure the conditions for the post-Fordist virtuous circle to operate. Among the relevant crisis-tendencies in the KWS are its stagflationary impact on the Fordist growth dynamic (especially where state economic intervention is too concerned with maintaining employment in sunset sectors), and its growing fiscal crisis rooted in the ratchet-like expansion of social consumption expenditure. The SWS would seem to address both problems. For not only does it adopt supply-side intervention to promote innovation and structural competitiveness, it also goes beyond the mere retrenchment of social welfare to restructure and subordinate it to market forces. Both functions match the dynamic of the post-Fordist regime.

To avoid the dangers of falling into a teleological analysis of the SWS as the functionally necessitated complement to an emergent post-Fordist labour process, accumulation regime, or social mode of economic regulation, the arguments presented above must be qualified by more concrete and complex analyses of Fordist modes of growth as well as by more substantive work on the crisis mechanisms of the KWS considered as a political regime (for an example of the latter analysis in this context, see Jessop (1992c)). Thus a more detailed analysis of the SWS would need to explore the structural coupling between each type of Fordism and the character of the nation-state and the problems this creates; the complexities of the capital relation in each regime type and its implications for the forms of economic and political struggle over crisis-resolution; the path-dependency of the trajectory out of crisis which emerges in and through such struggles; and the problems that arise when the pre-SWS lacks the capacities to manage the transition. It is in this spirit that the following section offers a brief and preliminary analysis of the British case.

POST-FORDISM AND THE STATE IN BRITAIN

I have argued elsewhere that Britain never had a truly Fordist economy but was characterised instead by 'flawed Fordism' (Jessop, 1989b). More precisely, not only did its economy fail to make a successful transition to a mode of growth based on the virtuous Fordist circle of mass production–rising productivity–rising wages–rising mass consumption–increased investment, by means of mass production; it also failed to find a niche within Atlantic Fordism or the wider global economy that could finance sustainable increases in mass consumption through the growing exports of other types of goods and/or services. In part this failure can be explained in terms of the institutional and organisational failures rooted in earlier periods in British political economy (Elbaum and Lazonick, 1986; Newton and Porter, 1988). But it is also attributable to a lack of core state capacities to contribute to an effective social mode of economic regulation for British Fordism (albeit from a different perspective (Marquand, 1988)). This was associated in turn with a flawed KWS state form which both reflected and helped to sustain this flawed Fordism (Jessop, 1989b; 1992c).

It was a dual crisis of flawed Fordism and a flawed KWS culminating in a deep-seated and far-reaching political crisis that helped trigger the attempts at economic and political transformation pursued in the name of Thatcherism in the 1980s (Jessop *et al.*, 1988). This raises the question whether Thatcherite Britain witnessed a movement towards a post-Fordist state which helped to overcome the contradictions of flawed Fordism and a flawed KWS and thereby consolidate post-Fordism; or whether, on the contrary, it has seen a movement from a flawed Fordism to a 'flawed post-flawed Fordism'. Given that our initial focus is a transitional regime, the key issue in this regard is how far Thatcherism has performed the appropriate tasks noted above.

At first glance a case could be advanced that Thatcherism involved a real attempt to effect a radical transition from a flawed Fordist accumulation mode of growth and a flawed KWS to an effective post-Fordist regime and a neo-liberal variant of the SWS. Once it was secure in power (mid-1982), Thatcherism undeniably, indeed explicitly, engaged in attempts to demolish Fordist regulation of the wage relation, to destroy the main forms of KWS crisis-management, and even to push back the frontiers of the normal form of the KWS. At the same time it gave strong voice to a post-Fordist rhetoric of flexibility and entrepreneurialism in place of the earlier Fordist discourse of productivity and planning. Mere destruction without creation is not enough, however, to create the conditions for post-Fordism. Instead, disembedding and deregulating a crisis-ridden economic order must be accompanied by its re-embedding and re-regulation. Otherwise the destruction of the old social mode of economic regulation would produce an unregulated economic (dis)order which could be defined chronologically as 'post'-Fordist but would nonetheless lack the capacities to resolve for any significant period the crisis-tendencies of its precursor. Radical Thatcherism also attempted such a re-regulation and re-embedding of the accumulation regime. Its principal chosen instruments in this regard were the expansion of purportedly self-regulating markets and the creation of an enterprise culture sustained by a state-sponsored popular capitalism. In short, the social democratic Fordist KWS, with its commitment to full employment and social welfare, was to be replaced with a neo-liberal post-Fordist SWS, characterised by 'market opportunities for all and popular capitalism'. It is my contention that pursuit of this project has signally failed to resolve the interlinked structural crises of British capitalism and its state inherited from a flawed Fordist past. Indeed, the Major government is now confronted with a more deep-seated structural economic crisis but has a much reduced and seriously weakened set of state capacities with which to address it. It is in this context that we can now see some hesitant moves towards a different vision of the SWS.

One creative element in radical Thatcherism was its self-declared aim to complete the blocked modernisation of Britain. In this regard successive Conservative governments pursued a distinctive neo-liberal strategy intended to marketise social relations and create an enterprise culture so that individuals could operate in (and embrace) a market-oriented society. Such a strategy clearly cannot be confined to the (expanding) market economy alone; it must also be extended to the whole ensemble of social institutions, organisations, networks, and norms of conduct which regularise economic relations. This all-embracing tendency is especially clear from 1986 onwards when a near-fatally drifting Thatcher regime rescued itself with a wide-ranging radical programme to re-invigorate civil society as well as regenerate the economy and restructure the state (Jessop *et al.*, 1988). This extended key elements of the neo-liberal accumulation strategy and also supplemented them by an ambitious hegemonic project for the wider society. What had previously been hesitant and halting accompaniments to economic regeneration were accelerated and given a more coherent ideological justification.

In narrow economic terms, the neo-liberal strategy demands changes in the *régulation* (governance) of both the public and private sectors. For the public sector, it involves privatisation, liberalisation, and an imposition of commercial criteria in any residual state sector; for the private sector, it involves deregulation and a new legal and political framework to provide passive support for market solutions. This is reflected in government promotion of 'hire-and-fire', flexi-time, and flexi-wage labour markets; growth of tax expenditures steered by private initiatives based on fiscal subsidies for favoured economic activities; measures to transform the welfare state into a means of supporting and subsidising low wages as well as to enhance the disciplinary force of social security measures and programmes; and the more general reorientation of economic and social policy to the perceived needs of the private sector. Coupled with such measures is a disavowal of social partnership in favour of managerial prerogatives, market forces, and a strong state. Thatcherite neo-liberalism also involves a cosmopolitan approach that welcomes internationalisation of domestic economic space in the form of both outward and inward investment and also calls for the liberalisation of international trade and investment within regional blocs and more generally. Innovation is expected to follow spontaneously from the liberation of the animal spirits of individual entrepreneurs as they take advantage of incentives in the new market-led climate and from the more general government promotion of an enterprise culture. In turn national competitiveness is understood as the aggregate effect of the micro-economic competitiveness of individual firms. Hence there is little state concern to maintain a sufficiently deep and coherent set of core economic competences in the domestic economy and/or adequate national or regional innovation systems to provide the necessary basis for structural competitiveness. In this context local and international state apparatuses are expected to act as relays for a market-led approach to innovation and workfare rather than to play an active and independent role in enhancing and guiding the competitiveness of domestic economic forces in the new world economy.

Even when viewed in relatively narrow economic terms, it is remarkable how wide-ranging has been the neo-liberal onslaught on the legacies of Britain's flawed Fordism. Among many areas which central government targeted for change are: research and development, new technologies, product design, quality control, marketing, industrial relations, labour markets, forms of competition and cooperation, financial and business services, taxation regimes, social security and welfare delivery systems, and education and vocational training. There is also growing interest (not always in neo-liberal form) among local states (and typically subject to centrally imposed constraints) in labour-market policies, education and training, technology transfer, local venture capital, innovation centres, science parks, and so on. In this context the Thatcher government seems to have expected that the newly privatised utility companies would play a key role in building local and regional growth coalitions and thereby act as a relay to take Thatcherite enterprise into local communities.[9] Similar hopes were invested in local business people as they assumed leading roles in the plethora of local quangos and voluntary bodies concerned with economic regeneration and welfare service delivery. In addition to these shifts at central and local level, with their greater emphasis on the supply-side, Thatcherism has also attempted to defuse the political repercussions of the crisis of Fordism and to allocate the economic and social costs of the transition in such a way that its own political base is secured.

The above-mentioned trends in the social mode of regulation have been most important for the halting emergence of neo-liberal SWS activities in Britain. But highlighting these new or stepped-up functions should not blind us to how they are linked to the reorganisation of the state itself. For the latter is also acquiring a radically new form. In part, corresponding to the first criterion for a post-Fordist state, this involves systematic attempts to introduce post-Fordist elements into the state's own *labour process*. This can be seen in the development of new forms of flexibility at work and in the labour market, localised bargaining, decentralisation of functions, etc. But, corresponding in addition to the second criterion for a post-Fordist state, it is also reflected in the changing role of the *state economic sector* and the more general reorganisation of state apparatuses and agencies. This involves more than the abolition of tripartite bodies (such as the National Economic Development Organisation), social-democratic quangos, or labour-controlled metropolitan authorities. It is also evident in such matters as the creation of new supply-side agencies (such as the Training Agency or urban development corporations); the acquisition of new supply-side capacities by existing apparatuses (e.g., Department of 'Enterprise'); the transfer of traditional functions to more enterprise-minded ministries (e.g., urban policy from the Home Office and Environment to Industry, education to Employment); the insistence that local government exercise its newly restricted powers in partnership with business and the 'third sector' (opted-out and voluntary bodies) within limits set by central government; and, accompanying privatisation, new regulatory bodies to supervise private sector monopolies (e.g., Ofgas, Oftel). It is precisely such structural changes in the state system (and not just its functional reorientation) that might justify a claim that a new, strategically selective post-Fordist state was emerging in Britain (Jessop 1989b; 1993b).

Finally, we should note the number of state-sponsored shifts in the wider society intended to promote post-Fordist *societalisation* (corresponding to the fourth possible criterion for defining a post-Fordist state). Some of these are side-effects of the emerging neo-liberal mode of social regulation. This is the case, for example, with the restructuring of education at all levels and its reorientation towards vocational training and 'enterprise'. But other shifts have been the object of explicit state strategies intended to provide a social and cultural basis for a neo-liberal regeneration of the British economy. This pattern is illustrated in various attempts to sponsor popular capitalism through widespread changes in housing tenure, pension provision, wider share ownership, small enterprise schemes, and so on; in the wide range of measures to remodel social institutions along the lines of commercial enterprise, including a concern with value for money and satisfying the demands of consumers, and to encourage the acquisition of enterprising qualities; in the recent emphasis on the potential contribution of 'workfare' to re-integrating the long-term unemployed into a post-Fordist labour process. Also, we can see various measures intended to cope with the social costs and repercussions of the crisis of Fordism and to facilitate a move to a post-Fordist mode of growth. The initial creeping authoritarianism of Thatcherite Britain and the subsequent attempts to legitimate many of the political changes through citizens' charters, league tables, and other demonstrations of 'value-added' can both be included here. So can the displacement of many welfare functions to the 'community' (i.e., voluntary organisations, the patriarchal family, or single women) to reduce the burden of restructuring on the exchequer. However, although some shifts can be partly attributed to deliberate state-sponsored strategies, it would be quite wrong to treat them all as inter-related parts of some well-defined and comprehensive hegemonic project. Instead they often involve small-scale, molecular changes in social organisation and values which emerge as unintended consequences and/or hoped-for side-effects of economic and political restructuring. Many other current changes, of course, are irrelevant, marginal, or contradictory to the consolidation of post-Fordist societalisation.

If many of these changes (especially in the state's role in the social mode of regulation) exemplify the trend towards a neo-liberal SWS, they also illustrate certain features of the 'hollowing out' of the nation-state. They clearly involve the re-articulation of the powers of central and local government in a complex and contradictory process. This combines the centralisation and concentration of some powers (at the expense of elected local authorities – especially those with social-democratic pretensions or a 'loony left' image) and the devolution and fragmentation of others (in and through new non-elected, competitive, and often single-function agencies). The latter often perform significant supply-side functions in economic and social policy, with or without supplementary input from local authorities (Stoker, 1989a). Indeed, especially in more autonomous bodies such as the Welsh and Scottish Development Agencies, they have often departed markedly from neo-liberal prescriptions. But all such bodies are beset to a greater or lesser degree by constraints originating from the centre. Even localised neo-liberal strategies have been undermined by the lack of a supportive national framework, inadequate integration of regional and local economic-development frameworks, short-termism in funding, the volatility and *ad hoccery* of policy-making, and demands that locally determined economic initiatives do not undermine national economic policy (Bovaird, 1992).

The other two dimensions of 'hollowing out' are also discernible in Britain. Thus, notwithstanding Thatcherite hostility to the centralising predilections of the European Commission and the threats of a European super-state, the EC has still come to play a key role in regard to economic and social policy in the intensifying battle for international competitiveness. The Conservatives under Thatcher were enthusiastic supporters of the 'neo-liberal' project to create a single market; they were also somewhat more reluctant partners in various neo-statist initiatives to strengthen (or, at least, defend) Europe's technological competitiveness relative to North America and East Asia; and they have been keen to draw upon (if not to publicise the fact) regional and structural funds to underwrite economic and social spending at home, whether to cushion the impact of the crisis of Fordism in Britain or to finance the infrastructure for an integrated, post-Fordist Europe. There are also signs of increasing interest in collaboration between local and regional authorities in Britain and the Continent for the purposes of urban regeneration and local economic development. In these respects too we find 'hollowing ut' is closely related to supply-side concerns and the promotion of flexibility and competitiveness (Cooke, 1990b; Dawson, 1992; Dyson, 1989).

In concluding this discussion of possible indicators of the restructuring and reorientation of the British state towards a post-Fordist SWS, I would like to stress the real limitations to this transformation in Thatcherite Britain. These are partly rooted in the unpromising terrain of an already flawed Fordism and weak state capacities. But they also stem from the frequent subordination of neo-liberal economic policy to political priorities. Indeed, given the much enhanced decisional autonomy of the Thatcher governments and their support for conviction politics, considerations of party advantage or partisan ideology have often proved incompatible with effective economic intervention. I have argued elsewhere that the economic failure of Thatcherism was related to the increasing primacy in its third term of party political and 'two nations' redistributive considerations at the expense of productivist concerns. Similar problems are now besetting the Major government as it finds itself squeezed politically. On the one hand, it is faced with demands for intervention to counteract a prolonged recession with mounting unemployment and stubborn trade deficits rooted in earlier Thatcherite exacerbation of the structural economic crisis; and, on the other, it needs to cut a growing budget deficit without resort to higher income taxes or interest rates. This is reflected in the inversion (if not yet rejection) of earlier neo-liberal policies. Thus privatisation is once again being driven forward less by long-term productivist concerns than by a short-term desire to limit losses or to raise cash (e.g., coal, rail, mail, and the government's art collection). And, although Major has recently put 'workfare' on the political agenda, his aim seems less to promote labour-market flexibility and competitiveness than to further reduce the drain of unemployment on the exchequer. Short-term political expediency rather than long-term productivist strategy is now in charge and the result is a sense of political drift and economic decay. This is associated in turn with renewed Establishment chatter about the graceful management of national decline rather than the Thatcherite celebration of Britain's economic miracle.

Thatcherism (including 'Thatcherism with a grey face' in the form of Majorism) is presiding over a transition from flawed Fordism to flawed post-Fordism and from a defective KWS to an ineffective SWS.[10] In large part this is attributable to the general unsuitability of a neo-liberal strategy for a transition to post-Fordism in the British context; but it has been made worse by Thatcherism's systematic destruction of alternative state capacities and modes of policy-making and implementation which might well have served to flank, supplement, or substitute for the neo-liberal strategy as the latter's crisis-tendencies and contradictions became evident. Instead Major's government is bereft of supportive social partners and effective dirigiste powers, and thus obliged to fall back on moral exhortation, petty corruption, and prerogative powers to pursue its ideologically muted, *faute de mieux* neo-liberalism.

CONCLUDING REMARKS

The results of my deliberations can be stated quite briefly. First, I have attempted to show that there are serious theoretical difficulties in the currently fashionable fascination with the concept of post-Fordism and, even more obviously, with the notion of a post-Fordist state. Even so, second, I have tried to introduce some conceptual clarification into the discussion of Fordism and post-Fordism and, in this context, to suggest several approaches to the definition of the post-Fordist state in both its transitional and its consolidated guises. In particular, and third, I have suggested that the normal form of the latter can be described as the 'Schumpeterian workfare state'. To some extent this deliberately magnifies, for heuristic purposes, the discontinuities between the Fordist and post-Fordist states. In many cases the contrast will be less marked. Fourth, I have indicated that there can be various forms of post-Fordist state as well as various transitional routes from Fordist to post-Fordist regimes. This is important if one is to avoid the impression that 'there is no alternative' to the neo-liberal variant essayed under Thatcher and Major – especially as the latter has recently been flirting with the idea of 'workfare' in its least claimant-friendly form. Elsewhere we can find neo-corporatist and neo-statist attempts to pioneer the road to post-Fordism. Finally, I have attempted to show that, whatever the prospects may be elsewhere for a successful transition to a post-Fordist welfare state, they are less than bright in Britain. Rather than moving towards an efficient and competitive post-Fordist regime, we seem to be moving further down the international economic hierarchy as flawed post-Fordism replaces flawed Fordism. However, as will be quite evident from the somewhat speculative form of the arguments on this point, much work remains to be done on this issue. But I hope that the various criteria for assessing the development of post-Fordist regimes will provide a useful basis for subsequent work in this area.

The arguments presented above have veered from the highly abstract to the apparently concrete. Thus the first sections of the chapter took the form of a thought-experiment to determine theoretically what would constitute a normal post-Fordist welfare regime. The penultimate section was concerned to apply the arguments presented earlier to the case of Britain during the Thatcher years. There is still much work to be done both theoretically and empirically before the rather heroic (if not foolhardy) claims advanced here can be provisionally accepted. Nonetheless I think there are good grounds for believing that there really is a widespread tendential shift in Europe and 'Europe abroad' from the sort of Keynesian welfare state regimes associated with Atlantic Fordism to the dominance of the sort of Schumpeterian workfare state regimes found in the paradigmatically post-Fordist economies of East Asia and successful regions in other growth poles. The grounds for this belief are twofold: the self-evident crisis of Fordism and the KWS and the remarkable economic success of societies with more flexible accumulation regimes and supply-side oriented states. It is this combination of Fordist crisis in Europe and North America with East Asian success which is reinforcing pressures in the first two triadic growth poles to abandon KWS for Schumpeterian workfare strategies. The growing importance of structural competitiveness is the mechanism which leads me to believe that we will witness the continuing consolidation of the 'hollowed-out Schumpeterian workfare state' in successful capitalist economies. Economic spaces which fail to make this transition in some form or other will fall down the global hierarchy of economic spaces and/or be marginalised. This does not exclude struggles over the future forms of the post-Fordist SWS: it makes them even more imperative.

NOTES

1 On the French regulation approach see Boyer (1990), Dunford (1990) and Jessop (1990a); on 'strategic-relational state theory' see Bertramsen *et al.* (1990) and Jessop (1990b). I am grateful to Colin Hay for comments on an earlier version of this paper.

2 I prefer the term 'social mode of economic regulation' to both the usual French regulationist label (mode of regulation) and that suggested by Peck and Tickell (social mode of regulation) on the grounds that only the first highlights both the manner of regulation and its object. Tickell and Peck's usage conflates the mode of regulation of the economy in its integral sense and the mode of regulation of the wider society in which a specific integral economic order is dominant (Tickell and Peck, 1992).

3 Fordist and post-Fordist societalisation effects will be ignored below. In general they can be seen as derived effects of the dominance of an 'accumulation regime in regulation' and/or as contributing to that dominance.

4 This is one version of the general problem in theories of the bourgeois state: is it a state in capitalist societies or a capitalist state? On this general issue see Jessop (1990b).

5 An exceptional Fordist state would exist where an *ad hoc*, more conjunctural rationality enables state managers to promote Fordist expansion despite major structural discongruities and relatively weak state capacities.

6 This does not exclude other characterisations from different perspectives and/or at different degrees of theoretical concreteness or complexity.

7 Flexibility alone is insufficient to define post-Fordism: all accumulation regimes contain elements of flexibility and, indeed, flexible specialisation

regimes also pre-dated Fordism (Piore and Sabel, 1984). The novel element in post-Fordism is the way in which flexibility is shaped and enhanced by a new techno-economic paradigm which institutionalises the search for permanent innovation.

8 To posit two distinct types of post-Fordist state that succeed one another (transitional and consolidated) would repeat the structuralist fallacy of positing a transitional mode of production between successive normal modes of production, with the former defined by its structurally inscribed function of securing the transition between the latter (cf. Hindess and Hirst, 1975: 262–87). This is why I refer to transitional *regimes* with indeterminate form and a determinate normal *state*. Even the latter, however, can have variant forms (see below).

9 I owe this point to discussions with John Goddard.

10 There may still be a residual functionalism in so far as it is assumed that post-Fordism and the SWS are the most appropriate forms of economic and political organisation for the future. This establishes a fixed reference point from which to calculate the dysfunctionality of some state forms.

3 The politics of the modernisation of the UK welfare state

Paul Hoggett

INTRODUCTION

In 1987 I wrote a brief essay which, along with a piece written by Robin Murray in the same year (Murray, 1987), appears to have been the first attempt to link the emerging debates around economic restructuring to developments in the public sector. My decision to make the link was prompted by two factors. First of all I had been interested in long wave theory since the 1970s, when Mandel's (1975) work on the matter had obtained some impact upon what was then the revolutionary left in the UK. The importance of long wave theory to some of the Left at that time (Tarbuck, 1991) was that it provided a framework to think the unthinkable – the possibility that capitalism, far from moving towards internal collapse, contained the possibility of revolutionising itself, that is, for embarking upon new eras of development and modernisation. Even then, however, it was clear that the predominant accounts of long waves, past and present, tended towards a technological determinism (Hoggett, 1979). What was required was an analysis through which the human subject could be envisaged as both determined and self-determining. The answer seemed to lie in the concept of crisis, for if each downswing of a long wave corresponded to a period in which structural contradictions were acute and in which previous solutions had become current problems, then periods of crisis were also periods of uncertainty, innovation and experimentation in all realms of life. To put it another way, periods of crisis are always periods in which the potential for change based upon human choice is at its maximum.

The second, and more immediate, factor which prompted me to think of the possible link between developments in the public sector and broader processes of social change, was my experience of working alongside councillors and officers in Islington for much of the early and mid-1980s as they attempted to introduce their decentralisation programme. The problem

I encountered was that by about 1986 the initiative was already losing its cutting edge. The concept of a new form of participatory democracy was beginning to wither as the programme of change met not only with opposition from trade unionists and managers within the bureaucracy itself but, more importantly, began to fade as a vision held by several of the key change agents in Islington. Yet again I found myself having to face the unthinkable – that this remarkable innovation may in another ten years resemble nothing much more than a particularly modern and progressive form of public service management. For it seemed to me that this kind of internally decentralised, team-based organisation was one to be found increasingly in the private sector. The essay I wrote in 1987 (Hoggett, 1987) drawing upon some of the early literature on private sector restructuring processes, attempted to draw this analogy in a persuasive manner. With hindsight one could say that it was less a work of analysis than a work of the imagination. It probably did make me sound like a technological determinist (Cochrane, 1991; Painter, 1991b) – a possibility that I hope I may have corrected in a later article I wrote on the same theme (Hoggett, 1990). However, there are a number of issues which I feel require further clarification and a number of arguments put forward by Cochrane and Painter that I would like to take issue with.

FORCES AND RELATIONS OF PRODUCTION

Several analyses of contemporary developments (e.g., Painter, 1991b) draw heavily upon regulation theory. This approach draws its name from the idea that the capitalist mode of production contains within itself modes of regulating its own internal contradictions. One sometimes senses a certain abstractness and woolliness, however, in some of this work – sometimes the regulatory forms are perceived as more or less synonymous with the state, sometimes they are not. Moreover, there often appears to be a certain coyness in specifying the concrete contradictions which require regulation – are they timeless or contingent to a particular regime of accumulation, are they really contradictions in the Hegelian sense or merely oppositions and conflicts? Perhaps more importantly, however, I am concerned that by focusing upon the mode of regulation our attention is drawn to contradictions within the social relations of production (i.e. ultimately between capital and labour) and away from the contradiction between the forces and relations of production. It is often forgotten, but when Marx and Engels reflected upon the 'contradictions of capitalism' they were concerned to include both. There is a danger that we lose sight of this. It is quite possible to place regulation theory within an analytical framework which includes the forces and relations dialectic (Dunford, 1990).

Many writers appear to have shrunk from an exploration of the role of productive forces in social and economic development, no doubt out of fear of being accused of technological determinism. Certainly, there is a danger that 'productive forces' can be conceptually reduced to technology, that is why it is necessary to think of 'technique' in its broadest sense. Marx's position was simply this, that under capitalism our knowledge of how to do things always tended to outstrip our aesthetic and moral knowledge.

A number of writers (Giddens, 1979; Meiksins-Wood, 1984; Young, 1976) indicate that this tendency for the productive forces to constantly develop is specific to capitalism; it was not a characteristic of any previous mode of production. As Young demonstrates, this dynamic is inherent to the logic of capital accumulation:

> the drive to produce capital and produce surplus-value on an extended scale . . . [This] is the law for capitalist production, imposed by incessant revolutions in the methods of production themselves, by the depreciation of existing capital always bound up with them, by the general competitive struggle and the need to improve production and expand its scale merely as a means of self-preservation and under penalty of ruin.
>
> (Young, 1976: 229)

No preceding society carried within its heart this maniacal tendency towards growth and development.

This does mean that under capitalism productive forces tend to push ahead of productive relations. But this is not always the case. The Russian revolution, for example, catapulted a social form way beyond the productive forces which surrounded it – hence no doubt the Bolsheviks' desire to introduce electrification as rapidly as possible. Hence also their desire to introduce Taylorist methods of production – an unfortunate confusion of modernisation and a particular form which capitalist modernisation assumed. As I have argued recently, which kind of technique is adopted by a given society is always a matter of social choice:

> the development of the productive forces themselves is not arbitrary or serendipitous, that is, it is not the outcome of some endogenous logic presumed to exist within the process of scientific discovery. Not only does the dynamic of capital accumulation fuel scientific discovery, but, moreover, it influences the form of the discovery process itself. Take Taylorism/Fordism as an example, such a 'technological style' is only conceivable within certain forms of society. This is only partly to do with the level of development, it is also to do with 'form of culture' – what kind of culture is able to conceive of, and champion, the reduction

of living and creative human powers to the inanimate and programmed reflexes of a machine?

(Hoggett, 1991a)

From a long wave perspective, each periodic downswing (for example the inter-war years) is equivalent to a situation in which the existing mode of regulation has become an obsolete container for the new productive forces. Dunford (1990) and Clegg (1990) point out that a variety of industrial trajectories and corresponding modes of regulation will be compatible with the new productive forces. Clegg likens the latter to a kind of template from which the new trajectories can be moulded. Which trajectories are adopted will depend upon social choice and struggle. This is not just a question of the ability of labour to insert its requirements into the restructuring process, it is also a broader social issue for familial and kinship traditions, enduring cultural patterns and customs, etc., which will have a crucial bearing upon the kind of trajectory 'chosen' (Clegg refers to this in terms of the concept of 'cultural embeddedness' (see Granovetter, 1985)).

The key question for an analysis of developments in the public and private sectors in the UK is, therefore, which trajectory are we embarking upon?

THE LOCAL STATE AND THE WELFARE STATE

As Painter (1991b) points out, the 'local state' is not straightforwardly a part of the mode of regulation nor a part of the organisation of production, it is clearly an element of both. We should be careful, however, about the terms we use. One of the problems with the notion of the 'local state' is that it sometimes tends to separate out local government from the rest of the welfare state – e.g. the National Health Service, the social security system, etc. If our primary concern, as I believe it should be, is to understand how both the organisational form and role of the welfare state is changing during these times, then we need to understand that the 'local state' is just one element of the phenomenon we are seeking to study. However, irrespective of whether our focus is the local or welfare state, it is clear that such institutions are both in the business of producing goods and services and are an element of the mode of regulation. They are also, crucially, an aspect of the hegemonic structure of society playing an important ideological and legitimatory role. It is not clear to me whether regulation theorists include such hegemonic structures within the mode of regulation; Dunford (1990) argues that they should be treated separately.

Painter (1991b) suggests that during the Fordist era the sphere of collective consumption became socialised precisely because human and other services were not amenable to mass-production techniques. Both he and Cochrane doubt, therefore, that local government services ever really were organised upon mass-production lines. I would agree with Painter's initial premise here but this did not mean that progressive attempts were not made to model public service organisations upon the lines of the industrial bureaucracies of that period. The concept of management came late to the public services of all developed countries and when, in the 1970s, it did arrive, the assumptions and methods it brought were deeply bureaucratic and mechanistic (see Alford (1975) and Heydebrand (1977) on the USA). In the context of British Local Government, the 1974 reorganisation and the introduction of corporate management practices in the following years can be seen as part of this process. The irony of this was that British local government was busily engaged in adopting the form of the modern industrial bureaucracy precisely at the moment when in the private sector it was entering a period of crisis and supersession.

However, I do not feel we can fully understand the massification of public services in the UK during this period simply in terms of the impact of Fordist methods and assumptions. Traditions of centralisation, standardisation and uniformity were a crucial element of Labourism (Hoggett and McGill, 1988) and contributed greatly to the receptiveness of the welfare system to bureaucratic approaches. On the other hand, that Labourism drew some of its character from Fordism can also not be doubted. We need to think of an interactive, if not iterative, relationship between the two, out of which the peculiarly statist model of UK welfare emerged. Chamberlayne (1992) usefully reminds us that, with the exception of the Nordic states, no other European nations manifested a state monopoly of welfare service provision to the same degree as post-war Britain.

To summarise, it was precisely because human services were difficult to rationalise, that, if costs were to be kept under some kind of control, the need to rationalise them was so great. But the attempt to control professional service workers in this way was almost doomed to failure, given the discrepancy between the bureaucratic and professional modes of control. The point about the latter is that, in its strong form, described by Johnson (1972) as 'collegiate', professionalism resembles a pre-Fordist mode of organisation of the labour process. Hence my view that the welfare state was a 'mongrel' form of organisation 'based on an uneasy marriage between a pre-Fordist craft (professional) productive system and a Taylorised (rational-bureaucratic) system' (Hoggett, 1987: 223). In a later paper (Hoggett, 1990) I attempted to extend this line of analysis by suggesting that the failure to develop bureaucratic methods of controlling professional labour within the state was partly responsible for the inability to keep state spending under control. In the context of the UK, one can make a strong argument to say that the overriding objective behind the development of competition legislation, internal markets, devolved agencies, and so on has been cost control – certainly, the evidence available tends to suggest that, of all the possible impacts (e.g. extending choice, creating a share-holding democracy, increasing competition, etc.) of government legislation, the impact on containing costs has been the least ambiguous (Marsh, 1991; Walsh, 1991). It seems to me that the new strategy of control is quite different to the previous bureaucratic one: rather than try and control professionals by managers, you convert professionals into managers (i.e. by giving them budgets or by setting them adrift as quasi-autonomous business units).

INTERPRETING NEW DEVELOPMENTS

One of the methodological problems we face in this area, and one I am not sure I have any answers for, concerns the difficulty in knowing which of three possible interpretive schemas to use when considering a particular development. On the one hand, there is the danger of confusing the underlying template with one of its particular forms. For example, is financial deregulation a basic characteristic of post-Fordism or simply an expression of the neo-Liberal form of post-Fordism? And what about the withdrawal of state intervention in economic development, for as Clegg (1990) indicates, state interventionism appears to have been crucial to Japanese economic progress in the 1970s and 1980s and continues to be so.

Another possibility is that developments (such as mass unemployment) may simply be the expression of crisis and recession. Again, the advantage of long wave theory is that it indicates how the downswing will always be a period of slow growth, stagnation or even regression. The last great downswing during the inter-war period was also a period of mass unemployment and social upheaval. We should, therefore, be wary of announcing that the age of full employment is over; it could be that, if and when the new upswing occurs, the present forms of mass unemployment evaporate.

The third possibility is that developments are simply attributable to deliberate governmental intervention. A key analytical task is, therefore, to distinguish the particular way in which political strategies intersect with underlying processes of restructuring. In a previous paper (Hoggett, 1990) I tried hard to distinguish between what I felt to be three characteristics of the basic template of post-Fordism – 'the progressive decentralisation of production under conditions of rising flexibility and centralised strategic control' (Hoggett, 1990: 5) – and the particular way in which successive

Conservative administrations in the UK have sought to shape the process of restructuring. Specifically, I suggested that they had given emphasis to:

1 the development of time and pay flexibilities (but not skill flexibilities) by breaking down national pay bargaining structures and creating a secondary public service labour market;
2 the promotion of forms of external rather than internal decentralisation or, where the latter was undertaken as in the Local Management in Schools (LMS) initiative, seeing this as the prelude to externalisation; and
3 the weakening and residualising of local government and the rudimentary democratic structures residing at district level within the NHS, by concentrating strategic control within central government or dissipating it into a myriad disaggregated local agencies and service units (Hoggett, 1990: 49).

Of these three strategies, it is the latter I would like to briefly focus on. It now seems quite clear that the aim of the Conservatives is to abolish entirely the strategic role of district-based health and education authorities, as formal planning systems become displaced by the market behaviour of parents, schools and GPs.[1] I have a strong suspicion that, even under the new forms of post-bureaucratic control, such arrangements will prove organisationally untenable, that local education authorities (LEAs) having been abolished, will have to be re-invented.[2] In our desire to discern underlying patterns, there is a danger that we interpret everything as an expression of deeper trends. The creation of markets in health care and education – are they internal or external markets, who knows any longer whether opted-out units are inside or outside the boundaries of the state? – does not appear to borrow from the new organisational logics at all. Can you imagine a private firm relinquishing its strategic control over devolved operational units in the same way that District Health Authorities (DHAs) and Local Education Authorities (LEAs) are having to do? It may well be that at this point (and there may prove to be others) the ideological predilections of the Conservatives have taken them into forms of experimentation which lead only to chaos.

STRUCTURE AND ROLE

Cochrane and Painter pointed to a weakness in my early papers, which were preoccupied with understanding changes occurring in the structure of the state to the detriment of an analysis of changes to its role. Thinking about this, what has most interested me is not so much changes in structure (for example, decentralisation) but rather changes in the technology of control. I am becoming increasingly convinced that it's not so much devolved control as 'remote' control which appears to be superseding bureaucratic control as the preferred method of regulating institutional life.[3] That is why radical processes of internal and external decentralisation can occur at the same time as the centralisation of command (hence LMS and the National Curriculum). I am not convinced that the Conservatives have the ability to make a success of this strategy, nevertheless their intent seems clear. Wherever you look now in the welfare state, semi-autonomous units appear to be springing up.[4] Give managers and staff control over resources, make them accountable for balancing the books, add a framework of performance targets, and perhaps a few core values and mission statements, finally add a dash of competition and there you have it – a disaggregated, self-regulating form of public service production. Bearing in mind this possibility of a radical shift in the technology of control, I wish to switch my line of analysis away from changes in the organisation of the labour process within the state to changes in the role of the state. I found Cochrane's (1991) notion of the local state as the defender of enterprise a rather narrow concept and not very convincing. It does seem as if the brief splutter of the enterprise culture is now over, at least in the UK. My feeling is that with hindsight, perhaps in a decade's time, we shall see this as a brief and fairly ephemeral blip upon an otherwise consistent process of deindustrialisation. The theme of 'the decline of Britain' has re-emerged on the left recently. In a series of recent articles in at least one journal, Britain has been described in terms of a 'rentier economy' (MacShane, 1990), a 'regressed economy' (Hoggett, 1992) and even as a 'Newly Deindustrialising Country' (NDIC) (Lee, 1992). The point is that, whilst all of the developed capitalist economies may be going through a prolonged wave of crisis and relative stagnation, within the UK this conjunctural crisis simply compounded the organic crisis of British capitalism which has been underway for several decades (viz. the 'British disease' of the 1960s and 1970s).

This brings us to the issue that I touched upon at the very beginning of this chapter, namely the different forms of industrial trajectory possible within the template of 'post-Fordism'. Here I was particularly struck by Lane's (1988) comparison of flexibility strategies emerging in (what was) West Germany and the UK in the 1980s. I felt that she gave a convincing account of the way in which, in Britain, flexibility strategies have given emphasis to time and pay rather than skill flexibilities, something she describes as a kind of neo-Taylorism. Such a strategy certainly fuels the impulse towards the creation of a dual labour market but within the context of general social decline and deindustrialisation – and this seems to be the crucial difference between Britain and the USA. As a consequence, social divisions are less pronounced than in the USA, not because social groups dependent upon secondary labour markets are not impoverished, but because many of those working within the primary labour market are themselves relatively impoverished.

In this light, I would concur with those, such as Stoker (1989b), who point to the creation of a two-tier welfare system as a possible direction for the post-Fordist state in Britain. However, because of the relatively low skill levels, low educational requirements, poor wages and conditions of many within the primary labour market, I feel that it may well be less easy to create a dual welfare system because of the relatively large social layers still without any capacity to exercise effective choice within a more market-orientated and pluralistic system. In this context, the defeat of the poll tax as a result of direct action by millions of people (see Bagguley, this volume) may well prove to have been a significant block to the further exacerbation of inequalities within the welfare system. However, initial attempts to evaluate the impact of government reforms in education and health do suggest that the creation of a two-tier welfare system remains a real possibility (Le Grand, 1992).

If such forms of social polarisation are an inherent feature of the post-Fordist mode of regulation, then we must develop an appropriate way of conceptualising that social layer which becomes increasingly excluded from primary labour, housing and educational markets. Many object that the concept of the 'underclass' is too tainted by its usage by the political right in the USA; this may be valid but it is incumbent upon such critics to develop an alternative. Whatever analytical devices we use to describe this socially excluded layer, the issue of social control in relation to it appears to be a key problematic for the coming period.

Now the interesting thing about technologies of control, of course, is that they are potentially as pertinent to the way in which social order on the streets is exercised as they are to the way in which control over the labour process in maintained. That is why there is value in insisting upon the intimate link between the nature of a society's productive forces and the character of its social relations of production. Could it be that the basic paradigm of social control in the coming period will also draw upon models of self-regulating systems, and of remote rather than proximate monitoring and intervention?

It strikes me that in both Britain and the USA the dominant paradigm of social control in the 1960s and 1970s was incorporational – that is, the state dealt with 'dangerous elements' primarily through attempts to *include* them (culturally, politically and administratively). This no longer seems to be the case. The new forms of social control seem to be based much more upon processes of political and spatial *exclusion*. I was struck by a comment made recently by Alibhai-Brown (1992:12): 'it was in America, a couple of years ago, that a Harvard professor said to me: "We are starting to get rid of the race problem. We are swallowing up the bright ones, and building high fences around the rest so they will eat each other up"'. In his study of Los Angeles, Mike Davis (1990: 223–60) uses the phrase 'spatial apartheid' to describe the exclusion of Blacks and Latinos from desirable business and residential areas, a process which literally includes the construction of walls and other physical barriers to keep what he calls 'the underclass "Other"' out. The biggest paradox, of course, is the nature of the commodity – drugs – which has brought a certain kind of perverse self-regulation to many of these communities.[5]

Clearly, in Britain the underclass is less racialised and the drugs economy does not yet play the role that it does in many USA cities. Nevertheless, the spatial isolation and exclusion of the underclass in Britain is quite striking. In a city like Bristol, for example, the 'cordon sanitaire' around the inner area of St Paul's is stronger today than it has ever been, whilst the outer city estates of Hartcliffe and Lawrence Weston are literally physically decoupled from the rest of the city. Such places are out of sight and therefore out of mind; there is virtually no social or physical mobility here, people are 'locked-in' to such spatial communities. My hypothesis is that rioting and lawlessness in such areas is seen less and less as a social problem requiring policy action. It may soon be useful to think in terms of 'collapsed communities'.

The underclass therefore appears to have become beset by processes of social implosion and fragmentation. At the same time, processes of globalisation (of production, capital, communications and culture) appear to coincide with their opposite – the explosion of what Bauman (1990a) described as 'neo-tribalism' (see also Castells (1983) for the notion of 'metropolitan tribalism'). For my part, our recent analysis of neighbourhood participation in Islington and Tower Hamlets has convinced me that to speak of 'empowerment' in the context of fragmented city communities is plain daft. But the project of creating public spaces in which communication might occur across group boundaries seems to me to be more vital than ever in the coming period. There is a grave danger that both government policy and broader patterns of social change will lead to a situation where the notion of 'the common good' is lost altogether amidst the uproar of defended groups, particular interests and incommensurable identities.

NOTES

1 Since the 1992 election it does seem that the government intends to focus the 'purchasing role' at the GP level rather than the district level.

2 It is interesting to note in this light that in Bromley, where the majority of secondary schools have now opted out, the heads of the opted-out schools now meet on a regular basis and it is not unknown for the Head of Schools in the Borough to attend also.

3 Since completing the first draft of this chapter I was intrigued to note that a recent Audit Commission (1993) review of the Housing Benefit system was entitled *Remote Control: the Administration of Housing Benefits*!

4 For example, hospital trusts, GP budgets, the decanting of central professional services into quasi-business units, locally managed schools, internally decentralised service departments, the newly devolved district structures within the already devolved Benefits Agency and so on.

5 The 25,000 plus black males who were murdered in the USA last year is an extraordinary statistic!

4 Social relations, welfare and the post-Fordism debate

Fiona Williams

INTRODUCTION

At a simple level the application of the post-Fordist analysis to welfare suggests that changes in the organisation of both production and consumption in the wider economy have influenced and even been reproduced within the provision of welfare: mass production to flexible production; mass consumption to diverse patterns of consumption; production-led to consumer-led; from mass, universal needs met by monolithic, bureaucratic/professional-led provision to the diversity of individual needs met by welfare pluralism, quasi-markets, reorganised welfare work and consumer-sovereignty. This idea offers us an important analytical leverage. It can provide us with an understanding of the restructuring of welfare grounded in economic changes operating at both global and local levels. It has the capacity to take us beyond the nation-bound analyses of welfare which have seen this restructuring simply as the consequence of new right or neo-liberal policies and ideologies which can be simply resolved by a return to Beveridge-type policies. It also forces us to think about the new demands upon welfare that have emerged. Ideally it should enable us to disentangle the social policies of the new right from the economic forces which both impel and constrain them (Jessop, 1991b; this volume; Pierson, this volume). And the conceptual shorthand of post-Fordism which signifies the economic changes occurring at the international level may in addition provide a useful reference point for a comparison of the variety of responses of different welfare regimes to these changes (Esping-Andersen, 1990).

However, the application of post-Fordist analyses to social institutions and social changes has yielded a number of methodological and substantive problems. This chapter aims to develop the critique of the analytical limitations of the post-Fordist debate in its application to developments in welfare since 1945. It examines the two main ways in which the Fordist/

post-Fordist dichotomy is applied to welfare and argues that neither provides an adequate account of the social relations of welfare. One of the reasons for this, it will be argued, is because most post-Fordist analyses have emerged from an unreconstructed political economy approach to the organisation of labour which is then carried into an understanding of the welfare state. By 'unreconstructed' I mean the inability to account for (except perhaps in a functionally consequential way) the significance of social relations other than class, particularly the social relations of gender and of 'race'. This omission is particularly serious for any study of the welfare state (or welfare regimes) for it is in this area that the social relations not only of class, but of gender and 'race' – not to mention age, disability and sexuality – are most apparent. These relations underpin welfare policies, their outcomes, the organisation of labour within the welfare state, the delivery of services, political pressures and ideologies, and patterns of consumption. The final part of the chapter examines the conditions and discourses of diversity within recent developments in the British welfare state. It will be suggested that we need to be aware of these developments as the result of more complex and contradictory forces than simply those identified by post-Fordist analyses.

DIFFERENT THEORISATIONS OF POST-FORDISM AND WELFARE

Post-Fordism is marked by its own diversity of approaches from the normative to the critical to the prescriptive (Bagguley, 1991a). In this section I briefly summarise different theoretical approaches to post-Fordism before identifying the different ways these approaches take account of, or apply their analyses to, the welfare state.

Theories of post-Fordism

Bagguley (1991a) and Elam (1990) both provide useful classifications of the different approaches to post-Fordism. Bagguley identifies three schools of theory. The first is the French 'regulation school' of Marxist political economy exemplified by the work of Aglietta (1979). The focus of this work is an analysis of the ways in which capitalism at an international level survives its self-destructive crises and the implications for this of capital–labour relations. This process involves two dynamics: the regime of accumulation and the mode of regulation. The first dynamic refers to the way in which capital is accumulated and, put simply, the second represents the protective measures taken to ensure the first, or to overcome the crises with which it is faced. In these terms Fordism represented a particular combination of these dynamics through the introduction in the immediate post-war period of mass-production techniques along with the development of mass consumption and mass trade unionism. By the late 1960s and early 1970s, however, a crisis of Fordism developed where the dynamics of some of the key features of the Fordist regime locked together to produce an inflexibility of capitalist development and a rigidity in the movement of labour which inhibited continued accumulation. Post-Fordism (or neo-Fordism as Aglietta terms it) represents an attempt to overcome this crisis by creating new forms and areas of production and consumption, more specialised and flexible working patterns, new forms of management and limited union negotiating power.

The second school – the 'institutionalist school' – is based on the work of Piore and Sabel (1984). The focus here is on the way markets change. So, according to this school, Fordism is characterised by mass markets and the crisis of Fordism is marked by the fragmentation of the core markets in the major capitalist economies. This economically determinist view is tempered by an emphasis upon technological change which is seen as being shaped by social struggles. Unlike the regulation school which identifies new forms of technology with new possibilities for capital accumulation, the institutional school sees here the possibilities for new forms of innovation and communalism.

The 'managerialist school' is the third approach. Here, the development of the 'flexible firm' is associated with the emergence of core and periphery workers – the former highly skilled, well-paid and permanent and the latter part-time, short-term, temporary and low-paid. Atkinson and Meager (1986), representatives of this school, identify technical change as the key agent for this new flexibility: new technologies and production systems force into existence new forms of the organisation of labour and more efficient labour processes. However also crucial, in this view, is the development of a new managerialism able to initiate flexibility and respond quickly to new opportunities.

Elam's three-fold classification of Fordist/post-Fordist theories follows similar lines, but he is more concerned to elicit the theoretical adequacy of each approach. In his view, the second two of the approaches described above are found wanting. The institutional school because of its economic determinism – markets feature as the central agent of change. The managerialist school (Elam's nearest equivalent is what he calls the Neo-Schumpeterian perspective) because of its technological determinism – changes in technology are deemed to herald changes in the organisation of production. By contrast the regulation school is able to juggle with the shifting relationship between economic changes, political forces and institutional transformation as the key factors determining change. It does this through its conceptual inclusion of both a regime of accumulation and a mode of regulation. By articulating these two dynamics it becomes possible to create an analysis which can, on the one hand, describe the international dimensions of changes in the economy and, on the other, the specific responses of national economies. It can analyse, Elam (1990: 24) suggests, 'the conjuncture of general and particular determinants of crisis and transformation'. Furthermore, in keeping with its more politicised analysis, rather than seeing the features of post-Fordism as inevitable necessities or pre-givens, the future shape of post-Fordism is left open-ended: 'the new rule-book of capitalist life [is seen] as only partially-written with room for many co-authors' (Elam, 1990: 34). However, is even this theoretical adequacy sufficient when it comes to an analysis of the 'post-Fordist welfare state'? What rules and which authors are referred to? These are questions I shall return to.

POST-FORDIST APPROACHES TO WELFARE

There have been two main ways in which the welfare state has been drawn into post-Fordist theories. The first has been to use Fordism, the crises of Fordism and post-Fordism as the framework in which to analyse the development of the welfare state in various industrialised countries since 1945 and, more particularly, the restructuring of welfare in the 1980s and 1990s. This approach is best exemplified by the work of Jessop (1990a; 1991a,b) and others (Hirsch, 1991; Kosonen, 1991). The second approach has examined how far the key features of post-Fordism are being reproduced within welfare institutions and the local state as part of welfare restructuring. The work of Hoggett (1987; 1991b) and Murray (1991b) is significant here. I have identified these two approaches as first, the neo-marxist approach and second, the radical technological approach.

The *neo-marxist approach* attempts to provide an understanding of the restructuring of welfare states which has taken place in the different industrialised countries since the 1980s in relation to the crisis of Fordism. The key steps of the analysis, as represented by Jessop are as follows: the Keynesian welfare state played a central role within Fordism, for through it the interests of capital and labour were secured by a system of welfare which guaranteed a minimum social wage, full employment and health and welfare provision. However, the welfare state was also implicated in the crisis of Fordism – the crisis, that is, to establish a new regime of accumulation regulated and secured through not only economic but social, political and ideological means. One reason for this was that whilst the economic growth of Fordism created the tax revenues to fund welfare expansion, this very expansion contributed to some of the rigidities of capital and labour which were from the late 1960s central to Fordism's crisis. For example, in so far as welfare provision gave the working class greater economic security, it also strengthened organised labour. This in turn meant wages grew faster than productivity and made attempts to restructure labour processes, move labour or restrain rising wages difficult. In addition, the costs of welfare provision also grew as did the range and articulation of needs which the welfare state was set up to meet.

The restructuring of welfare, which in Britain has been developed by a neo-liberal government, is therefore seen not simply as a way of cutting social expenditure costs nor merely of ensuring conditions of economic growth and accumulation, but as part of a search for a new mode of regulation. For example, two key features of the shift to post-Fordism – the flexibility of labour and labour processes and the polarisation between core and periphery workers – have major implications for the reorganisation of social security and taxation systems. At the same time, these two processes are also associated with the fragmentation of the working class and a limited potential for full, continuous employment, and with that any possibility for the sort of class compromise upon which the Keynesian Welfare State was based.

At this point, since according to this analysis, post-Fordism has not yet arrived, it is only possible to speculate what forms the post-Fordist welfare state might take. Jessop suggests three possibilities based on neo-liberalism, neo-corporatism and neo-statism. What is common to all of these, though delivered in different ways, is a subordination of social policies to economic ends – for example, in the neo-statist model, there would be an increased role of the state in promoting labour market and skill flexibility.[1] Finally, Jessop considers in a rather conjectural way, the possibilities of post-Fordism being introduced into the welfare state in terms of new labour processes, new products, and shifts in the balance of private and public sectors.

Below I shall look in greater detail at Jessop's understanding of the welfare state and particularly at his (limited) account of the role of gender and 'race' in the development of welfare through the post-war period. At this point however, I want to pick up the last point about post-Fordism within welfare, for this is the focus of the second approach to post-Fordism and welfare, to which I now turn.

The *radical technological approach* exemplified by Murray's work shares with the 'institutionalist school' mentioned earlier an optimistic view of what post-Fordism might bring, particularly in relation to the welfare state (Murray, 1991b). According to Murray, the post-war welfare state borrowed the ideas and methods of industrial Fordism:

Progressive architects tried to apply Ford's methods to housing, schools and hospitals. They designed basic models, and then standardised the components and the process of construction. The lack of variety was justified in terms of economy and equality and became bound up with the welfare principle of 'universality', the availability of standard rights and services for all . . . Alongside the standardisation went the ideal of scale, the bigger, the cheaper. London's mental hospitals looked like large factories in the green belt.

(Murray, 1991b: 22)

In terms of the organisation of work, the bureaucratic, hierarchical and centralised structure of management and the remoteness of services to users – all followed the Fordist model. Murray also notes the problems in applying the model wholesale to welfare services – for example, in the resistance of autonomous or semi-autonomous professionals and unionised administrative and technical workers to job standardisation, or in the highly centralised and remote power of ministries and parliament – and so prefers to describe this traditional form of the modern state as 'semi-Fordist'. In this analysis, the neo-liberal restructuring of welfare is seen, not as a post-Fordist response to the crisis in Fordism, but rather as an attempt to roll back the state and cut costs by strengthening the Fordist elements of welfare. Part of this project includes the de-skilling of jobs, systems of performance-related pay, restructuring of management control, the shift of the role of the local authority from provider to purchaser and, essentially, the introduction of the contract. The limitations of the new right project thus lie in its attempt to create a new-style state based on an outdated and discredited model of management. By contrast, Murray suggests that a socially valued, decentralised and equitable, democratic, and user-led public service could be possible through the development of some of the elements of post-Fordist methods of management and production – an open system of organisation, a skilled and cohesive labour force, decentralised autonomous working groups, accessible methods of information gathering, processing and reporting.

Hoggett's work (1987; 1991b) also attempts to use the Fordist/post-Fordist dichotomy as an interpretative schema through which to understand the changes taking place within welfare. His particular focus is on the way productive *forces* (as distinct from productive *relations*) develop. These forces refer to the methods, techniques or technologies used in production and are determined not simply through the development of methods or technologies themselves, but by the nature of existing social and economic conditions and conflicts.[2]

In terms of these productive forces, the shift from Fordism to post-Fordism within industry is characterised by a shift from bureaucratic supervision to 'delegation, participation and team work organised within a subtle framework of increasingly computerised control systems' (Hoggett, 1987: 222). And it is this shift that Hoggett sees mirrored within the restructuring of welfare. One example he gives in this earlier work is of the contribution of new technologies to programmes of decentralisation in the early 1980s within Labour-controlled local authority housing departments. Whilst on the one hand acknowledging the competing ideologies contained within the notion of 'decentralisation' (from cost-cutting and rationalisation, to an attack on institutional power of the bureaucratic unresponsiveness of the welfare state), Hoggett sees in this move the new organisational and managerial forms attributed to post-Fordism (neighbourhood offices, devolved budgets, powers over selection and recruitment, etc.), with one of its chief functions being the collecting, processing and distribution of information. He also acknowledges that there is nothing intrinsically progressive in these new administrative and productive forms, because the struggle to tie them to a political objective still has to be waged. Thus, paradoxically,

> Decentralised systems could become a vehicle for the exercise of greater *control* over front-line staff, consumers and communities unless the secondary political objective (the redistribution of power between provider organisation and consumers) is given much greater priority than it has been so far.
>
> (Hoggett, 1987: 226)

More recently, Hoggett (this volume) offers a more qualified view of the nature of post-Fordism, noting that the characteristics attributed to post-Fordism are themselves subject to variation, but his analysis is similar: that changes in the 'technology of control' mirror, and are mirrored by, the new controlling aspects of welfare. The new semi-autonomous organisational units of the welfare services – hospital trusts, locally managed schools, GP budgets etc. – operate as disaggregated and self-regulating forms of welfare production. However, since these decentralised forms operate within an increasingly centralised system of command (e.g. the National Curriculum) this results in a form of 'remote' control. Hoggett speculates that this remote control is reflected in the way social control is exercised over an increasingly alienated section of society who are part of the impoverished secondary labour market. Increasingly such communities are subject less to direct control and more to social and spatial exclusion and the expectation of self-regulation. In this way he attempts to connect changes in the nature of Britain's productive forces to changes in the social relations of production.

DEVELOPING A CRITIQUE

The variants of the Fordist/post-Fordist analysis have been subjected to a number of different criticisms, some of which apply to one variant rather than another. Some of these criticisms are levelled at the misuse of what is essentially an ideal-type methodology: for example, Cochrane (1991) argues that as an ideal-type analysis it cannot tell us about the dynamics of change. Others suggest that the method may prevent us from allowing for the diversity of (non-post-Fordist) responses to the crisis in Fordism either internationally or regionally (Painter, 1991b) or where apparently post-Fordist methods have not given rise to post-Fordist characteristics (Cochrane, this volume; Pierson, this volume). In addition, it has been argued that the analysis is reductionist: it reduces changes in welfare (or social and cultural change) to economic and technological imperatives and ignores the significance of political struggles and shifts in the balance of power in generating, resisting or permitting change (Rustin, 1989).

Pollert, in an argument mainly directed at the 'managerialist' school suggests that the post-Fordist model is drawn from the manufacturing sector rather than the service sector; it fails to identify the continuities in labour processes and, in particular, it confuses what is in effect a 'repackaging of well-worn employment patterns and practices' (Pollert, 1988: 310) aimed at raising productivity and profit, with a conscious management strategy aimed at developing flexibility though a core and peripheral workforce. Instead, she suggests other factors need to be brought in to account for these developments: intensified continuities in employment inequalities in 'race', gender and age; new social forces like the feminisation of the workforce; and new right policies in employment, such as the youth training schemes, weakening of trade-union and wage-bargaining powers (Pollert, 1988).

In relation to the public sector she also claims that here employment restructuring may be more developed than in the manufacturing sector, not merely following it. This is the consequence not of economic or technological change, but of budgetary constraints, uncertainty over future funding, and new-right policies aimed at encouraging a mixed economy of welfare, especially private welfare.[3]

The drift of these criticisms have relevance to the problems I have with the way post-Fordist ideas have been applied to the welfare state. First, Pollert brings in the relevance (within production) of other social divisions. Second, she suggests that since the post-Fordist model is drawn from the experience of manufacturing it tends to universalise a white, male experience of work; it assumes a gender-neutrality in its use of terms like core, periphery and skill, which are in fact profoundly gendered and racialised. In common with many labour-market theories, no adequate conceptual bridge is provided to allow an understanding of the relationship between the production and the domestic spheres (Beechey, 1988). And third, by bringing in the possible factor of the 'feminisation of the workforce' she gives gender a power of explanation in the argument.

All these observations and more can be applied to the way the welfare state has been brought into the post-Fordist model. I will summarise these before elaborating them in greater detail. First the conceptualisations of the welfare state, or welfare regimes, used in post-Fordist analyses are rooted in a white, male, able-bodied experience of welfare which ignores or marginalises the significance of other social relations. In particular, the relevance of social relations other than class is ignored in relation to: the organisation of *paid* and *unpaid* work in welfare; the consumption of welfare; conflicts and struggles over the distribution and delivery of welfare provision; the ideological content of welfare policies and practices; and the outcomes of welfare policies. In so far as issues of, say, gender or 'race', are brought in then they are either seen as the consequence of the organisation of welfare in relation of production or to class–capital relations, or they are subsumed under a more generic concept such as 'inner-city problems', 'underclass', 'New Social Movements' or 'family'. In particular rarely is the power of explanation or the power of agency granted to gender, 'race' or any social relation other than class.

In some ways these criticisms both cut across and highlight the more general criticisms made above of economic determinism, technological reductionism and production-orientation. But they also point to another area of weakness in applying post-Fordist ideas to welfare systems and that is what some have identified as the complex and distinctive history of provider-user relations within welfare regimes which has involved the provision of welfare services by (often competing) groups of professionals within bureaucracies. There is, in the eagerness to identify more overriding trends of much post-Fordist writing, a failure to grasp the complexity of these 'social relations of welfare' and, from my perspective, a failure to acknowledge the attempts of the movements around gender, race and disability which have sought to challenge and change them. Let me now explain these points in greater detail and with specific reference to the two approaches – the neo-Marxist and the radical technological – I outlined earlier.

The first problem of the neo-Marxist approach lies in the way the welfare state is defined and conceptualised. According to Jessop (1991a) the welfare state involves four elements: (1) the tensions, conflicts and contradictions between welfare policies and market forces; (2) a relation not only to the market but to the family as the core unit of social reproduction; (3) a 'historical and moral dimension' – that is, a particular ideological commitment to welfare; and (4) a particular political arrangement or model of welfare provision. In relation to the last point Jessop draws on the work of Esping-Andersen (1990) on the variations in political welfare regimes in post-war industrialised countries – for example, social-democratic; conservative and liberal models. These models are seen as developing from and subsequently influencing the balance of class forces. In these terms, the Fordist welfare state 'linked the interests of capital and labour in a programme of full employment and social welfare' (Jessop, 1991a: 87).

The first difficulty with these ideas is that gender and gender relations are subsumed under the notion of the family or family change. Thus, rather than attribute any change in forms of social reproduction to the agency of women or gender relations – through struggles, or changing expectations in employment or personal relationships or to power relations within the family and the effect of welfare policies on these – Jessop identifies these as emerging from the family itself: 'Changes in the family form and its stability must also be included when explaining the changing forms of social reproduction' (Jessop, 1991a: 83). In addition, Jessop's definition of the welfare state is based on a definition which refers to the recipients of guaranteed minimum income and sickness unemployment, and old age benefits as 'individuals and families'. In the post-war settlement, Beveridge defined a woman's primary role as wife and mother which meant that in national insurance terms she was to be treated as a dependant of her husband or, if she worked, as eligible for a lower rate of contribution and benefit (this was only abandoned in the 1970s). This suggests that most women are not 'individuals' but just part of 'families'. The notion of the individual here is implicitly defined in terms of access to independent wage-earning.

This problem, which is really a problem of generalising from a particular experience – in this case the white, able-bodied man's experience – also runs through Esping-Andersen's analysis of welfare regimes, on which Jessop draws. A number of critiques of Esping-Andersen's work have emerged recently and these are relevant to the application of post-Fordist analysis to welfare regimes. Here I summarise some of the most pertinent points.[4]

The first problem is the concept of decommodification which is central to Esping-Andersen's understanding of the welfare state. Decommodification occurs when social rights exist to insulate the working class from the pressure to participate in the labour market. Esping-Andersen argues that these social rights, guaranteed by a universalistic welfare state, are the necessary pre-requisite for political mobilisation. However, taking a gender perspective, decommodification can mean different things to men and women. Whilst decommodification may enhance male workers' capacity to enter the labour market on their own terms, this capacity is also enhanced by the unpaid domestic and caring work that women carry out in the home (Orloff, 1992). As Orloff points out:

> If we make the mistake of assuming that women who work for pay like men are largely freed from domestic and caring labour, we might be persuaded that decommodification alone can enhance their freedom as it does men's. But this very notion depends on someone else doing the housework and minding the children (or caring for grandparents . . .).
>
> (Orloff, 1992: 26)

Similarly the rights associated with decommodification may not be extended fully to women: in Britain many women have traditionally worked part-time with less access to work-related benefits – a phenomenon intimately related to the sexual division of labour in the home, access to the labour market and lack of social care provision. Elsewhere, for example in Denmark and Sweden, where women have been brought more fully into full-time work, the actual take-up of benefits which facilitate this (e.g. parental leave) has been one factor (along with continuing domestic responsibilities for women) contributing to the creation and maintenance of a highly sex-segregated workforce. This has resulted in the Scandinavian countries in what Borchorst and Siim (1987: 152) describe as 'a shift in the locus of oppression from the private to the public sphere' – the weakening of family patriarchy and the strengthening of social patriarchy.

Second, the social rights associated with decommodification do not apply to all social groups in the same ways. For example, men may make some claims on the basis of their paid work, whereas for women these rights may be based on their marital or maternal status. In addition such claims can also be dependant upon nationality or settlement and exclude minority ethnic groups.

Third, the welfare benefits associated with decommodification may in different ways reinforce woman's role as an unpaid carer and as dependent (if not upon a partner, then on the state). For example, until the mid-1980s, the invalid-care allowance in Britain was not granted to married women caring for a sick or disabled relative on the basis that this was part of her normal duties. What is missing in the notion of decommodification (and this is also true for the analyses of the Fordist/post-Fordist welfare state) is any reference to the inter-relationship between the state, paid employment and unpaid domestic and caring work. 'We need . . . to supplement the dimension of decommodification with an analytic dimension which taps into the extent to which the state promotes or discourages women's paid employment – the right to be commodified, if you will' (Orloff, 1992: 27).

A second key concept in Esping-Andersen's distinction of welfare regimes is stratification, that is, the effect that different welfare regimes have upon class divisions and class solidarity or integration. Yet the provision of welfare can also have both a mitigating, reinforcing or compounding effect upon *other* social divisions: not only gender, but 'race', age and disability too. Further, the pattern of these effects may cut across Esping-Andersen's distinction of existing regimes. Lewis's analysis of Ireland, Britain, France and Sweden suggests that it is possible to identify a 'male-breadwinner family model' existing historically in all of these countries but one which in the case of France and Sweden has been modified in different ways (N. Lewis, 1992). Similarly, rights won through the capital–labour nexus may not *necessarily* enhance the social rights of all social groups equally, for example, reproductive rights for all women, or rights to freedom from violence for women and minority ethnic groups, or rights to personal autonomy for disabled or older people. In addition, even by recognising the value of women's caring work by socialising it, or by paying individual women to carry it out, this may not necessarily challenge the sexual division of labour nor meet the rights for independence of disabled or older people whom women care for. In other words, an approach which privileges class and class relations

> implies a unity of working class struggle and purpose which fails to explain why many welfare reforms resulted in gains for some sections rather than or even at the expense of others. The white skilled male working class in the 1920s gained from National Insurance, for example, whilst 'aliens' and women were denied access.
>
> (Williams, 1989: 142)

We need instead to understand the struggles and settlements over welfare regimes as influenced not only by class relations but also, and relatedly, by the relations of other forms of social power – racism, nationalism, male domination and so on – which influence both the demands of the working class and the response of capital and the state.

To go back to the question of the development of the Fordist welfare state, then we need substantially to qualify the statement that it simply 'linked the interests of capital and labour in a programme of full employment and social welfare' (Jessop, 1991a: 87) with an understanding of the gendered and racialised nature of these 'interests' and this 'programme'. As Ginsburg (1992: 6) explains: 'patriarchal social insurance based on the family-wage model was a cornerstone of the New Deal welfare reforms in the US and the Social Democratic reforms in Sweden in the 1930s, and the Beveridge and Adenauer Welfare reforms in Britain and the FRG in the 1940s and 1950s'. Similarly, as I have demonstrated elsewhere in relation to Britain (Williams, 1989), and as Ginsburg has in relation to the FRG, the US, and Sweden (Ginsburg, 1992), racialised processes are historically embedded in different ways in the development of welfare-state policies and practices. In addition, both patriarchal and racialised processes have historically been challenged not necessarily by class struggle but by emancipatory movements of women and black and minority ethnic groups.[5]

So an understanding of mass-producing, mass-consuming Fordist Man, however overstated, requires an acknowledgement that Fordist Woman and Fordist Family were also part of the deal. The assumption of a family wage, women's domestic labour and, in Britain, the part-time employment of working-class women, made possible the way production and consumption were organised. Similarly, the post-war welfare settlement depended upon women's unpaid caring work in the home (and to that extent welfare was never entirely state-provided) and reinforced both this and their economic dependency. Furthermore the development of mass provision was also made possible through the availability of low-paid labour from the colonies and ex-colonies. At the same time the 'universalism' of many of the post-war services and benefits was based on the norm of the white, British, heterosexual, able-bodied Fordist Man, and often excluded women and black people upon whose paid and unpaid labour it depended. In different ways, in different industrialised countries a welfare settlement was struck according to a combination of the balance of class forces, the availability of cheap labour, cultural and political traditions and expectations which themselves were rooted in specific interrelations of capitalism, patriarchy and imperialism.

The effective reproduction of labour power by the British welfare state had not only its class, but also its gender and 'race' components. For example, women and black men and women played an important role as labour within the post-war welfare state in keeping down the rising costs of welfare expansion. Indeed in many ways the expansion of the post-war welfare services depended on drawing in cheaper female and formerly colonised skilled and unskilled labour. Since welfare services are labour-intensive and have, traditionally, provided less possibility for automation than manufacturing industry, a cheap and flexible labour force came to play an important role in limiting rising costs. For women the welfare state became a significant source of employment, though they found themselves in the lower and less well-paid grades of the welfare workforce. The fact that for many of these jobs, women brought with them skills – cleaning, cooking, and caring – which had been developed in their homes meant that it could be labelled as unskilled, but also much of that work, in keeping with the post-war ideology of a woman's primary role as mother and housewife, was also part-time, and therefore low-paid. This was even true for professional jobs like nursing and teaching. Part-time work was not every woman worker's destiny though. Many Afro-Caribbean women in the 1950s and 1960s had themselves and families to support and were often forced into low-paid, full-time jobs in welfare with unsocial hours. Since the 1980s the trend has been to casualise even more women's work in the welfare services, and this has also made contracting out and privatisation easier to put into effect.

Black and migrant workers also played a specific role in maintaining lower social expenditure. The study by Doyal *et al.* (1981) shows how the NHS has been dependent upon overseas workers, both as contract labour and settlers, from the Caribbean, India, Ireland, and Malaysia since the 1950s. One third of the doctors and 20 per cent of student nurses in Britain in 1981 were recruited from overseas. In spite of immigration controls, the NHS has continued to recruit skilled overseas labour and, until fairly recently, unskilled labour.

In this situation, costs are also cut by virtue of the fact that many of those doctors' and nurses' training has been paid for by their own country of origin. Indeed the justification for recruitment of workers from the black Commonwealth countries by the British governments in the 1950s and 1960s was calculated on the basis that few of their social costs would need to be borne by this country. As they were British passport holders, the recruitment of workers from the black commonwealth was relatively simple compared with European immigrant workers. They were deemed to have come 'individually and on their own initiative' and no provision was considered necessary. When black migrants did use welfare services they were often portrayed as scroungers, as in the case of council housing or income maintenance, or, in health, education and social services, treated as 'problematic' with little sensitivity to different social and cultural experiences or, subsequently, as pleading for 'special treatment'. The main point in relation to post-Fordism is that since gender and 'race' played a significant role in the creation, provisions and policies of the Fordist welfare state then it would seem to indicate that these issues might have some relevance in the move towards a so-called post-Fordist welfare state, in terms of changing patterns of patriarchal and racial domination and the use of female, minority and migrant labour.

However, there is still another aspect of the picture of welfare development which most post-Fordist analyses miss and that is the role that women and black people and other welfare constituents, as workers and users, have played in challenging the social relations of welfare. In many of the post-Fordist analyses women and black people as agents of political change are often brought into play in three, rather limited, ways: first, as part of a general phenomenon – the so-called New Social Movements; second, as part of some future political scenario; and third, as a consequence of the shifts related to post-Fordism, most notably the fragmentation of the working class. None of these are usually spelt out. So, for example in Jessop's account of the welfare state in transition, little mention is made of the way gender and 'race' are inscribed within the Fordist settlement or the crisis over Fordism, but they are brought belatedly into a future possible neo-statist scenario, indeed as key political agents: 'A significant shift in the post-Fordist society will none the less be the enhanced role of organisations and groups rooted in the new social movements which developed in response to the social structure of accumulation' (Jessop, 1991a: 99).

Whilst the second half of this statement is partly true, the failure to spell out the precise ways in which this happened, leads, I think, to a misleading view of those social movements and of the social relations they challenge. These all have an enduring history pre-dating the 1970s crisis of Fordism. Bagguley has argued a similar point elsewhere (Bagguley, 1992): that many of the theories of post-Fordism, 'disorganised capitalism', post-industrialism and postmodernism, in different ways, relate the development of new social movements with the various forms of class fragmentation or new class formations associated with these different processes. Rather, he suggests we should understand these movements, not simply in terms of changes in class relations, but in terms of changes in the structure and form of social relations they seek to challenge. If we do this in relation to the role of these social movements within welfare then we begin to unravel a more complex analysis of the patterns and balances of power in the restructuring of welfare taking place now. Of course this also means that our comparative analyses of welfare regimes would have to take this on board too, as I argued earlier in relation to Esping-Andersen's work.

The working class stands and has stood in a contradictory relation to welfare provision. The welfare state provides protection against the inequities of the market within a capitalist society whose structured inequalities it both modifies and reproduces. Arguably the most significant social divisions within capitalism in Britain are class, gender, 'race' and sexuality, but the welfare state is also centrally involved in the modification and reproduction of disability and age inequalities. In other societies, including parts of Britain, ethnic, religious, national, cultural and regional divisions are also significant. For many of the social groups affected by these inequalities, welfare provision is a particularly important aspect of their lives especially where access to independent wage earning is restricted or denied, but also for other specific reasons (for example, health care for women, or older people). In this way, for many of these groups the contradictory elements of welfare are more acute than they are for the working class as a whole. Similarly, the struggles of many of these groups against relations of dominance have themselves focused on welfare provision. So, for example, the struggles in black communities in Britain from the 1950s onwards were not simply over wages, but over housing and education. Similarly, the demands from the development of the second wave of feminism particularly focused on welfare provisions (child-care, health care and reproductive rights, education and training etc.). The autonomous nature of these struggles was also partly a result of the economism of the labour movement's exclusive focus on wages and work conditions, and of its failure to acknowledge the significance of social relations other than class. What was also important about these social movements was that they were not simply concerned with the distributional politics of welfare, but with the very way welfare was organised. Racism and sexism operate at state, institutional and personal levels and in so far as these specific movements struck a new universal demand it was over who controlled welfare and in whose interests. In these terms the campaigns of the Women's Movement not only linked conditions within the private sphere of domestic and personal relations to the public sphere of paid work and politics but also sought to replace the bureaucratic and professionally controlled relations of welfare with non-hierarchal, non-sexist, non-racist relationships where users of welfare exercised control over the nature and delivery of welfare services.

What is significant about this history is that it developed not as a post-Fordist response to the crisis of Fordist mass-production techniques, but as a common link in the struggles over the social relations of gender, 'race' and disability. These demands entered the welfare state through the development of alternative voluntary provision (women's refuges, Saturday schools, well-women clinics), through the radicalisation of welfare professionals (the development of anti-racist and anti-sexist teaching and social work) and through the development of local authority equal opportunities strategies. All of these constitute a significant set of political forces which the new right in Britain has attempted to accommodate, undermine and challenge in its restructuring.

On the face of it, the work of Murray and of Hoggett would seem to give more acknowledgement to this aspect of welfare development since they both focus on the social relations of welfare. But, in my view, both these writers pay far too little attention to either the complexity of political relations and struggle involved in the shift to new organisational forms within welfare or to the specific outcomes for different social groups. On Murray's part, this is partly because the key force for change he identifies is post-Fordism harnessed to collectivist social values. Where these might come from (and how) is not addressed. This also causes him to over-characterise (semi-)Fordist and post-Fordist models of welfare. Thus large-scale mental hospitals of the post-war period are seen to epitomise the Fordism of the semi-Fordist welfare state: large, cheap and standardised. Yet, in fact, these large institutions (mostly all built before the 1930s) were already under attack from different quarters by the 1950s. Civil liberties groups opposed segregation, doctors were beginning to use new drug technologies which required only outpatient attendance, the shortage of unskilled labour meant many of the more able patients were able to live independently outside institutions, and the post-war government – less concerned with the politics of eugenics than with social expenditure – had by 1957 declared its commitment to the closure of institutions. In this way then, to understand one significant element of welfare restructuring in Britain – community care – just in terms of Fordism/post-Fordism would be to omit the complexity of political forces involved. This is explored later.

In Hoggett's work there is more acknowledgement of such complexity. He analyses decentralisation in terms of the different forces involved, which range from the

centralisation of institutional power to managerialist cost cutting and rationalisation, from the incorporation of urban social movements within the tentacles of the local state to Eurocommunist and Libertarian Socialist strategies aimed at the transformation of state, economy and civil society.

(Hoggett, 1987: 217)

He also describes how these forces constitute a challenge to the existing social relations of welfare.

Decentralisation has constituted an attack upon the massivity and remoteness, inflexibility, inefficiency and unresponsiveness of the welfare state . . . The social and political development which has thrown this ideology into crisis finds its expression today in the legitimate demand for a more differentiated state product. This demand comes directly from a new actor whose appearance over the last decade corresponds to another important change in the environment of most welfare state organisations – the 'differentiated consumer'.

(Hoggett, 1987: 224)

Yet, somehow, in spite of Hoggett's careful and insightful writings, these complexities fall from view in his main focus – the changes in productive forces. Though he is committed to an analysis of technology which is both determined by, and determining of social forces, it is not clear to me in Hoggett's analysis what role either 'urban movements' or the 'new actors' play in determining or struggling over the new technologies of control in welfare. How far, for example, can organisations of disabled people take over and control technologies and put these to their own use? How far can communities audit their own needs? And in what ways, given the history of the labour force within the welfare state, are the new organisational forms within welfare also gendered and racialised? Is there room in the new 'leaner and flatter managerial structures' (Hoggett, 1987: 225) for the plumper, rounder sex?

More recently Hoggett has linked the outcome of the introduction of technologies of control to social control in a broader sense, particularly to the laissez-faire policies of government in the early 1990s around 'the underclass' (Hoggett, this volume). There are many problems associated with the concept of 'underclass', not least of which is its appropriation by the new right to stereotype poor communities as 'welfare dependants' devoid of moral responsibility. However, what the concept and its usage here has in common with concepts like 'new social/urban movements' or 'citizenship' or 'decommodification' is a capacity to obscure the specific class, gender and 'race'-related ways in which such processes or phenomena operate. In the case of 'underclass' it obscures the elements of gender, 'race', age and disability that are caught up in the creation of poverty and so-called welfare dependency.

To summarise: my main criticisms of the applications of the Fordist/ post-Fordist dichotomy to welfare are that they have, first, focused on the relationship between the state, production and class relations to the exclusion of the relationship between the state, production, the domestic sphere and other significant social relations of power, most notably gender and 'race'. Second, there has been a tendency to generalise and conceptualise from the basis of the white, male experience of work and of welfare. Third, in so far as gender or 'race' relations are brought in to the picture, then these references tend to be non-specific (using general terms such as 'family' or 'inner-city'), ahistorical, class-determined, and consequential. In particular, no power of agency is given to either gender or 'race' or other social relations.

Does any of this matter? Isn't the Fordist/post-Fordist analysis merely a schema, signposting in an abstract way the most generalisable of economic, technological and social shifts over the past fifty years? Am I simply raising specific questions of societalisation which lie outside the scope of these analyses? I do not think so. In so far as these analyses abstract and generalise the concrete histories of the organisation of paid work and of welfare then such generalisations need to be informed by the significance of gender and 'race' in the constitution of work and welfare and in the ways these have changed over time. In so far as these analyses, in common with postmodernism, invoke the social movements around gender and 'race' (and more) as key points in the future political landscape, then it is as well that we are clear about the histories of such movements, the social relations from which they emerged and which they seek to change.

Finally, I suggested that the post-Fordist description of welfare, whilst partly true, tends to elide a number of different and contesting forces which have all contributed to the way in which welfare has been restructured in Britain – notably: demographic changes; budgetary constraints; new right ideology (not only its supremacy of the market but its attitude to questions of family and nationhood); and radical movements amongst both professionals and welfare-users. It also tends to oversimplify what is, in fact, a complex and contradictory picture of welfare where notions of consumer-sovereignty, diversity and choice represent different and competing interests, and where notions of efficiency and equity, managerialism and professionalism, corporatism and localism, needs and budgets sit very uncomfortably with each other (Clarke and Newman, 1993). By way of conclusion and as a brief illustration of this complex and contradictory picture, I want to focus upon some elements of diversity and difference within the current restructuring of welfare in Britain.

THE RESTRUCTURING OF WELFARE IN BRITAIN: THE DISCOURSE AROUND DIVERSITY

Two concepts that have been central to both post-Fordist and post-modernist descriptions have been *diversity* and *difference*. This is the way in which Stuart Hall connects post-Fordism to a development of cultural and political diversity:

> consider the proliferation of models and styles, the increased product differentiation which characterises 'post-Fordist' production. We can see mirrored there wider processes of cultural diversity and differentiation related to the multiplication of social worlds and social 'logics' in the West – the pluralisation of life expands the potentialities and identities available to ordinary people in their everyday working, social, familial and sexual lives.
>
> (Hall, 1989: 129)

Such an observation is important but how can it be translated into welfare terms? Does welfare pluralism expand the 'potentialities and identities' available to people? Does welfare provision relate to the 'multiplication of social worlds and social logics' in any way? What forms of diversity and difference are represented in welfare policy, provision and practice? Does, to use Hoggett's (1991b) phrases, 'the differentiated consumer' find 'a differentiated state product'? Are there possibilities for 'a new form of collectivism founded upon the celebration of diversity rather than its disparagement'?

First of all, it is important to understand the restructuring of the welfare state not only as a neo-liberal response to the crisis of Fordism, not only as a shift away from mass, monolithic forms to prepare the ground for a post-Fordist economy, but also a reflection of challenges and accommodations to a balance of power especially around class, race, and gender. For example, in some areas of new right policy there has been a clear attempt to reassert traditional family values against the incursion into these by an increase in women's aspirations, and the development of a diversity of non-traditional family forms (e.g. the 1991 Child Support Act, community care policies, increased dependency of young people upon family financial support). In other areas, such as education, traditional values have been asserted through the National Curriculum to counter, amongst other things, developments in anti-sexist and anti-racist teaching strategies. This has also been accompanied by the disempowerment of the trade unions, of local authority power and funding and with that an attempt to discredit anti-discriminatory strategies by local authorities. Yet in other areas there has been an acknowledgement, if tokenistic, of the need to acknowledge cultural and family diversity (e.g. the 1989 Children Act). Nevertheless the overall effect of new right social policies has been to intensify inequalities of gender, race, disability and age, especially where these are compounded with class inequalities or marginalisation from paid work (Williams, 1993).

If we take one major policy intervention in Britain in the 1980s and 1990s – the NHS and Community Care Act 1990 – we cannot make complete sense of it by seeing it simply as a policy vehicle for a shift to post-Fordist conditions. We have to see community care policies as playing out all sorts of contested issues in the field of welfare within the specific social, political and cultural relations of Britain in the 1990s. In this way community care policies in the 1990 NHS and Community Care Act represent, among other things:

- an assertion of the primacy of family, particularly female, care and self-help;
- a recognition (but only this) of the needs of carers for support;
- a shift in the power and responsibilities of local authority Social Services Departments from providing care to facilitating the development of care services from the private and voluntary sectors;
- a shift in the balance of power away from professionals to managers;

- a reordering of skills from management skills through to care skills;
- an attempt to give service users a say through choice and consumer-sovereignty;
- the introduction of a 'needs-based' service, though within strict financial controls.

As such, community care in Britain represents an attempt by the new right to generate self-help, the traditional role of the family, the introduction of markets into welfare, the stimulation of the private sector, the residualisation of the state sector, the reduction of local authority powers and of the powers of welfare professionals, and the limitation of state spending within a context of rising needs from older people. At the same time the policies represent pressure from professionals and user-groups for deinstitutionalisation and independent living, pressure also from user-groups for representation and pressure from carers and women's groups about carers' need for support.

To return to the question of diversity and difference: within the restructuring of welfare these concepts have taken on different and competing meanings. Here I identify three. The first two are part of what might be called 'diversity from above'.

1 First, the notions of diversity of choice and differentiation of services have entered the language of welfare through the advocacy of a mixed economy of welfare. Here diversity and difference are counterposed to the monopoly, universalism and uniformity of the Keynesian welfare system. The opening up of the private and not-for-profit sectors have been seen as crucial in meeting the differentiated choices and needs of the population. However the whole notion of difference here is underexplained – it is seen as belonging to the individual and expressed through consumer choice. This imposes a market model upon the organisation of welfare in which consumer choices and preferences determine the nature and range of provision.

2 The second way diversity and difference appear in recent restructuring programmes is through the introduction in health and social care of a needs-based service. The separation of the roles of purchaser and provider in health and social care has been accompanied by a requirement that purchasers assess the needs of potential service-users and arrange for the provision of services on a needs-led basis. Here again diversity and difference are recognised largely in individual terms: individuals have different needs for which individual care packages can be organised. On the one hand, the encouragement of individuals to articulate their specific needs breaks with past practice where services were based on providers' definitions of needs. On the other hand, professional assessment of needs –

whilst acknowledging differentiation in individual circumstances – financial, social support, housing and so on – still remains fairly firmly planted within professionally defined categories of vulnerability – the old, the sick, people with learning difficulties, disabled people, the homeless, people deemed to be mentally ill, victims of violence, abuse or neglect and so on. However alongside this individual approach to difference, there is also a requirement for local authorities to draw up Community Care Plans, in consultation with users and with health authorities, which meet their population's needs. Clearly here opportunities exist for the collective articulation and audit of needs in which different patterns of diversity emerge. Whether such opportunities are grasped will probably depend upon the strength of organisation of what constitutes the third meaning – the expression of diversity 'from below'.

3 A third way in which difference has entered welfare organisations, this time (though not always) from 'below', is through equal opportunities policies, particularly in gender, 'race' and disability. These have been significant for raising issues of discrimination within welfare organisations and, where they have been translated into anti-discriminatory practice, for service-users too. Alongside the development of equal opportunities, has been the emergence over the past decade of local, national and international movements operating outside the statutory services, based on the identities of groups as specific users of services – for example, 'Survivors Speak Out' for users of psychiatric services, or 'People First', the self-advocacy organisation for people with learning difficulties, the Derbyshire Centre for Integrated Living for disabled people. These groups, like the equal opportunities movement, have their roots in longer standing social movements for women, black people and disabled people, particularly in some of the self-help welfare initiatives that emerged in the 1960s and 1970s such as women's health groups or refuges. Common to these social movements and the self-help and campaign groups from which they emerged, is an understanding of difference as first, the basis for political mobilisation and second, the reflection of existing social relations of power and inequality.

There exist, then, in the restructuring of health and social care, at least three discourses around diversity and difference: one based upon notions of the exercising of consumer-choice; another based on the creation of services based on the assessment of different individual needs; and a third rooted in difference as a form of political identity and a challenge to existing relations of power and inequality. In so far as the second category also appeals to the involvement of local people in establishing the basis of an assessment of local needs, then it creates spaces for the involvement of groups in the third category operating with a more politicised notion of diversity and difference.

However, recent experience in two areas – the development of equal opportunities and welfare provision for disabled people – suggests that such spaces may be fairly circumscribed. Equal opportunities policies have often been the first to be dispensed with in drives for economic efficiency, in organisational decentralisation, in sub-contracting and in developing the private sector (Newman and Clarke, 1994). In addition, there has been a tendency to organise such policies around discrete categories of oppression – 'race', disability, gender etc. Within the context of financial rationing this has slipped easily into competing claims. It has also led to an inability to adapt to people's experiences of the interrelatedness of oppression, to a tendency to ossify difference as rigid and essential, and therefore to a difficulty in linking common needs (for improved housing, transport, health, education, etc.) to specific and different needs (for well-women centres, black women's refuges, disabled access to transport etc.).

Over the last ten years there has been a significant development in the collective organisation and influence of disabled groups (Oliver, 1990). Indeed they could be said to represent one of the 'New Social Movements'. Their understanding of the difference they experience is that it is constructed by the processes of marginalisation and oppression in society. The situation of disabled people is understood as a particular form of compounded oppression where they are both marginalised and discriminated against by social institutions and able-bodied people, and this is compounded by the creation of dependency by welfare professionals. Their demands include therefore rights to employment, housing etc., anti-discriminatory legislation, but also to control over and rights to welfare provision – to access to information, accountability and direct payments.

So how have recent developments in welfare diversity affected this group? According to research by Glendinning (1992) policies since the 1980s have not served disabled people well. First, the diversification of a mixed economy has not found a growth area in the development of services for disabled people. Consequently this group has found itself increasingly dependent on dwindling state services. Second, with the streamlining and downgrading of welfare benefits which was intended to produce both winners and losers, many disabled people have been losers, losing out on extra benefits intended to cover the extra costs incurred by disability. In addition, particular forms of targeting have divided disabled people by awarding particular benefits to those with a lifelong disability but not those disabled in old age. Poverty and disability, especially in old age, go hand in hand. Furthermore attempts by social workers to assess needs are seen as both a form of gatekeeping, and therefore a potential denial of rights, and as a form of unnecessary personal scrutiny. In this way these developments are regarded as quite contrary to disabled people's own definition of their difference and the needs which flow from this – the right to develop independence, self-reliance and a charter of rights. In other words the development of a notion of diversity from above does not appear, in this situation, to match the diverse needs articulated by the users below.

The emphasis in recent welfare policy upon differentiated needs and welfare diversity may well mirror the product differentiation which characterises post-Fordist production. But these developments are also the consequence of, and the vehicles for, competing discourses around diversity and difference. These discourses emerge from modified neo-liberal welfare ideologies, from competing managerial and professional approaches to service delivery, and from the challenges to old and new welfare regimes made by social movements and user movements. At a conceptual level, if we are to take the issues of diversity and difference within welfare seriously then we have to be able to identify the ways in which identities are constructed, and also recognise the extent to which the structured conditions of people's existence create different identities and diverse needs. In other words, the individual consumer of welfare is not someone who is free to choose but someone whose needs and choices are constituted, articulated and structured by a variety of social divisions and individual differences. In order to examine diversity and differences in relation to welfare needs, rights and demands, it is important that we reconnect these concepts to the struggles from which they have emerged, the conditions in which they exist and the social divisions and social relations they reflect and challenge.

To submit post-Fordist analysis to critique and to assert the greater complexity of social relations and social forms in the restructuring of welfare should not detract from the important directions in which post-Fordist analyses can take us. The question of what will or can replace the core of the post-war settlement – the male breadwinner social insurance scheme – is a crucial one, and one which has raised renewed interest in the guaranteed minimum wage and more inclusive and dynamic notions of welfare citizenship. My point in this chapter is to insist that these issues and debates need to take account not only of the changing conditions of work but of the changing conditions of family, culture and nationhood too, and that these should be understood in terms of the changing relations not only of class, but of other social divisions, including gender and 'race'. Furthermore, what is important for the study and future of welfare is the intersection between these divisions and the changing relations of welfare.

NOTES

1 The concept of a Schumpeterian workfare state is more developed in Jessop (this volume).
2 In this particular way Hoggett's theoretical intentions are more rooted in a neo-marxist analysis.
3 Pollert's arguments have recently been supported by McGregor and Sproull (1992).
4 See Langan and Ostler (1991), Chamberlayne (1992), Ginsburg (1992), Lewis (1992), Orloff (1992) and Shaver (1990). Most of these critiques deal with gender, only Shaver and Ginsburg address the issue of 'race'.
5 My shift from talking about the social relations of gender and 'race' to concrete references to the experiences of women and black people within the welfare state should be qualified by an insistence on the heterogenity of these experiences in terms of class, ethnicity, religion, sexuality, age and more. For a discussion see Anthias and Yuval-Davis (1992) and Williams (1992).

5 Prisoners of the Beveridge dream?

The political mobilisation of the poor against contemporary welfare regimes

Paul Bagguley

INTRODUCTION

What is absent from many discussions of the transition to 'post-Fordism' is a consideration of what Marx called events 'written . . . in letters of blood and fire' (Marx, 1977: 669). The changes wrought by recent economic restructuring and the correlative transformation of welfare regimes are too often seen in structural terms, as the expression of all-embracing logics of social transformation. Alternatively they might be seen as simply the impact of policies pursued by dominant collective agents. It would be too easy to see the old days of Thatcherism as such phenomena. But the agency of the insubordinates has an impact as well, sometimes a fundamental one.

In this chapter I am concerned with the response of the poor to the Thatcherite restructuring of the welfare regime. What is striking is the divergence of responses to the changes in unemployment benefits on the one hand, and the poll tax on the other. A theoretically informed analysis of these two cases – at the opposite ends of an empirical continuum from acquiescence to protest – might tell us something about collective action generally, but also something quite fundamental about the nature and forms of the state under a 'post-Fordist' welfare regime.

After the recent restructuring of the state, the state–civil society connection is now more complex than ever, if anything the simple Gramscian dichotomy is dissolving. The very *form* of the state, the *form* of civil society and the forms of relationship between them involve radically new political technologies distinct from Foucault's disciplinary power of the modern state. These new forms of power and political technologies one might call *market power*.

Whereas disciplinary power was aimed via the body at the psyche to produce a 'bureaucratic personality' inside a docile body, market power is aimed at the *calculus* of the subject inside a proactive body. The goal is to displace the *zoopoliticon* of the modern state with a *homo economicus* basing political decisions on value for money and quality at a low price. As always Thatcher herself has put it most succinctly: 'Economics are the method. The object is to change the soul' (Margaret Thatcher, *Sunday Times*, 7 May 1988, cited in Roberts, 1992: 15).

The Thatcherite project was partly concerned with displacing a 'dependency culture' with an 'enterprise culture' (Keat and Abercrombie, 1991). But the consequences of market power are to produce a 'contract culture'. Market power operates with the discourse of the contract. Everything, it sometimes seems, is organised through market 'contracts'.

The case studies I am concerned with here are at opposite ends of two redistributive circuits. The poll tax as payment for local services, not all of which are 'welfare'. Unemployment and related benefits are cash transfers that are increasingly 'targeted' and means tested through criteria of 'eligibility'.

Both may be seen as examples of what we are calling post-Fordist types of restructuring of welfare. The poll tax aimed to create local 'political markets' – to an academic's eyes in retrospect it was an incredibly incompetent application of public choice theory. For the unemployed there has been a reinforcement of labour-market discipline through various financial and bureaucratic mechanisms (Bryson and Jacobs, 1992). There has also been the central state's concern to reduce the costs of deindustrialisation and mass unemployment. Again a blanket term like *marketisation* captures some of what is happening, but not all of it. I feel we are still at the stage of empirical description and generalisation, but some attempt at linking these generalisations to some theoretical issues might enable us to move forward.

IS THERE A POST-FORDIST WELFARE STATE?

Post-Fordist writing on the welfare state remains largely schematic. The typical discussion is to point to recent changes in the welfare state as one dimension along several where societies are becoming post-Fordist (see for example Jessop, 1989b: 264). In the case of Jessop's analysis all that follows is a list of the more obvious changes in welfare introduced by the Thatcher government, giving rise to a 'two-nations' society (Jessop *et al.* 1988: 177–80; Jessop, 1989b: 275–6).[1] A more explicit discussion, of particular relevance to the poll tax, is Stoker's (1989b) analysis of changes in local government reflecting a Thatcherite strategy for a transition to post-Fordism. Other discussions (Painter, 1991b) also consider the relationship between post-Fordism and the local state.

Stoker outlines the development of the Fordist local state, involving the shift from an emphasis on infrastructure, poor-relief and policing to collective consumption such as education and housing. The local state's internal organisation became functionally differentiated, providing mass services through a hierarchical bureaucracy, effectively mimicking the Fordist corporation.

Within the local state the production and provision of welfare becomes increasingly post-Fordist through sub-contracting, new information technologies and flexible labour market and pay systems. The consumption of welfare is increasingly characterised by dualism and organised through markets rather than bureaucracies. Within the new post-Fordist local state, discourses of consumer sovereignty and market differentiation become dominant. The nature of political institutions is also transformed with a limited scope for local democracy, and changes originating from the centre. Local political institutions are restructured to fragment power bases through Urban Development Corporations, TECs and HATs and so on (see Byrne, this volume). Finally, the core state institutions increasingly relate not to departments but to agencies and sub-contractors through contracts (Stoker, 1989b: 149–58).

The main problem I have with these discussions is that given the level of abstraction these authors are often operating at, I fail to see the causal mechanism that links post-Fordism as a regime of accumulation and the welfare policies that are discussed. It seems that they are conflating levels of abstraction, since if it is the case that, as Jessop insists, post-Fordism is a regime of accumulation that can only be conceptualised abstractly, then others such as Stoker are making a gigantic leap between the concept of post-Fordism and the empirical trends that they list. *If* there is a causal mechanism on view then it is Thatcherism as a strategy for transforming the state. However, even if this were the case then its status as a causal mechanism linking post-Fordism and the welfare state is asserted rather than demonstrated.

A major theme of post-Fordist and related writings on the welfare state has been recommodification as originally signalled by Offe (1984) and more recently discussed by King (1989). However, I want to argue that this account is too limited for our present uses, largely because empirical reality, in Britain at least, has moved beyond it.

King argues that recommodification has definite social and political limits, the welfare state and the local state are in effect irreversible.[2] For King, what might be termed a 'power bloc' of producer interests within the welfare state limit the possibilities of radical reform. In the core institutions of the Fordist welfare state, such as the NHS, that operate on principles of universal citizenship there is unlikely to be radical change. On this account we would expect post-Fordism to have only minor implications for the welfare state.

However, an entirely contrary interpretation by Pickvance (1991) argues that there has been radical change in the local welfare state institution for the following reasons:

> the lack of public opposition to spending cuts is due immediately to the concealed nature of many cuts and the defensive position adopted by local government around the notion of 'local autonomy' which was unattractive to service consumers. But more fundamentally it is due to the whole style of public service provision in Britain with its lack of participatory structures, and to the ambivalence in people's attitudes to local government. The local government power bloc thus claim qualified rather than unquestioning public support.
>
> (Pickvance, 1991: 79)

Pickvance is also dismissive of post-Fordist economic restructuring as a sufficient explanation of recent changes in the local state (Pickvance and Prétèceille, 1991: 197–8). In his explanation economic restructuring is only one factor, along with neo-liberalism, operating in the context of a British local state with extensive decentralised welfare functions. In this context he shows that while Thatcherism has successfully pursued structural reforms of a centralising character in areas such as capital spending and the abolition of metropolitan councils, it has been comparatively unsuccessful in reforming day-to-day practice. Some features, such as competitive tendering and consumer power in education and housing, he sees as yet to succeed or fail (Pickvance, 1991: 79).

So the recommodification strategy does have limits, but they are structural and technical rather than political. One can only sell so many council houses to their tenants, as many are too poor to buy them. In response to these limits Thatcherism developed an alternative model. One which I am calling marketisation, which directly transforms producer and consumer interests. The recommodification model suggests a turning back, a case of simply returning to the market. Whereas in fact the past was a multi-faceted regime of welfare, a mix of forms of provision in mutualist, market, patriarchal-familial and local state variants. This was not a simple dualism, but a complex social division of welfare shot through with intra-class, gender and ethnic divisions (Mann, 1992).

The recommodification strategy essentially reasserts labour-market discipline and re-introduces some kind of market rationality in the consumption of welfare services. Recommodification consists of cuts and sales. However, the structural and technical–economic limits to this strategy have led to a shift in focus. This shift in focus has two principal dimensions. One, the development of market rationality in the internal organisation of state welfare, and two, the development of market rationality in the politics of welfare.

Nevertheless, marketisation and the development of a welfare regime and state form organised through market power captures only certain aspects of the current changes. Older 'Fordist' forms of action and organisation continue alongside recommodification.

I also have reservations about construing contemporary economic restructuring as post-Fordist. The critical literature on this question is now burgeoning (Gilbert *et al.*, 1992). But there are two claims I would like to make very briefly. First, I think that post-Fordist forms of restructuring in the economy are restricted to specific locales and sectors. A better characterisation of contemporary change is in terms of post-industrialisation. The fact that more people are manipulating symbols or servicing other people directly in the context of wage labour has more implications for forms of consciousness and patterns of class-based collective action, than does flexible specialisation. Furthermore, most post-industrial labour operates under poor conditions in exchange for very low wages. Second, to think in terms of a post-Fordist welfare state is to begin to move towards a functionalist and economistic mode of thinking. It implies that there is some kind of state provision of welfare that corresponds to, or is caused by, 'post-Fordism'.

So is there a 'post-Fordist' welfare state? I think not, because I worry about buying both the post-Fordist and the state parts of the package. One way through the jungle is to focus on the changing form of power, as I have already indicated. The other route is to follow Esping-Andersen (1990) and focus our analysis on *welfare regimes* rather than the welfare state:

> the concept of the welfare-state is too narrowly associated with the conventional social amelioration policies ... contemporary advanced nations cluster not only in terms of how their traditional social welfare policies are constructed, but also in terms of how these influence employment and general social structure. To talk of 'a regime' is to denote the fact that in the relation between state and economy a complex of legal and organizational features are systematically interwoven.
>
> (Esping-Andersen, 1990: 2)

Those who refer to the welfare state are basically conceptual prisoners of the Beveridge dream; the very idea of the welfare state is a peculiarly ethnocentric term. Furthermore, the idea of a welfare regime enables one to capture 'non-state' forms of welfare. Although Esping-Andersen's approach broadens in a significant way many contemporary theories of the welfare state, I still feel that there are significant problems with his model of welfare regimes.[3]

First, it is in a sense ahistorical, since his aim is to classify countries, or statistical clusters of countries into the three welfare regime types – liberal, conservative or social democratic. This is compounded by his desire to emphasise the role of institutional and political traditions in shaping contemporary welfare regimes (Esping-Andersen, 1990: 38–41). One effect of this desire is to ignore the possibility of movements from one regime type to another, which is why I think that Britain is frequently the odd one out in his classification exercise. Counter-intuitively, perhaps, Britain appears in the liberal category in terms of decommodification, albeit on the margins, and in terms of pensions Britain is the 'only one really mixed case' (Esping-Andersen, 1990: 52, 87). He further notes that the British system 'failed to progress further' along the road of decommodification after 1950 (Esping-Andersen, 1990: 53–4). Put this along with the fact that the USA, Germany and Sweden are discussed as the concrete ideal types of his three worlds of welfare capitalism, and one begins to suspect that the British case constitutes the cognitive limit of his model.

The way to move beyond this cognitive limit is to locate the concept of welfare regime within a broader restructuring approach.[4] By applying a restructuring methodology to welfare regimes we can begin to tease out the ways in which the various layers of welfare innovations, expansions and contractions become combined into the contemporary composite picture. It also enables us to examine the possibility that over the past fifteen years Britain has embarked on a major restructuring of welfare provisions which differs fundamentally from that of the imediate post-war period, and how this contemporary restructuring transforms and/or combines with the already existing institutions. To quote from Massey's analysis of local economic restructuring:

> the structure of local economies can be seen as a product of the combination of 'layers', of the successive imposition over the years of new rounds of investment, new forms of activity . . . Spatial structures of different kinds can be viewed historically . . . as emerging in a succession in which each is superimposed upon, and combined with, the effects of the spatial structures that came before . . . Each new layer, each new round of investment, brings with it potentially new economic bases of social organization, new 'structural capacities' . . . The actual implications will depend, not just on the nature of the new round of investment, but also on the existing character of the areas affected. The combination of layers is a form of mutual determination.
>
> (Massey, 1984: 118)

What I wish to distil from this is the logic of its methodology. One could insert 'welfare provision' in the place of 'local economies' and 'spatial structures' to get a quick sense of what I intend here. At any particular point in time a welfare regime will be the residue of successive layers of restructuring. Not of the economy, but of institutions and legislation in the context of social struggles. However, Massey's methodology has been strongly criticised by Warde (1985: 199) for failing to provide adequate 'rules' for how layers are combined. I have two responses to this problem. The first is that the restructuring methodology is precisely that – a methodology. It is an especially useful way of operationalising theoretical models in a historical context. Specifying rules is a theoretical not a methodological task. Secondly, I feel that Massey sets up a metaphor of 'combination of layers' which is too strongly phrased. An *imbrication* of layers might be a better term. This refers to the surface as one of over-lapping tiles, rather like a slate roof. Some aspects of the layers are combined, others merely sit alongside each other, yet others are partially hidden. One can flesh this out further using the roof metaphor. When the roof is partially repaired, new slates replace old broken ones (crisis ridden or politically unacceptable welfare institutions). The new slates sit alongside old ones, with their insertion perhaps damaging these old slates and instigating their decline (opted out hospitals alongside NHS hospitals). Gradually most or all of the old slates are replaced or become degraded and limited to those parts of the roof where the drips from the rain do not matter too much! A welfare regime is formed by the imbrication of layers of welfare provision. Over time, it may be gradually transformed or radically re-roofed into a different kind of welfare regime. Beneath this lies an articulated structure of class, gender and 'race' relations – the timbers of the roof etc. Since this articulated structure is very general in its effects on the welfare state, by setting limits on the state and its institutional forms, it fails to cover the details of the recent restructuring of the welfare state. It is fundamental in an abstract sense, but trivial for detailed explanations.

The second major area of concern I have with Esping-Andersen's model relates to his conceptualisation of class struggle. Admittedly he is much more sophisticated than most in his account of class struggle emphasising coalition formation, but it is still focused on the classic trade unions plus the working-class party of industrial society (Esping-Andersen, 1990: 16–18, 108–11). This has two consequences. He overlooks the significance of *intra-class* conflict for the development of welfare regimes. He sees this as merely weakness on the part of labour, whereas the coalitions he refers to are frequently between particular fractions of the working class and other classes. Indeed, Mann (1992) has shown that collective action by fractions of the British working class are central to explaining the British welfare regime. Intra-class division and intra-class struggle are as important as class coalitions in accounting for national peculiarities.

A third related point concerns Esping-Andersen's treatment of what in contemporary popular language would be the 'underclass'.[5] Here he seems to condone – or at least not criticise – nineteenth-century Marxist accounts of a dangerous politically suspect 'lumpenproletariat' (Esping-Andersen, 1990: 65–6). My argument here is very much contrary to the implicit drift of Esping-Andersen's approach. Whereas he is concerned about the impact of welfare regimes on social stratification in general and the power of the 'organised working class', I am concerned with the impact of welfare regimes on the possibilities for collective action among those who are not directly part of the organised working class.

This approach I am advocating which focuses on how the institutions which shape the everyday lives of the poor was originally developed by Piven and Cloward (1977). This has been subsequently developed and used in modified forms by other authors (Bagguley, 1991b; Schmitter-Heisler and Hoffman, 1989). Piven and Cloward have been criticised for being too structural and deterministic and playing down or misrepresenting the political resources of the poor (Bagguley, 1991b: 23–9; Valocchi, 1990). Nevertheless, their core idea that welfare institutions structure protest among welfare clients seems conceptually sound as a starting point and, I have argued, has considerable empirical support in the British case (Bagguley, 1991b). As a result my principal aim in this context is to attempt to theorise how different elements of welfare regimes structure the opportunities for collective action and resistance to them.

One important advantage of the welfare regime approach is that it enables us to re-frame the *social* division of welfare within our analysis (Mann, 1992), and it also 'de-centres' the state and class from the analysis, but hopefully not into obscurity! On another level it is still fundamentally concerned with the 'three fs' of welfare – forms, functions and finance and their complex interrelations. Consideration of private market forms of provision become central, and we can more easily consider what one might call 'private patriarchal welfare' – the caring work of women in the home. I propose that we examine societal regimes of welfare structured by *intra-class* divisions rather than a welfare state with private alternatives. Welfare regimes should be analysed within a restructuring methodology. I am proposing a rather different conceptual map, but what are its empirical referents?

If one were to think in terms of a post-Fordist tendency in Britain's welfare regime, the empirical trends might include the following:

1 A shift from a state-centred to a market-centred regime in terms of the *mode of provision*. I have in mind here changes that are not directly associated with privatising state welfare, but which are related to restructuring of the remuneration package in the private sector. Welfare

'dependency' – and I use that word with great caution – shifts from the state to occupational welfare.

2 Within the overall welfare regime there has been a deepening of class, gender and racially based divisions constituting the overall social division of welfare. This is often erroneously, and in my view ideologically, represented as the growth of an 'underclass' (Bagguley and Mann, 1992; Smith, 1992).

3 Within the 'state sector' (if it still exists as a coherent institutional ensemble) market power is increasingly important, and is expressed in a number of ways:

(a) Internal contracting, agencies working to contracts and institutional coordination through cash transfers or 'electronic money', e.g. higher education and health care.

(b) Market power increasingly characterises the relationship between professionals and clients in areas such as dentistry.

(c) Outright sales of welfare infrastructure such as council houses either to consumers or 'welfare capitalists'.

4 Processes of de-institutionalisation, community care and the 'normalisation' of groups such as those with learning difficulties. This fits less well than some of the other changes, but could be conceived as the end of the 'Fordist asylum'.

5 Post-Fordist style labour relations within the state sector: flexibilisation in both functional and numerical terms; increased sub-contracting; decentralised wage bargaining; performance-related pay; and other managerial techniques such as 'total quality management' (see Pinch, this volume). These are often forms of market power.

6 A shift in forms of decision-making from corporatism to bureaucratic statism; insider pluralism; and attempts to create the political market of the poll tax.

All of these tendencies in the contemporary British welfare regime have been shaped by social struggles. Less often by 'clients' – but my guess is they will increase – than by organised sections of labour that produce and provide welfare services. In another sense, class struggle at the point of production has also restructured welfare provision, extending fringe benefits to organised manual workers. It is clear that market power is only expressed in some of the trends discussed above, but it is central to understanding the two case studies that follow, and even the notion of market power needs fine tuning to grasp the empirical specifics. What I would like to emphasise at this point is that there is currently a wide range of processes of change underway that cannot be cognitively captured by an all-embracing portmanteau concept such as post-Fordism.

In the following sections I want to indicate how unemployment and the poll tax illustrate different aspects of contemporary welfare restructuring. Unemployment and income support benefits are still essentially part of the Fordist state form, although their internal organisation is being restructured in a 'post-Fordist' direction. The Fordist state is essentially sealed off from influence by collective action among the unemployed. In contrast the poll tax is a wholly new form of state. A marketised form of state, not concerned with producing disciplined subjects, but market subjects. Individuals who would see local politics as a market place.

'PRISONERS OF THE BEVERIDGE DREAM': THE UNEMPLOYED IN THE 1980s AND 1990s AND THE REMNANTS OF THE FORDIST REGIME

The politics of the unemployed during the 1980s reveals many of the features of the Fordist disciplinary forms of power embedded in the practices of the state's income maintenance system. My argument, in short, is that the form of the relationship between the unemployed and the state acts as an effective block against the mobilisation of collective action among the unemployed. They are politically trapped by the welfare state. Political prisoners of the Beveridge dream.

The unemployed are dependent on the state for their means of existence, so it is the state's income maintenance system that they principally seek to influence if they become politically organised. In particular it is the *changing* forms of the state's income maintenance institutions that require some further analysis.

The state form is the institutional means through which social forces are represented in the state, the structure of decision-making and administration within the state, and the ways in which the state 'intervenes' in civil society and the economy. The state form has biased and asymmetrical effects on the political forces that are attempting to influence state policies (Jessop, 1982: 228–30). Consider for example the extension of the franchise, or the rise and subsequent decline of corporatism. With the extension of the franchise individuals in the working class and women were able for the first time to have some, albeit indirect, influence over parliamentary decisions. In the instance of corporatism only those who were members of the functional organisations rooted in the division of labour, namely trade unions and employers' organisations, were able to have influence over state policies.

However, this form has not been historically constant, and its variations are part of the explanation for historical variations in political movements of the unemployed. Initially in the early nineteenth century, for the unemployed to receive benefits, they either had to be part of a voluntary insurance scheme, or had to accept 'relief' under the poor law, in which case they came into direct contact with the state. Such relief was in theory supposed to be given in the workhouse as 'indoor relief'. However, in practice local political circumstances often determined that relief, to the unemployed at least, was not in the stigmatised workhouse (Knott, 1986). These institutions were not always offering legally codified cash benefits in a large-scale bureaucracy. Local state institutions under conditions of local democracy had some autonomy in setting the levels of benefit until the 1930s. This meant that they were 'open' to pressure from the local electorate and local social movements. However, after the effective centralisation of decision making and its insulation from democratic control in the 1930s, *there was no effective way for political organisations of the unemployed to have clear access to these institutions.* This centralisation and insulation from democratic processes occurred in part through the successes of the struggles of the unemployed themselves (Bagguley, 1991b). My periodisation of the forms of the state's institutions of unemployment relief are summarised in Table 5.1.

Table 5.1 Periodisation of state forms of unemployment relief

Features of state form	Period		
	Early 19th century	*1880s–1930s*	*1930s–present*
Democracy			
Level	local	local	central
Franchise	limited	extending	extensive
Decision-making			
Representative	high	high	low
Corporatist	low	low	medium
Pluralist	low	low	medium
Bureaucratic	low	medium	high
Intervention	cash benefits/ indoor relief	cash benefits/ indoor relief	cash benefits
Insurance	voluntary	state/voluntary	state

Source: Bagguley (1991b: 41)

During the contemporary period the form of state institutions responsible for unemployment relief means that the conditions for a political movement of the unemployed are now more limited than in the past. The democratic aspects of the institutions governing unemployment benefits are now entirely centralised. Local state institutions have no role in their administration. The process of decision-making is dominated by formal bureaucratic procedure, with civil servants and appointees, rather than elected representatives, taking the central role in the details of levels of benefits etc. since the middle of the 1930s (Whiteley and Winyard, 1987: 63–7). Even the role of appointees has all but disappeared since the abolition of the Supplementary Benefits Commission in 1980, and benefits now tend to be fixed in the midst of the government's budget in general. The dominance of bureaucratic and legal procedure means that political organisations which can respond in similarly detailed legalistic ways are more likely to influence policy. Centralised pressure groups, such as the Child Poverty Action Group or Shelter, staffed by middle-class professionals, attempt to influence policy by making a detailed documented case for reform on behalf of client groups who may or may not be members of the pressure group concerned (Whiteley and Winyard, 1987). Into this category I would also place bodies such as the Institute of Directors or the Institute of Economic Affairs, which, although quite different kinds of organisations politically from the poverty lobby, essentially seek to influence policy in the same way as the more conventionally understood poverty lobby. During the 1980s it seems these 'new right' pressure groups had more influence than others over social security policy (Penna, 1990). Most recently agencies have been created, but these appear to be mechanisms of financial control within the state. So the creation of the Benefits Agency, for example, is an important change in the state form, but one which has little direct impact on the unemployed. Specific attempts to reform policy such as genuinely seeking work clauses are more important in affecting their experience of the state (Bryson and Jacobs, 1992).

During the late 1970s and early 1980s the few remaining features of local discretion were exploited by representatives of the poor and the unemployed, but in a legalistic fashion. Local DHSS officials still had some discretion over exceptional needs payments, although these were tightly bound by centrally determined rules (Prosser, 1981: 148–9). Organisations such as the Child Poverty Action Group and some claimants' unions were able to extract considerable sums of money for some individual claimants. However, these gains were for individuals rather than the unemployed or claimants as a whole, so it was difficult to present them as incentives for wider collective action. In any case the Fowler reviews of the mid-1980s replaced the remnants of local discretion, and the scope for successful welfare rights action, with the more tightly regulated social fund, which gave loans rather than grants (Penna, 1990). However, more recent genuinely seeking work legislation seems to leave considerable discretion in the hands of local offices, and uncertainty in policy outcome may increase (Bryson and Jacobs, 1992).

When it comes to influencing policies, it is the *structural biases* of the forms of state institutions that systematically favour different forms of political strategy, organisation and mobilisation at different periods in history. Currently the structural bias for outside influence is towards centralised pressure groups, rather than collective action by the unemployed. However, this structural bias of the state form is the product of social struggle. The historical evidence is quite clear that a principal reason for setting up the Unemployment Assistance Board (UAB) in the 1930s was to remove the administration of relief from local democratic control as part of the more general aims of rationalisation and modernisation. Conceivably it could have been modernised without the loss of local democratic control (Briggs and Deacon, 1973).

The relationship between the unemployed and the state is *individual* rather than *collective*. However, this individualisation is mediated by the patriarchal form of households, or rather the way in which the practices and legal codes of the income maintenance institutions presume that men are single sources of income for households. In so doing, through the rules relating to co-habitation, the state contributes to the maintenance of such household forms. Unemployed woman are subjected to the disciplines of the state's social security system in a quite different way to men. So the state does not have a simple straightforward 'isolation effect' on social relations as authors such as Poulantzas suggest (Poulantzas, 1978: 130–7). There is a systematic gender bias in the individualising practices of the state in relation to the unemployed.

This relationship is not all one way, with the state's institutions dominating their unemployed 'subjects'. In relationship to the state the unemployed have certain legally codified *citizenship rights*, and the contestability of these changes over time and varies between categories of claimants. The contest over these legal rights forms the content of most political projects of movements of the unemployed, albeit shaped by the institutional forms of the state. This has been restructured in the context of social struggles, such that there is currently less space now then say in the 1920s and 1930s for social struggles by the unemployed. The detailed application of citizenship rights during the 1920s and 1930s was open to contestation at the local level, whilst it is now much more tightly codified in technical legal discourses which are less open to influence by popular social movements. Consequently this places contemporary political organisations of the unemployed in something of a dilemma. If they can no longer *collectively* influence the levels and forms of unemployment benefit, what indeed can they do on a day-to-day basis in terms of political struggle?

During the 1980s the unemployed were effectively integrated into the trade union movement through the TUC's centres for the unemployed. Because of the local variations in the politics of these centres there was no effective collective action by the unemployed. There were of course 'marches for jobs'. But how many did they mobilise? What did they achieve? Similarly the 'poverty lobby', which doesn't mobilise the poor, but acts as a self-appointed representative, has largely been excluded from influence over policy such as the Fowler Reviews. As Penna (1990: 325) states:

> with only the support of a number of right-wing think tanks ... and particular representatives of capital ... the government was able to transform significant basic principles of welfare provision and significant basic rights of social citizenship. This capacity of a centralised administration to achieve broadly *unpopular* aims indicates the extent to which the restructuring of the institutions and relations of social democracy has ... severely curtailed the ability of popular movements to effect change.

These key policy changes affecting the unemployed and their benefits during the mid-1980s followed upon reforms during the early 1980s. The broad trend of changes during the 1980s has been to reduce the value of benefits, exclude certain groups from eligibility, and introduce a 'sense of responsibility' among claimants (for example, the social fund and genuinely seeking work clause). In response to these changes there has been no widespread collective action by the unemployed, despite the considerable resources of the labour movement apparently being available through centres for the unemployed (Bagguley, 1991b). This is in complete contrast to the inter-war period, when action by the unemployed, then largely isolated from the labour movement, achieved increases in benefit and other changes. It is also in complete contrast to the fate of the poll tax, another state attack on the incomes of the poor.

'LIBERATED FROM THE BEVERIDGE DREAM': ANTI-POLL-TAX PROTEST AND THE LIMITS OF THE MARKETISED REGIME

The poll tax was concerned with local taxation and therefore the form of the local state. The form of the local state has been analysed in terms of both neo-Weberian (Saunders, 1986) and neo-Marxist (Duncan and

Goodwin, 1988) theories of the local state, and state forms have been discussed more generally by neo-Marxist authors (Jessop, 1982; 1990b). However, the most influential theorist of the form of state power is Foucault (1977). It is Foucault who has written most insightfully about how power is exercised and the consequences of the forms that power takes. So can we analyse the poll tax as an instance of modern disciplinary power?

The poll tax aimed to create a political body of disciplined citizens who were to act in accordance with public choice theory. The focus of taxation was shifted from property under the rates to the individual, it was thus radically individualising in its effects. As in Foucault's analysis of disciplinary power we might pick out three dimensions of the poll tax. The poll tax may be seen as involving *hierarchical observation or surveillance*. We all had to register for the poll tax, we had to make ourselves visible to the unseen poll-tax bureaucracy. It is not surprising, then, that one strategy of opposition to the poll tax has been to make oneself 'invisible' to the poll tax bureaucracy.

The poll tax possibly involved an element of *normalisation* in attempting to make us all equal tax payers. It took the liberal ideal of citizenship – an exchange of taxation for voting – quite literally. Even the poor were to pay, but with an 80 per cent discount. In order to make us all normal and responsible political subjects, we had to see, and feel, financially, the consequences of our political behaviour in local elections. Furthermore, housewives who were not in employment would have to pay the full poll tax if their husbands were employed.

Arguably there are also elements of Foucault's idea of the *examination* in the poll tax. There are records of all our individual registrations, payments and non-payments. If we do not submit to the poll tax we become subject to fines and/or imprisonment.

However, I think Foucault's analysis of disciplinary power is somewhat lacking as the basis for an analysis of the poll tax. This is not because the idea of disciplinary power is inherently flawed, but because it is concerned with the production of disciplined subjects *within* bureaucracies; that is within prisons, hospitals, factories, workhouses etc. Any wider effects outside the physical location of the institutions of modern disciplinary power, are due to diffusion effects. Foucault's wider concept of a disciplinary society is thus problematic. The poll tax was concerned not to produce disciplined subjects to follow explicitly formulated rules, but to produce subjects who would become market subjects in the arena of local politics. *The poll tax was the means through which 'market power' was to become the 'political technology' of the local state.* One might say that certain disciplinary 'techniques' are used in the form of the poll tax, but the effects are to produce a different kind of political subject. In short, the poll tax was *universalising, individualising*, and *marketising*. We can thus retain the broad methodology of Foucault's analysis of power, but conceived as *'market power'* rather than disciplinary power.

The effects of the poll tax were supposed to be twofold: to produce market subjects among the local electorate, and also to discipline profligate local politicians. The poll tax was to be the last stage of a long-running saga of conflict between the central Conservative state and local Labour states. The poll tax seemed the ideal solution; control would no longer be from the centre, but from the newly marketised local electorates. But the outcome was far from what was intended. In Foucauldian terms the poll tax produced docile bodies of local politicians, but a rebellious body of the poor!

Foucault frequently mentions resistance, indeed his accounts in *Discipline and Punish* might be seen as written from the perspective of the condemned and the disciplined. Power is always 'relational' for Foucault. His analysis of the shift from sovereign to disciplinary power could be seen as a 'class struggle' theory of social change, but he largely fails to theorise resistance, as many commentators have complained. Ironically, his critique of theories of power that see power as something possessed by or done by individuals or groups as missing the significance of the forms of power, that is, how power is exercised, might also apply to his discussions of resistance. One can see why people resist, and resistance is always something that people do in response to the exercise of power. But Foucault neglects the analysis of *how* people resist. In order to understand how people resisted the poll tax we have to move on from Foucault. Where do we move from here? Well our discussion has highlighted the universalising, individualising and marketising effects of the poll tax. These shape the opportunities and forms of resistance. The principal analysts of marketised individualised collective action are *rational choice theorists*.

RATIONAL CHOICE THEORY AND THE 'CAROL THATCHER STRATEGY'

Ask any activist organising against the poll tax about non-payment, and they will tell you it was easy. This is because most people pursued what I shall call the 'Carol Thatcher strategy':

> Bailiffs were today trying to contact the daughter of the former premier Margaret Thatcher over the late payment of her poll tax. Although freelance journalist Carol Thatcher settled the bill before the date of her court appearance, the bailiffs were asked to recover £32.32 legal costs. Miss Thatcher was quoted in a national newspaper today to have

answered a question on what the ex-prime minister would think with the words: 'My mother wouldn't give a s***, my dear.'

(*Yorkshire Evening Post*, 27 November 1991: 1)

This quote illustrates a number of wider features of opposition to the poll tax. Like Carol's mother, most people didn't give a 'shit'. More importantly, many people calculated that they did not have to pay any poll tax until half way through the financial year, when legal action began to be taken against non-payers. Unfortunately, Carol Thatcher left her payment that little bit too late and incurred legal costs, and the small amounts that people were and still are being chased for in both unpaid poll tax and legal cost make the poll tax excessively expensive to administer. This kind of Foucauldian rational choice analysis of the poll tax reveals it to be inherently 'self-destructive'.

By making simple short-term cost-benefit calculations any individual poll-tax payer would see that they certainly would not lose, and may gain financially by not beginning to pay their poll tax until October of each financial year. Non-payers of the poll tax were also very well informed of the consequences of non-payment due to the information campaign run by the anti-poll-tax movement. The currently available statistical data supports this interpretation in that in the 1990–1 financial year 28 per cent of the poll tax had been collected by December 1990, and in the 1991–2 financial year 28.5 per cent had been collected by December 1991. In short, millions of people have been involved. The effect of so many people pursuing this Carol Thatcher strategy of non-payment is that local authorities have to borrow to meet ongoing costs, and they incur additional costs of sending reminders and instituting legal actions etc. against the Carol Thatchers.

This increase in local authority costs is further exacerbated by the fact that those non-payers who are charged at the 20 per cent rate – the poor, students etc. are probably disproportionately represented among the non-payers. In many cases the cost of collection from these groups may exceed the income achieved. These extra costs, combined with the need to cover the uncollected poll tax, lead to increases in the overall level of the poll tax and consequently the 'hard' incentives not to pay in the following year.

Most people did not pay the poll tax, because there were immediate financial benefits to them as individuals. However, the material and cultural dimensions of popular opposition were closely related, that is, the inability to pay was closely reflected in popular notions of a natural justice, a sort of 'natural rights critique of the tax'. A 'moral economy' of taxation is a peculiarly apt term for describing the nature of popular opposition to the poll tax. In this instance the moral dimension – 'it's unfair!' – fits closely with the economic dimension – 'I can't afford it!'. Furthermore, most people opposed it, and the costs of non-payment to individuals only emerged six months or more after the bills were sent out. By this time the financial and political damage had been done. Several anti-poll-tax activists appreciated this point:

> I think basically it was the extra cost that got people up in arms . . . and the fact that the rich people were getting away lightly and they were all having to pay more, the so called poor people, that was what they objected so strongly and a lot of them said 'if people are entitled to housing benefit and rate benefit on the basis of ability to pay they should get some sort of poll tax benefit' and they weren't gettin' it. I think that was it and the fact that everybody who seemed to speak at rallies used to quote the Earl of Harewood, you know, it's going to cost him something like £700 per year for his 4,000 acres of big mansion, and there are people living down here in this two-bedroomed house who are going to pay twice as much. I think that got home to a lot of people, because that more or less came out at every meeting that we went to . . . the difference between the rich people and their big houses and the poor people in the small houses.
>
> (Brian, Halton)

> there's all sorts of reasons why people are going to be involved in the struggle against the poll tax; the common factor is the fact that the majority of people who are involved in our campaign cannot afford to pay it, right, and need to defend each other against the consequences of not paying. I think moral outrage goes hand in hand with that, if you see that you are worse off . . . Then of course there is a feeling of moral outrage that what is happening is wrong.
>
> (Ian, Leeds Federation Secretary)

> Well, I think a lot of people simply can't afford to pay it and probably would pay if they could, and then other people, like me I mean, why it's been scrapped is because of mass non-payment, so that's not just the people who can't afford to pay it. I think a lot of people in this county obviously thought this is unjust, this is just not fair.
>
> (Pat, Gipton)

These quotes are in complete contrast to those from middle-aged former shop stewards involved in an unemployed centre in Brighton in the early to mid-1980s (Bagguley, 1991b: 146–7). In this case there is a strong sense of 'powerlessness', no material basis of solidarity, and no incentives for immediate collective action:

I would have thought that the most vocal body against this government would be unemployed people. Er . . . because I think you only have to look at your direct conditions that you're living in, that you're forced to face . . . But because of the nature of unemployment, the way it makes people sign on the dotted line every two weeks, and then go back into poverty . . . away from sharing the experience with other people.

(middle-aged man, former shop steward)

So while the relationship between a social group and the state is central to structuring the potential for collective action, that collective action requires mobilisation and organisation. The impact of mobilisation, organisation and protest by anti-poll-tax groups on the non-payers can be seen to be threefold:

1 The bolstering of a popular anti-tax moral economy. For example, through leaflets and speeches elaborating on the injustice of the rich and the poor paying a flat level tax.
2 The sheer economic inability to pay was seen as being justified since the government had introduced an unjust tax.
3 Detailed information and knowledge of the consequences of not paying disseminated by the anti-poll-tax unions. This last point was crucial, because people could have been 'picked off' individually. But this has been prevented by providing all households with information on their legal rights, and a constant presence at the courts by anti-poll-tax activists providing on the spot advice. Non-payment by those who could not pay has probably been much more widespread and sustained for a longer period as a result.

For many individuals the two sets of incentives – economic and moral – were mutually reinforcing. Many people did not pay because they were opposed to the tax, and only paid up when legal action and costs were threatened. The benefits of participation, however passive, were *both* individual and collective. They got away with not paying the tax and the tax was defeated. It was defeated because of the financial and administrative impact of non-payment on local authorities, and the electoral consequences for the Conservatives.

CONCLUSIONS

These two case studies reveal not just the factors explaining collective action in specific historical circumstances, but they also offer a way into theorising the social forms of the contemporary welfare regime and some of the factors propelling its restructuring.

First, thinking about contemporary welfare regime restructuring in terms of post-Fordism, a dual society or recommodification points our gaze in particular directions. It directs us away from the form of welfare, and sometimes away from the struggles which reshape it. Such approaches are often embedded at their roots in an older economistic class-theoretical paradigm. They seek to explain welfare regime restructuring in terms of responses to economic crisis tendencies and their resolution.

Second, there is no unitary form to a welfare regime, rather it is an imbricated structure with diverse forms within it. This is clearly revealed when one examines collective action against the various state forms of welfare. Changes in welfare regimes refashion this imbricated structure in unpredictable ways. Some are marketised, yet others are recommodified. Complex interactions of technical, institutional and political factors decide these outcomes.

Third, democratic class struggle theorists such as Esping-Andersen come out of the 1980s British experience in severe difficulties as a result of their neglect of collective action among the poor. In this approach the organised labour movement is seen as a principal bulwark against the restructuring of welfare. In Britain at least it is nothing of the sort. It was and always has been a factor preventing the unemployed and the poor from influencing the welfare state. Ironically, perhaps, its opposition was a factor aiding the anti-poll-tax movement. A related point also applies to those who postulate the existence of a 'welfare state power-bloc'. It may act as a partial obstacle to narrow recommodification, but marketisation alters social relations more fundamentally. One is now tempted to ask – what power-bloc?

What these recent approaches have in common is an out-dated concept of power – an essentially instrumental one. The form of power matters at least as much. In understanding contemporary welfare restructuring it is not just who is doing what to whom that matters, but *how* they are doing it.

ACKNOWLEDGEMENTS

I would like to thank the many anti-poll-tax activists who were very generous with their time for my silly questions, and who have provided considerable documentary sources. Jess Maslen, Debbie Hook and Carolyn Weaver grappled with incomprehensible tapes of interviews. The Nuffield Foundation provided financial support under its small grants scheme.

NOTES

1 But see Jessop (this volume) for an attempt at a rather tighter specification.

2 See Mishra (1990) for an extended discussion of the irreversibility thesis.
3 Esping-Andersen is not the only writer to use the term welfare regime, but his discussion seems to be the most developed and influential. See the discussion in Pierson (1991: 182–93).
4 See for example Bagguley *et al.* (1990) and Massey (1984).
5 See Bagguley and Mann (1992) for a critical discussion.

6 Continuity and discontinuity in the emergence of the 'post-Fordist' welfare state

Christopher Pierson

INTRODUCTION

Much of the discourse of 'Fordism, 'neo-Fordism' and 'flexibilisation' still bears the imprint of its origins in the evaluation of changes in the nature of the labour process. However, it has long been recognised that Fordism and its transformation involve far more than simple modifications in the organisation of production. Theorists of the regulation school, for example, have concerned themselves with the overall structure of 'regimes of accumulation' or 'modes of regulation' and, more particularly, with the 'modes of societalisation' or patterns of mass integration and social cohesion within which specific strategies for economic growth may be pursued (Aglietta, 1979; Jessop 1988; Lipietz, 1988; 1992a; Nielsen, 1991). In the latter context, increasing attention has come to be focused upon changes in the nature of the welfare state in the transition from Fordism to post-Fordism (Albertsen, 1988; Hirsch, 1991; Jessop, 1991a). At its simplest, the argument is that the Keynesian Welfare State, with its characteristic commitment to full employment, macro-economic demand management and a growth-funded expansion of public welfare, was appropriate to the broadly Fordist regime of accumulation that dominated from the end of the Second World War until the late 1960s. However, the crisis of Fordism which developed in the early 1970s was at the same time (and, for some commentators, above all) a crisis of the Keynesian Welfare State. The present transition towards a new regime of accumulation built upon 'flexibility' will bring with it a transformation in the nature of the welfare state and whilst few have argued that the welfare state is going to 'disappear', there is widespread support for the view that under a new regime the state's provision of welfare will be quite different (Hirsch, 1991; Offe, 1987). According to Albertsen, what we are witnessing is a 'fundamental restructuring of state interventionism' in which 'Keynesian policies aiming at full employment through national regulation of general social demand' are increasingly giving way to 'austerity policies aiming at international competitiveness in wage levels and directed primarily against the public-sector service class and the lower strata of the working class' (Albertsen, 1988: 349).

It is this general argument about the transformation of the welfare state and the evidence that is taken to support it that I consider in this chapter. I shall not discuss arguments about the *cultural* transformation of Fordism and will only very indirectly address the question of whether Fordism and especially post-Fordism are appropriate categories with which to explain current developments under advanced capitalism. I can also only do limited justice to the emergent literature on the nature and consequences of the gendered construction of the transition to post-Fordism (Bryson, 1992; Ginsburg, 1989; Langan and Ostner, 1991; J. Lewis, 1992; Munro and Smith, 1989; Watson, 1988). In the first part of the chapter I give a schematic account of the major changes which it is suggested the welfare state undergoes in the passage from Fordism to post-Fordism. Nearly all of those who have written about this change are careful to stress that the transformation of the welfare state is an open-ended and as yet incomplete process, and that the experience of the welfare state under post-Fordism is likely to be just as varied as it was under Fordism. Jessop, for example, writes of three ideal-typical state strategies in response to the challenge of neo-Fordism: the neo-liberal, the neo-corporatist and the neo-statist, (Jessop, 1988: 10; 1991a: 95). However, there is some evidence that the changing *international* context for welfare practices has tended to privilege the neo-liberal response, and since I am principally concerned with recent changes in the welfare state in Britain, I shall concentrate in what follows upon the parameters of neo-liberal strategy. My principal concern is to establish whether recent changes in welfare state policy can properly be understood as part of a transition to a new and post-Fordist 'regime of accumulation'.

CLASSICAL FORDISM AND THE KEYNESIAN WELFARE STATE

Whilst it is impossible to find amongst those who work within the Fordist paradigm a uniform definition of what is to count as Fordism, there is surprisingly broad agreement, both about the generic features of the 'classical' Fordist regime and about the circumstances of its demise. In essence, the 'Golden Age' of Fordism is seen to have covered the quarter century between the end of the Second World War and the turn of the 1970s. Very broadly, this was a period of unprecedented and sustained economic growth, based upon the dominance of mass production and mass consumption (especially of consumer goods) and massified, semi-skilled labour. It saw an enhanced status for the collective bargaining of wages and conditions (increasingly upon a national basis), and a correspondingly increased role for both large-scale capital and organised labour. At the international level, it was built upon a commitment to 'free markets' and stable exchange rates, both under American military and economic leadership. Domestically, the new order was secured around:

1 Keynesian economic policies to sustain demand, to secure full employment and to promote economic growth;
2 the development of a more or less 'institutional' welfare state to deal with the dysfunctions arising from the market economy, 'to establish a minimum wage, to generalise mass consumption norms, and to co-ordinate the capital and consumer goods sectors' (Jessop, 1988: 5); and
3 broad-based agreement between left and right, and between capital and labour, over these basic social institutions (a managed market economy and a welfare state) and the accommodation of their (legitimately) competing interests through elite-level negotiation.

Thus, the welfare state under Fordism was shaped by both the accumulation needs of capital (including mass consumption as an important component in the valorisation of capital) and the defensive strength of the organised working class. It provided not only the class basis for mobilisation behind the welfare state, but also the corporate basis – in the rise of both organised labour and capital – and the institutional basis with the rise of the inter-ventionist state (Albertsen, 1988; Bowles and Gintis, 1982; Harvey, 1989a; Hirsch, 1991; Jessop, 1988, 1991a, 1991b; Kavanagh, 1987; Nielsen, 1991; Pierson, 1990, 1991; Roobeek, 1987; Taylor-Gooby, 1985).

'THE CRISIS OF FORDISM'

There is also fairly widespread agreement about the circumstances under which this epoch of 'classical' or 'high' Fordism drew to a close. For many commentators, 'the crisis of Fordism', increasingly apparent from the early 1970s, was itself a product of the cumulative rigidities built into the post-war Fordist settlement. Those very same Fordist arrangements which had secured the stability that made renewed capital accumulation possible in the period after 1945 had now grown 'sclerotic' and become a fetter upon continued economic growth. According to David Harvey, 'the period from 1965 to 1973 was one in which the inability of Fordism and Keynesianism to contain the inherent contradictions of capitalism became more and more apparent (and) these difficulties could best be captured by one word: rigidity' (Harvey, 1989a: 141–2).

The economic consequences of 'rigidity' could be seen in the deployment of both capital and labour. On the one hand, there was increasing difficulty in finding new opportunities for the profitable investment of capital and an especial problem with the inflexibility of long-term and large-scale fixed capital investments in mass production systems, the demand for whose standardised products was said to be approaching 'saturation'. At the same time, there was a range of associated problems with the supply of labour. In Nielsen's paraphrase of the new economic orthodoxy of the 1970s,

> Wages were seen as too high and too rigid, wage differentials as too small, and legally based labour rights, employment protection schemes, and social security systems as taken too far. The consequences were seen to be that workers priced themselves out of jobs; labour mobility, and thus structural adjustment, was hindered; and hiring of workers was discouraged while voluntary unemployment was encouraged . . . Inflexibilities in capital markets and government regulations were said to discourage risk-taking and implied a bias against the small entrepreneur and venture capitalist who had difficulty obtaining funds.
>
> (Nielsen, 1991: 4)

The welfare state was seen to be deeply implicated in this self-precipitating 'crisis of Fordism'. First, there was the burden of funding a constantly expanding welfare budget. Social expenditure grew rapidly in the post-war period, rising across the OECD countries from 12.3 per cent of GDP in 1960 to 21.9 per cent in 1975. Britain saw slightly below average growth as its social expenditure rose from 12.4 per cent in 1960 to 19.6 per cent in 1975 (OECD, 1985, 1988). Increasingly, this expenditure (especially in the case of social security and pension payments) was regarded not as an investment in 'social capital' or the meeting of a social obligation, but as an 'unproductive' cost, which diverted resources away from the (shrinking) productive sectors of the economy. Rapidly rising levels of social expenditure were seen not as a way of generating 'human capital' or sustaining demand, but as an economic disincentive to both capital and labour. High marginal taxation rates, bureaucratic regulation of business and the growth of public sector employment were seen to be 'squeezing out' productive private investment. Meanwhile, the commitment to full employment and to a rising 'social wage' strengthened the defensive power of the organised working class, driving up wage costs beyond corresponding rises in productivity, hampering the process of 'structural adjustment' and consolidating the veto powers of organised labour. As economic growth faltered, the costs of the entitlement programmes of the welfare state grew, while the revenues out of which these could be funded declined, generating the much discussed 'fiscal crisis' of the mid-1970s (O'Connor, 1973; Pierson, 1991). At the same time, the institutions of corporatist intermediation which had been established to reconcile the interests of state, capital and labour became increasingly an obstruction to economic reorganisation. In Harvey's account, 'big labour, big capital, and big government [were locked] into what increasingly appeared as a dysfunctional embrace of such narrowly defined vested interests as to undermine rather than secure capital accumulation' (Harvey, 1989a: 42). Thus, the institutions of the Fordist welfare state, which had once secured the grounds for capital accumulation by sustaining effective demand and managing the relations between capital and labour, had under new circumstances become a barrier to further economic growth. Governments' attempts to meet the crisis of Fordism with traditional Fordist solutions simply intensified their difficulties and, throughout the developed industrialised world, the politico-economic crisis of Fordism manifested itself in the historically unprecedented form of 'stagflation'.

'POST-FORDISM' AND THE WELFARE STATE

This crisis of Fordism and of its corresponding welfare state form is seen to have prompted a process of social and political restructuring in the quest to establish a new basis for sustained capitalist economic growth. According to Jessop, we can see this 'crisis of the welfare state as an opportunity for capital forcibly to re-impose the unity of economic and social policy in the interests of renewed accumulation' (Jessop, 1991a: 90). Theorists of post-Fordism are generally agreed that the present period is one of transition in which we are moving towards, but have not yet reached, a new and quite different 'regime of accumulation'. They are also generally agreed that this process of transition can be best summarised as the general displacement of the *rigidities* of Fordism with the logic of *flexibility* under a post-Fordist regime. At the global level, flexibility can be seen in the deregulation of international markets, the abandonment of fixed exchange rates and the introduction of new financial institutions which give capital a new international mobility, freed from tutelage to particular nation states. In the world of industry, Fordist mass production of standardised goods, typified by the assembly line and the minute division of semi-skilled labour, is increasingly displaced by batch production of diversified products, a growth in small-scale service industries and 'flexibility in the use of machines, materials, and human beings as well as in the inter-firm relations of production' (Albertsen, 1988: 348). The demands of batch production and 'niche marketing' taken together with the production possibilities afforded by the application of new technologies favour a 'de-massification' of the workforce. At its simplest, employment is polarised between a 'core' of well-paid, secure and qualified wage-earners with polyvalent skills and a 'periphery' of poorly paid, casualised and unskilled workers (see Pinch, this volume) who may move in and out of a category of still more marginalised 'welfare dependents'. There is a growth in sub-contracting, in 'atypical' work practices and in employment within the (largely unregulated) 'informal' economy. Trades unions, especially at the national level, lose much of the power that they exercised when industry was based upon the typically unionised semi-skilled worker of Fordist mass production.

These changes are seen to have profound consequences for the nature of the state, and especially the welfare state, under post-Fordism. There is, in fact, very limited support for the classical neo-liberal view that the problems of the welfare state can be effectively resolved by simply transferring functions from the (unproductive) state to the (value-generating) market. Indeed, there is a widespread recognition that, far from seeing a withdrawal of the state from intervention in the organisation and reproduction of labour power, the role of the state in training and the movement in and out of paid work may actually increase under post-Fordism (Offe, 1985). But such state intervention is likely to be increasingly concentrated upon the sphere of production, with even welfare provision being geared less towards the needs of clients than towards improving the international competitiveness of export-oriented industry. In Jessop's account, 'whereas Fordism facilitated a policy of full employment and welfare rights to secure demand and thereby created the basis for a class compromise between capital and labour, the new post-Fordist regime poses serious problems for full employment and the class alliances which this entails' (Jessop, 1988: 9).

Two changes in the general transition towards post-Fordism are of especial importance in recasting welfare state policy. First, there are the ways in which 'flexibilisation' of the *international* political economy has undermined the pursuit of Keynesian policies at a *national* level. Thus, the deregulation of international markets and financial institutions has tended to weaken the capacities of the interventionist state, to render all economies more 'open' and to make national capital and more especially national labour movements much more subject to the terms and conditions of international competition. In as much as the Fordist welfare state truly was a *Keynesian* welfare state, those changes in the international economy which have precipitated a decline of Keynesianism may be seen to have had a very material effect on the welfare state. The prospects for sustaining long-term corporatist arrangements within particular nation states (including the institutionalisation of a 'social wage') seem even less promising in a deregulated international economy. For many of its sponsors, (including Beveridge), the commitment to sustain full employment through government-induced demand was an indispensable element in the welfare state regime. Yet it is unclear that *any* government can now redeem this pledge and insofar as the deregulation of the international economy and its consequences lie outside the scope of even the most powerful governments, it represents a challenge to national welfare state settlements, *irrespective* of the varying political aspirations of national governments.

A second challenge to the bases of the traditional welfare state comes from changes in the labour process and the organisation of employment associated with flexibilisation under post-Fordist imperatives. We have already seen that the era of mass production and mass consumption in which the Fordist welfare state flourished has been identified with a central role for massified and semi-skilled labour and industrial unionism. Changes in patterns of employment and corresponding class formation bring with them modification in both the patterns of dependency and the patterns of political support within a post-Fordist welfare state. It has been argued for some time that, partly as a result of the growth of the welfare state itself, the advanced industrial societies in which Fordism was most effectively entrenched have seen the emergence of a new line of political cleavage drawn between those dependent for their consumption respectively upon the public and the private sectors (Dunleavy, 1980a; Saunders, 1986). The post-Fordist epoch is one in which the political power base of the public sector is increasingly out-powered and out-voted by the interests of the private sector. There is a consequent erosion of the basis of political support upon which the Fordist welfare state was built. For other commentators, it seems likely that division in the workforce between 'core' and 'periphery' will accelerate the transition from a 'one nation' welfare state, built around the 'objective of providing a high and rising standard of benefit . . . for all citizens as of right', towards a 'two nations' or 'Americanised' welfare state, in which there is 'a self-financed bonus for the privileged and stigmatising, disciplinary charity for the disprivileged' (Hoggett, this volume; Jessop, 1988: 29, 1991b: 151, 154; Lash and Urry, 1987: 229–31). At worst, it may lead to a wholesale residualisation of state welfare, as the securely employed middle classes and the skilled 'core' of the working class defect from public welfare, leaving the state to provide residual welfare services for an excluded minority at the least possible cost to a majority who are now sponsors but not users of these public services. Thus, Offe, for example, identifies, under the pressure of capitalist disorganisation, 'a self-reinforcing and self-propelling dynamic' of defection from all forms of support for the welfare state, concluding that 'the welfare state ... is rapidly losing its political support' (Offe, 1987: 534).

BRITAIN: TOWARDS A POST-FORDIST WELFARE STATE?

Of all the strategic responses to this 'crisis of Fordism', it is probably the prescriptions of the neo-liberals that represent the most fundamental challenge to the existing welfare state and nowhere has this neo-liberalism been more enthusiastically embraced over the past decade or so than in the UK. Certainly, the policy agenda of the Conservatives after 1979 contained many of the core elements identified with a neo-liberal strategy for transition to a post-Fordist welfare state. In terms of the 'mixed economy', there was a commitment to return publicly-owned industries to the private sector, to limit government interventions in the day-to-day management of relations between employers and employees and to 'redress' the balance of power between capital and labour. There was a commitment to sustained or enhanced economic growth, but this was to be achieved by *abandoning* Keynesian economics and the commitment to full employment in favour of monetarism and supply-side reforms. On the welfare state itself, there was to be a drive to cut costs by concentrating resources upon those in greatest need, to restrain the bureaucratic interventions of the 'nanny state' in the day-to-day life of its citizens, a greater role for voluntary welfare institutions and encouragement to individuals to make provision for their own and their families' welfare through the private sector. Overall, social policy was to be made much more explicitly subservient to the interests of the economy and wherever possible subject to the rigours of market-based competition. The first public expenditure white paper of Thatcher's first administration in 1979 maintained that 'public expenditure is at the heart of Britain's present economic difficulties' (HM Treasury, 1979). Since the single largest (and fastest-growing) element of this public spending was social expenditure, it seemed that reform of the Fordist welfare state along neo-liberal lines must be close to the heart of the Thatcherite project. In the second half of this chapter, I consider to what extent changes in the British welfare state over the past decade can be understood in terms of a transition from a Fordist to a post-Fordist welfare state and what these considerations might tell us, in turn, about the general nature of the transition to post-Fordism.

Given an uninterrupted tenure of office, the Conservatives had considerable success in pursuing their social policy agenda during the 1980s. Unemployment was allowed to reach unheard of levels (officially in excess of three million) and a string of major corporations and utilities were returned to the private sector. Mass unemployment and changes to the laws on employment and trade union rights were used to reimpose labour-market disciplines. There was a major (and popular) drive to sell off public-sector housing which saw (direct) public expenditure on housing cut by a half in real terms between 1979 and 1983. Under the first two Thatcher administrations, there were increases in some NHS charges, the 'contracting out' of some ancillary services in education and the health service, some curtailing of benefit rights, a less generous basis for the upgrading of retirement pensions and tax relief to encourage the private provision of pensions and health care. The 1986 Social Security Act was quite explicit in its concern with restraining costs, 'meeting genuine need' (which implied the more effective 'targeting' of available resources) and encouraging greater labour-force participation through the time-served principle of 'less eligibility'. The election of a third Thatcher adminis-tration has been described as ushering in 'the most decisive break in British social policy since the period between 1944 and 1948' in which the modern British welfare state was created (Glennerster *et al.*, 1991: 389; see also Le Grand, 1990). As well as the implementation of the government's 1986 Social Security Act, these years saw the passage of the 1988 Education Reform Act, the 1988 Housing Act, the 1990 National Health Service and Community Care Act and the implementation of a wholesale reform of the NHS following the publication of the 1989 White Paper *Working for Patients*. The unifying themes of these reforms of the late 1980s were the government's determination to divide welfare purchasers from welfare providers, the encouragement of private provision, the wish to relocate welfare 'within the community' and (wherever possible) the marginal-isation of local government. This has led both to a *devolution* of day-to-day authority into the hands of local managers and a *concentration* of formal powers in the hands of central government.[1] At the same time, there has been an expansion of 'private' – though often publicly subsidised – welfare for those who can afford it. There has thus been an enhancement of personal pension rights and private health care for those in secure and well-paid full-time employment. Rather than sketch the reform process in each of these important areas, I want to deal (though still quite briefly) with one key policy area, that of housing.

CONSERVATIVE HOUSING POLICY AFTER 1979

Housing offers a particularly useful example of government social policy, since the break with the prevailing order dates not from the late 1980s (as with health and education, for instance), but from the earliest days of the first Thatcher government. We may thus consider the consequences of policy change over a much longer period. Housing is also exceptional in that it is the one area of social expenditure where the government has achieved a real cut over the past decade. In real terms, the government's housing budget is now less than one half of what it was in 1979 (HM Treasury, 1991). It also bears many of the characteristic hallmarks of the neo-liberal version of post-Fordism: reduced dependence on the state, an enhanced role for the market and private initiative, diminution of the powers of local government and welfare professionals, and the residualisation of public provision.

Since 1979, Conservative housing policy has pursued the complementary ambitions of promoting owner-occupation as the preferred form of tenure and minimising the role of local authorities in the provision of housing. The 1986 public expenditure white paper of Thatcher's second government was particularly explicit in stating that 'the Government's leading housing policy is to encourage the widest opportunities for home ownership' (see Hills and Mullings, 1990: 137-8). In line with this policy, the Housing Act of 1980 gave local authority tenants the *Right to Buy* their properties at substantial discounts and during the 1980s almost 1.5 million local authority and new towns properties were sold to their occupiers, disposing of about one-fifth of the council-owned housing stock. New construction by local authorities dwindled to just 17,000 by 1989. The 1980 Act also changed the mechanism under which central government provides funds for local authority housing, effectively obliging councils to raise the general level of their rents. As general subsidies to local government fell and rents increased, the main burden of subsidising housing costs has fallen upon the means-tested Housing Benefit, which rose to £5.3 billion by 1990/1. The government also sought to revive the private rented sector which, while accounting for some 90 per cent of all households in 1900, had subsequently fallen to little more than 10 per cent (CSO, 1991; HM Treasury, 1991).

These policy intentions were reinforced under the Government's 1988 Housing Act. This had four main elements:

1   A further attempt was made to *encourage the private rented sector*, with rent deregulation and tax concessions.
2   Local authority tenants were encouraged to exercise a *'tenant's choice'* to enable them to transfer the ownership and management of their estates to a private landlord or housing association.
3   The government was given powers to create *Housing Action Trusts* (HATs) which will take over and manage on behalf of central government 'particularly difficult' local authority estates.
4   The Act legislated further central government control over local authority housing and identified *Housing Associations* as the preferred form of 'social' housing (see Glennerster *et al.*, 1991: 398–403).

The outcome of this latest range of reforms is as yet unclear. Given the current regime for owner-occupiers and the further fall in the private-rented sector to about 7 per cent of households by 1990, it is to be doubted whether the government can induce a major expansion of the private rental sector. Despite voting arrangements which are heavily weighted in favour of a change of status, tenants have shown remarkably little interest in a transfer away from local authority control or in favour of HATs (Duke of Edinburgh, 1991: 23). By 1990, housing associations accounted for about 3 per cent of all households, and the government hopes to see an expansion of about 40,000 homes per annum in this sector from 1992–3. However, the new financial regime is likely to see a steep rise in housing association rents, perhaps reaching twice the level of local council rents and it is not clear that housing associations will be able fully to meet the remit for social housing that the government has in mind (Duke of Edinburgh, 1991).

CONSERVATIVE HOUSING POLICY: POST-FORDIST REFORM?

The experience of Conservative housing policy is peculiarly instructive. It is clear that the Conservatives have had considerable success in realising their *formal* ambitions in the housing sector. Their principal objective of expanding owner-occupation has been widely realised. Owner-occupation, which accounted for 55.3 per cent of households in 1979, had risen to 67.6 per cent in 1990. Correspondingly, the public rented sector has fallen from 31.5 per cent in 1979 to just 22.4 per cent in 1990 (Council of Mortgage Lenders, 1991). The government has also succeeded in curtailing the role of local authorities in both the supply and the management of the housing stock. At the same time, there is evidence that as the public sector has shrunk (and the most desirable public properties have been sold off under the Right to Buy legislation), so it has come to constitute a more residual housing sector confined to those who are unable to take advantage of the inducements offered to take up owner-occupation (Hills and Mullings, 1990). The government's housing policy of the 1980s might also be considered an *electoral* success. It is widely argued, (though not to everyone's satisfaction), that many of the skilled manual workers whose shift to the Conservatives had helped them to win the election of 1979 were the principal beneficiaries of discounted council house sales and that this helped to cement their support for the Conservative party (for a critical review see Heath *et al.*, 1991). Meanwhile in the housing boom of the late 1980s, especially in the Tory heartlands of the south of England, owners made huge capital gains as house prices raced ahead of general inflation.

At the same time, these changes in housing policy, as in other areas of welfare administration, have clearly worsened the position of those excluded from the new opportunities. The 1980s saw an unparalleled rise in homelessness, with the figure doubling in England between 1978 and 1986. Given the decline in the public-sector housing stock, there was a still steeper rise in the numbers of households in temporary accommodation, often in extremely unsatisfactory bed and breakfast establishments. Whilst defining and measuring poverty is inherently controversial, it seems clear that this is just part of a general worsening of the position of the poor over the past ten years. Barr and Coulter, in a careful and measured analysis of the 1980s, insist that 'whatever the poverty line used, the number of poor individuals and families rose substantially . . . the number of individuals in poor households rose from 5.1 million [in 1979] . . . to 9.4 million in 1985' (Barr and Coulter, 1990: 333). It is clear that these changes in the area of housing, and in social policy more generally, have peculiarly severe consequences for women. Women's greater susceptibility to poverty and their greater reliance upon public-sector housing provision, (particularly in cases of marital breakdown), mean that this reconstruction of welfare opportunities has a distinctively gendered impact (Munro and Smith, 1989; Watson, 1988). Of course, the polarisation of welfare opportunities is fully consistent with at least some versions of post-Fordism. In expanding the private provision of housing, reducing subsidies to the public sector, halving the government's housing budget, curtailing the powers of local government and deregulating the market for housing finance, it may seem that the government has been pursuing (perhaps successfully) a coherent neo-liberal strategy of restructuring the welfare state to meet the demands of a post-Fordist order. However, this is not the whole story and I want to suggest that there are real difficulties in understanding Conservative social policy as part of such a post-Fordist reconstruction.

First, it has actually proven extremely difficult for government to reduce social expenditure. In fact, the housing budget was the one area in which the government made real cuts in the 1980s. Yet, the withdrawal of funds to local authority housing has probably been matched by the increasing costs of Housing Benefit (an element of the social security budget) and by tax expenditures on income tax relief on mortgages. Indeed, whilst owner-occupation is seemingly in tune with the neo-liberal themes of self-reliance and independence from the state, and certainly receives very little in the way of *direct* subsidies from government, owners benefit from a very favourable – if depreciating – tax regime. Mortgage holders enjoy income-tax relief on mortgages up to £30,000, a net cost to the public exchequer of £7.8 billion in 1990/1. Owner-occupiers pay no tax on capital gains in the value of their property. The temporary suspension of stamp duty on house sales either side of the 1992 General Election may have cost the public exchequer as much as £500 million. What is involved in the government's reforms is not so much a net saving of public funds but rather a *redistribution* of costs and benefits and, far from effectively targeting help, the comparative position of those most dependent on public services has clearly worsened.

Second, while the housing experience gives evidence of the *interconnectedness* of social policy with economic policy, it is not clear that the reform process has made these more mutually supportive. Britain has an unusually high level of home ownership and an unusual amount of the nation's (and most individual's) wealth is tied up in the housing stock. The housing market thus has an unusually powerful effect upon the general well-being of the national economy, not least in directing resources away from investment in industry towards investment in (domestic) property. The perverse consequence of the increased concentration upon home ownership and the boom of the late 1980s was to make it extremely difficult to revive the economy in the early 1990s. In a context of rising unemployment and consistently high real interest rates, many mortgage holders faced increasing difficulties in servicing their debt. Repossessions of houses by building societies and banks rose from an annual figure of 3,480 in 1980 to 36,607 in the first half of 1991 alone, and by the middle of 1991 more than 160,000 mortgage holders were at least six months in arrears with their payments (Council of Mortgage Lenders, 1991). In the year preceding the 1992 General Election, house prices fell by some 6 per cent across the country and by more than 8 per cent in the Conservative heartland of the south of England (Halifax Building Society, 1992). That the Conservatives, under the weight of all these disadvantages, and presiding over the longest economic recession in living memory, were still able to secure a fourth consecutive electoral victory tells us something remarkable about the nature of the British electorate and, possibly, something about the nature of the British electoral system. But it also demonstrates something about the economic inflexibilities to which the new housing market has given rise. For the government's desire to expand the economy was constrained, not only by the new discipline of membership of the European Exchange Rate Mechanism, but also by the depressed state of the housing market. While it has often been argued that subsidised council tenancies inhibited labour mobility, the evidence of the early 1990s suggests that the decline in housing values allied to high personal mortgage debt is now a much more substantial barrier to labour mobility. Whilst neo-liberal rhetoric has favoured redirecting spending power from government to consumers, high levels of personal debt, either directly associated with housing costs or secured against property, have made it extremely difficult to revive consumer spending in a period of recession. Government policies may have had some success in holding down wages, especially for the lowest paid, but the skill shortages of the early 1990s do not suggest that its education and training policies have been entirely successful in generating a highly-skilled and 'polyvalent' core workforce, appropriate to the requirements of a post-Fordist global economy.

Third, and more generally, it is important to stress, given the radical intentions of the Conservatives after 1979 and the burst of legislative activity of the late 1980s, that British social policy is marked quite as much by long-term *continuity* as by radical change. While the growth of spending was indeed restrained throughout the 1980s (a process which had already begun under the 1974-79 Labour government), social spending has proven to be remarkably resilient. In real terms it has risen by more than 20 per cent since 1979. Much of this increase has been required simply to meet the costs of rising and permanent mass unemployment and it certainly does not mean that there has been a matching improvement in the living conditions of those who are primarily dependent upon the state for an income. Nonetheless, wholesale cuts in social expenditure have been avoided and despite the government's enthusiasm for 'targeting' benefits, the state continues to be a provider of health, education and retirement pensions to a mass public. There has undoubtedly been some residualisation of public provision over the past decade, but this has been concentrated upon those who were already worst off, for example, those on state income support and in public-sector housing. This pattern of resources rather more generously directed towards the 'mass' welfare state, with retrenchment concentrated in the 'minority' or stigmatised areas, (such as unemployment benefit and one-parent benefit) is not a novelty brought on by the demands of post-Fordism but part of a longstanding British practice (Taylor-Gooby, 1985).

Of course, there have been significant changes, above all in the pattern of service delivery and there is certainly the possibility of reaching a watershed of 'mainstream' defection from public welfare which might move Britain towards an 'Americanised' or residual welfare state. But there are also some countervailing pressures. First, the expansion of private welfare is easily overstated. The rapid growth in private health insurance – often as an occupational benefit funded by employers (Calnan and Cant, 1992) – has slowed and private insurers face actuarial difficulties in extending their cover into a wider population which is both more prone to illness and less able to meet the rising costs of insurance. Again, while the numbers in private education have risen, this represents a long-term post-war trend and the overall numbers are still low (Papadakis and Taylor-Gooby, 1987; Taylor-Gooby, 1988). The character of public health care and education may be changed by the government's recent reforms, but the great majority of the population (some 90 per cent) still rely upon the public health and education services. Second, members of the middle class, who might be thought the most likely to defect from public services, still do rather well out of the welfare state. Spending on higher education, for example, tends to redistribute wealth *upwards* since the student population is disproportionately middle class and the more affluent majority may be less keen to defect from public education, for example, if reforms make it easier to deflect resources into their chosen institutions. Similarly, the extension of owner-occupation continues a long-term post-war trend and if we define the welfare state broadly enough to include fiscal policy, we see that owner-occupation is subject to a very substantial public subsidy (of about £8 billion in 1990/1). Third, opinion polls indicate a high, indeed a rising level of support for the welfare state across all social classes. In the 1990 British Social Attitudes survey, 56 per cent of voters favoured the option of increasing taxes to spend more on health, education and social benefits (compared with a figure of 32 per cent in 1983). The survey revealed a long-standing preference for increased spending on the mass-consumed (and most expensive) services (health, education and pensions), and a lower level of support for social security benefits, which were seen to be directed towards a 'less deserving' minority (Taylor-Gooby, 1990). Whilst some doubt has been cast upon the salience of these figures, there is as yet little evidence of a wholesale shift in public opinion away from state-funded welfare services. Finally, if the government were to succeed in delivering a more cost-effective, consumer-responsive (though less equitable and less egalitarian) service, we might expect not so much a wholesale residualisation of public welfare as a further bifurcation of the welfare state, in which the mass services enjoyed whatever improvements in funding were available, while the position of those poorest and most dependent upon the state declined further.

BRITAIN: FROM 'FLAWED FORDISM' TO 'FLAWED POST-FORDISM'?

How appropriate is it to understand this blend of continuity and change in British social policy as constituting the transition towards a post-Fordist form of the welfare state? Despite the elements of continuity which I have stressed, it is misleading to argue 'that nothing has really changed'. There has been a transformation of the organisation of public education and health, for example, and it seems clear that the division between welfare purchasers and welfare providers is unlikely to be reversed under any foreseeable political regime. Certainly, the government has sought to introduce some of the working practices associated with post-Fordism – sub-contracting, short-term contracts, casualisation, exclusion of trade unions and collective bargaining – into employment within the public sector. It has also sought to introduce within the public sector arrangements which mimic the allocational task of the market and taken steps to deregulate and diversify both the public and private provision of welfare services. However, it is perhaps more appropriate to think of these welfare reforms as a domestic response to characteristically 'post-Fordist' changes in the global political economy rather than as the inauguration of a distinctively post-Fordist welfare state.

There are a number of reasons for taking this rather cautious view of transformation in the British welfare state. First, there are many elements identified with the 'post-Fordist' welfare state which have long been generic features of British welfare arrangements. Those who wish to draw a sharper contrast with the past have generally given too benign an account of the decommodified or citizenship welfare state that is said to have preceded the recent epoch of reform. Elements of residualisation, of two-tier provision, of state reliance upon unpaid (female) labour within the family, of prejudice against particular minorities and of legislation subordinating welfare needs to the imperatives of labour markets are as old as the welfare state itself. Second, accounts of transformation rely upon an account of 'the crisis of the Fordist welfare-state' which is rather poorly borne out by the empirical evidence. There is a fairly broad consensus in comparative welfare state studies of the late 1980s and beyond that the logic of crisis which dominated studies from the mid-1970s to mid-1980s does not reflect the real fiscal experience of the advanced industrial societies over the past twenty years (Alber, 1988; Moran, 1988; Pierson, 1991). Whilst the welfare state has faced and will face enormous problems, many of them related to limited resources, it is a mistake to understand these problems and their potential resolution within the 'crisis' logic of the 1970s and 1980s.

Third, it remains quite unclear that the reforms associated with the post-Fordist welfare state can be generically understood as 'promoting *flexibility*'. Certainly, some reforms may have made wages more (downwardly) flexible and the reform of pensions, for example, will mean increased choice for some. But the exercise of greater consumer choice may reduce the options not only for public welfare providers but also for other consumers. For example, in the selling off of public sector housing, enhanced choice for some has effectively restricted the choice of others. Nor is this spectre of 'flexibilisation producing rigidity' confined to housing policy. 'Opting out' in schools will increase choice for some parents, but it reduces the flexibility with which those charged with the overall provision of public education within a given area can respond to changes in demand. New financial arrangements in the health service *may* increase flexibility for some purchasers of health services, but not without introducing new forms of rigidity in the overall allocation of resources. It is far from clear that the new welfare arrangements will always lead to an improvement in efficiency and flexibility. Of course, the main concern in post-Fordist accounts is with increasing flexibility in the rather narrower sense of making labour more flexible in the interest of capital. But even in this more limited sense, it is not clear that the reforms will always be successful. For example, we have seen how deregulation and flexibility in the private housing market may actually exacerbate *rigidities* elsewhere in the economy, inhibiting labour mobility and government macro-economic management. These conclusions should not be especially surprising. While popular sentiment may still see the welfare state as an expression of society's benevolent attitude to the less privileged, and the new right see it as a producer-dominated constraint upon the productive economy, neither of these amount to an adequate explanation of its (near universal) emergence in market-based societies. The welfare state exists in part to provide those public goods which markets cannot deliver or where market provision will have perverse outcomes. As Barr has observed, the welfare state has a 'major efficiency role' and, in a context of market failures, 'we need a welfare state for efficiency reasons, and would continue to do so even if all distributional problems had been solved' (Barr, 1987: 42). In terms of housing provision, for example, a more balanced tenure structure (similar to that of many of our European neighbours) might actually deliver greater *flexibility* and greater *efficiency* in terms of overall economic performance.

Fourth, we need to recognise that welfare policy, like policy in any other area, is driven by a political as well as an economic imperative. Studies of social policy in both its traditional and radical forms still suffer from the tradition of functionalist explanation in which welfare provision was 'explained' by the pattern of needs, either of the economy or of the 'social structure'. But throughout its history, British social policy has been shaped as much by political pressure, electoral and otherwise, as by 'the needs of the economy'. In the area of housing policy, for example, one could argue that very heavily discounted council house sales and the taboo upon reconsidering tax relief on mortgages are driven more by a political than an economic logic. Thus the *limits* of government policy may be set by a broadly post-Fordist international political economy, but within these limits government policy will be determined by a range of other considerations which may not always optimise, or indeed seek to optimise, flexibility.

CONCLUSION

Whilst it may be useful to think about changes of the past decade in the British welfare state in terms of the problems posed by the breakdown of a broadly Fordist regime, we need to be much more cautious in describing the new welfare regime as 'post-Fordist'. Certainly, if the policy aspirations of the Conservatives after 1979 are to be understood as post-Fordist, it must be said that they have met with very qualified success. To appropriate Jessop's classification, it may be that Britain is moving from 'flawed Fordism' towards a 'flawed post-Fordism'. Since 1979, Conservative social policy has been predicated upon reversing the failures it associated with the previous period of broadly social democratic government and which others have identified as the epoch of Fordism. Yet, after more than a decade of Conservative government, it is not clear that the transformation in the economy which a reformed social policy was to promote has really been achieved. The replacement of the 'nanny state' with the 'enterprise state' was supposed to unleash entrepreneurial skills, to galvanise investment and to transform the supply-side of the British economy. Yet, despite the undoubted economic and labour market changes of the 1980s, in the early 1990s many of the problems of the British economy look singularly untransformed. There is probably a keener understanding now, certainly compared with the consensus before 1979, that social policy and economic policy are intimately connected. But at the same time, the view that social policy has been a constraint upon successful economic policy is, following the evidence of the 1980s, rather less boldly and less frequently advanced. More often do we find the (rather bleak) recognition that only a more successful economic policy (or still more simply, a more successful economy) holds out the prospect of any substantial improvements in public welfare provision.

This sets British social policy in its proper and broader context. For all the rhetoric of choice, flexibility and enhanced efficiency, the single most important political consideration surrounding the welfare state over the last twenty years has been its cost. The major reforms of the late 1980s sought efficiency gains, so as to extract a greater welfare *output* from a welfare *input* which could not rise in line with either social expectations or demographically driven need. It is a process in which women, with their greater reliance upon public services and their much greater role in delivering unpaid welfare services within the family, have been disproportionately disadvantaged. The recent past and the foreseeable future of British social policy is thus dominated by the constraint of cost in a context of comparative economic decline. Indeed, it may be that the most important welfare initiatives of the 1990s will come not from Conservative governments at home, but from the neo-corporatist or neo-statist frame-work set by the European Community. As a part of the more general integration of the UK within the legal and economic ambit of European institutions, European law on social policy and European court rulings on British government practice are likely to have an increasing effect upon policy outcomes. Throughout the 1980s and into the 1990s, the British government has sought to avoid the enactment of European-wide reform of welfare policy and the labour market.[2] This will become increasingly difficult as integration progresses through the 1990s. Since European social policy is generally more comprehensive and more generous than UK provisions, and, in particular, since it gives much more extensive rights to workers, it will represent a very real challenge for any government that seeks to continue the policies of the Thatcher and Major administrations. Whatever the post-Fordist policy aspirations of British governments in the 1990s, the pressures for an improvement of public welfare services are likely to remain, and whilst there may be a new impetus for social policy reform and innovation from beyond these islands, the main barrier to reform will remain the sluggish condition of the British economy.

NOTES

1 As, for example, in the provisions of the Education Reform Act and in the centralisation of financial control over public-sector housing.
2 Note the reaction to the Social Charter, the Social Action Programme and the 'social chapter' of the Maastricht agreement for example.

Part II

Post-Fordism and the local welfare state

7 Restructuring the local welfare state

Allan Cochrane

INTRODUCTION

If pressed, most people would probably agree that local government in the UK is, and has historically been, part of the welfare state, but few have bothered to explore the broader implications of drawing this conclusion. Those (such as Cockburn (1977), Dearlove (1979), Saunders (1979) and Dunleavy (1980b)) who have attempted to do so have generally been sidelined in practice by the mainstream of local-government studies, even if the value of their contributions has frequently been acknowledged in principle. In practice dominant discussions of local government are still wrapped up in mythology about local democracy and infused with the notion that local government is best understood as a local version of central government.

Much of the controversy of the 1980s which focused on relations between central and local government (with the important exception of Rhodes (1988)) reflected this understanding, so that the conflict was often portrayed as being between different versions of the democratic mandate. Supporters of local government sought to produce evidence which showed that councils were more popular than central government and in some sense had more legitimacy in running their own 'communities' while critics took the view that central government had greater claims to democratic legitimacy (e.g. Adam Smith Institute (1989), Duncan and Goodwin (1988) and Jones and Stewart (1983)). One implication which could be drawn from these debates was that if only the appropriate framework for community government could be put together then problems would disappear (see Stewart and Stoker (1988), Young (1986) and the Widdicombe Report (1986) more generally).

These arguments are helpful insofar as they highlight the continued importance of local politics and the importance of conflicts over levels of expenditure, so they should not be dismissed out of hand. But if they are allowed to dominate discussion, as they have tended to, then they obscure some of the more important changes which have been taking place. They leave critical commentators cheering from the sidelines for whichever set of politicians or (to use the word generally favoured in local-government studies) 'practitioners' they support.

Dunleavy criticised much of the academic writing on local government in the 1960s and 1970s for having been written from the point of view of the 'inside dopester', based on information drawn from close relationships with political and professional actors, rather than on any attempt to analyse their behaviour from a more critical perspective. Such writing, he suggests, was 'fundamentally concerned with the same goals and operating in the same ideological frame as local government itself' (Dunleavy, 1980b: 7).

Dunleavy's criticism retains much force, and is reinforced by the extent to which much writing in the field continues to come from those who rely on close relationships with local government for training and consultancy contracts. Whilst there is no suggestion of direct corruption in this relationship, it does imply a rather narrow focus substantially driven by the concerns of those with whom continuing relationships have to be maintained (see also Dearlove's sharp critique (1979: 258-9)).

Locating local government explicitly as an integral part of the welfare state helps to bring out some of the key features of its development since 1945, as well as highlighting the ways in which it has been reshaped in the last twenty-five years. It makes it easier to explore and acknowledge some of the tensions between the different roles that it has been expected to play over the years. In the high days of the Keynesian welfare state, local government's spending rose and its sphere of influence increased. While it lost responsibilities for the provision of commodified services (such as gas and electricity) and for aspects of the health service in the immediate post-war years, it gained responsibilities for the provision of welfare services; that is, for the management of those aspects of the welfare state which required face-to-face 'professional style' involvement with people variously defined as clients, parents or tenants (in education, children's – later social – services, social housing and town planning). In many cities it also played the role of infrastructural investor, underpinning the schemes of private developers and construction companies, engaging in 'slum' clearance, reshaping city centres and constructing ring roads (see Byrne, this volume). Until the mid-1970s local authority expenditure as a proportion of national income seemed to be rising inexorably. In the late 1960s and 1970s local government's position at the heart of the British welfare state received official endorsement in a series of modernising legislative reforms, which culminated in local government reorganisation and the creation of new (generally larger) authorities designed to deal more effectively with the demands of managing social change.

THE CONTEXT OF RESTRUCTURING

It has recently become fashionable to suggest that the crisis of the Keynesian welfare state has been much exaggerated. Closer consideration of public expenditure figures has confirmed that welfare spending was not cut as much as might have been expected; indeed, it appears that most advanced capitalist countries continued to see real rises in expenditure in the 1980s, even if rates of increase were substantially lower than in the 1960s and 1970s (Hills, 1990; Pierson, 1991). More careful scrutiny of the promises made by political parties claiming the mantle of the new right and their programmes in government have also highlighted major gaps between rhetoric and the implementation of policy (Marsh and Rhodes, 1992). The extent of global consensus has also been questioned, with increased emphasis being placed on differences between states, rather than their shared features (Esping-Andersen, 1990; Pierson, 1991).

Despite these qualifications, however, there can be little doubt that the dominant assumptions of the first thirty years after 1945 which took welfare state expansion for granted have been called into question in an atmosphere of welfare austerity. In that sense there has been a significant change, since the political arrangements of those decades were based on such assumptions, whether (following Esping-Andersen, 1990) the welfare regimes they spawned are labelled corporatist, liberal or social democratic. However significant the differences were, there was a 'post-war consensus around the mixed economy and the welfare state, to which almost all advanced Western countries subscribed to a greater or lesser extent' (Mishra, 1990: 1) and it was unable to stagger on into the 1980s. In the UK at least, economic failure and political failure were closely linked (Gamble, 1985; Leys, 1989). Economic growth had made it possible to incorporate representatives of major economic groups (including the trade unions) and even to appease those formally allocated a marginal role in the system (including welfare recipients and those – mainly women – restricted to the domestic sphere). That was no longer possible after the mid 1970s and new arrangements began to emerge. Although neo-liberalism and the new right may have succeeded in constructing an effective (or hegemonic) alternative paradigm the area of acceptable political debate began to shift.

Even if the final outcome remains unclear, there can be no doubt that major changes are taking place. As Esping-Andersen notes:

> Ours is an epoch in which it is almost universally agreed that a profound realignment, if not revolution, is underway in our economy and society. The proliferation of labels, such as 'post-modernist', 'post-materialist', 'post-fordist' or 'post-industrial', often substitutes for analysis. But it mirrors the recognition that we are leaving behind us a social order that

was pretty much understood, and entering another the contours of which can be only dimly recognised.

(Esping-Anderson, 1990: 222)

There are direct links between the economic crises of the 1970s and late 1980s, the failure of social democratic approaches to resolve those crises and the state restructuring which has followed. Even if it is not possible to 'read off' political change from economic change the two are related in ways which confirm Jessop's understanding that the state still has to be understood as a capitalist state (Jessop, 1990b: 353–8). Elsewhere Jessop (this volume) suggests that it may be possible to identify a broader shift from a Keynesian welfare state to what he calls a Schumpeterian workfare state. This is a helpful suggestion because it highlights possible trajectories of change – in particular it points towards an increased emphasis on competitiveness and on a renewed role for the state in providing the context for continuing innovation. It emphasises the need to locate changes at local and national levels within wider processes of global change. The linkage between economic success and individual welfare is made increasingly explicit, not just at the level of the wider economy, but in terms of individual firms and at local level.

The key point of the emerging system is that priorities have shifted, so that welfare is explicitly understood as an almost incidental consequence of other ambitions rather than an aim in its own right. Of course, the needs of 'clients' or 'welfare dependents' were never paramount within the old structures of the Keynesian welfare state. On the contrary, one of the reasons it was so vulnerable to criticism from the right was that users frequently saw it as oppressive and tight-fisted, and it was already facing criticism from the left, from feminists and from anti-racist voices. But it is nevertheless important to highlight a couple of important differences in emphasis between the emerging system and its precursor. One is the rather peculiar feeling that the arguments of Marxists and neo-Marxists (such as Gough (1979)) that the Keynesian welfare state basically operated in the interests of the reproduction of capitalism (even if it could not always deliver what it promised) have become the unacknowledged orthodoxy of the 1990s, so that it has now become legitimate – indeed expected – for governments and business organisations to argue that this should be the case, even if they are less convinced that it already is.

The second is the extent to which it now seems to be accepted that welfare provision and welfare regimes are likely to vary between places, to reflect existing (and changing) spatial divisions of labour (Massey, 1984) and the extent to which different local formations of capital, interacting with other local social formations, may find expression in political regimes able to articulate and define divergent local 'needs' in the context of increased competition between places. It is not only possible to identify differences between the welfare regimes which dominate in different countries, but also to explore differences between urban and local political regimes which have implications for the operation of local welfare states.

RESTRUCTURING IN PRACTICE

Local government in the UK has faced particular problems as an institutional expression of the welfare state. What had been constructed was a national, comprehensive and standardised system locally delivered through multifunctional organisations with their own territorially based political pretensions. The form taken by the local welfare state in the UK, with its basis in elected councils, made the tensions particularly sharp since they gave the institutions of the welfare state a relatively autonomous expression. Welfare bureaucracies were defended behind an ideology of local democracy, however limited democratic control was in practice. Territorial politics was interwoven with the professional politics of policy networks in ways which made it difficult to completely transform existing structures, and which seemed to confirm the extent to which the welfare state tended to operate in the interests of those who ran it (Rhodes, 1988). As a result the crisis of the Keynesian welfare state in its British variant was also fundamentally a crisis of local government, which has led to a substantial restructuring of the local welfare state.

One aspect of the changes which has already been charted extensively is the expansion of local economic policy (Geddes, this volume), the revival of civic 'boosterism' and an increased orientation towards economic growth as a legitimate aim for local government. Cooke (1989) has emphasised the possibility of proactive intervention by localities; Harvey (1989b) has pointed to the emergence of 'urban entrepreneurialism'; Totterdill (1989) has sought to draw out wider lessons for economic policy; Harding (1990) has focused on the spread of public–private partnerships; in a series of case studies, Harloe *et al.* (1989) have highlighted the possible range of local economic policies; and there has also been a substantial increase in the self-help literature of economic development (see for example Campbell (1990a) for a collection which crosses the academic/professional divide). The new situation implies a significant change at local level, since competition between places intra- and inter-nationally provides the political driving force and the direction taken by local economic policy-making is one expression of this.

But explicit economic policy-making has always been and remains a relatively minor part of local government activity, still at the margins of local politics as it is popularly understood. If the local welfare state (and local government as part of that state) is being substantially restructured then it should be possible to identify a wider shift across policy areas more closely related to aspects of welfare provision. An increased emphasis on boosterism and on public–private partnerships to achieve growth may be an indicator of change, but an increased interest in the local economy in itself does not suggest a major shift in political approach or organisation. That would also require substantial changes in the core activities of the local welfare state. So it is on these that the remainder of this chapter shall focus.

The danger of overemphasising economic policy-making and growth-oriented politics is that it becomes easy to lose sight of the wider aspects of the 'business agenda' (Newman and Clarke, 1994) as it has developed at local level. This agenda has been constructed incrementally since the late 1970s and not as part of any clearly articulated grand plan of social change. Many of the direct pressures for change within the UK have certainly come from above; from initiatives sponsored by central government, particularly inspired by 'Thatcherism' and the ideas of the 'new right'. The key features have included attempts to reduce spending on welfare, helping to create a permanently beleaguered atmosphere of managing cuts within the local state; shifts in forms of provision, through attempts to create surrogate markets for example in the forms of privatisation, compulsory competitive tendering, the purchaser–provider split, fragmentation of providers, the removal of some forms of activity from local government responsibility and so on; and attempts to encourage business involvement in the civic arena (for example through TECs, Urban Development Corporations, City Challenge, support for enterprise agencies, direct involvement in schools and colleges through boards of governors and so on (Byrne, this volume)). The failure of the poll tax (see Bagguley, this volume) has ensured that the fiscal regime under which local authorities operate has become harsher and harsher in the 1990s. Not only are levels of local taxation limited through capping, but even where this is not the case few councils are able to use tax revenues to raise their budgets significantly, since income from council tax only covers around 15 per cent of their spending.

Although assisted by the initiatives of central government, business-based agencies at national and local levels have also been actively involved in the process of restructuring the local political agenda, as have many local authorities themselves desperate to generate social partnerships where none already exist. Jessop has noted the way in which the division between private economy and the state means that the latter remains dependent on the private sector as the source of economic well-being (Jessop, 1990a: 178–80). Although there is now no direct link between the success of local business and the tax income of councils, this wider dependence in the context of increased (global) competition between places helps to give the 'business agenda' its powerful resonance at local level.

Business interests have set out to influence the welfare agenda at local as well as national level, through Business in the Community, the Confederation of British Industry, and the work of Chambers of Commerce (expressed, for example, in Bennett and Business in the Community (1990), Bennett (1991) and Christie *at al.*, 1991; see also Jacobs (1992: ch. 9)). At local level individuals identified as the 'movers and shakers' of the business community (Fogarty and Christie, 1990: 94) have taken on the role of helping to shape this agenda, with the cooperation of the institutions of central and local government and, frequently, with 'messianic zeal' (Fogarty and Christie, 1990: 91). But the active involvement of such individuals (however widespread) is not an essential component of the new arrangements. Even where it is difficult to find active individuals or organisations from the business community, local state institutions increasingly attempt to act in line with what their agenda is assumed to be, forming 'alliances' with the shadows of local (and multinational) capital even in their absence. Private consultancy firms are only too eager to act as surrogates in preparing business-friendly policy programmes.

In extreme cases the whole issue is turned on its head, so that welfare provision is justified largely because of the way it make places more or less attractive to business. In one report (commissioned from consultants but sponsored by local government and the London Docklands Development Corporation) which focuses on the need to develop policies to ensure that London retains its status as a 'world city', for example, concern is expressed about the extent of urban deprivation experienced by the Bangladeshi community of Spitalfields, not because of the problems they face, but because it might reduce the quality of life for higher status residents and encourage businesses to relocate (Kennedy, 1991: 73–4). Similarly the discussion of the need for affordable housing has less to do with those who can be expected to live in it and more to do with the needs of employers, since 'the market's inability to provide housing for lower income households should be recognised as an impediment to London's development prospects' (Kennedy, 1991: 209).

Even where attempts are made to incorporate social regeneration more centrally into programmes of change the emphasis shifts because it is integrated into a business-oriented vision. Sheffield's strategy for the year 2000 was prepared through the Sheffield Economic Regeneration Committee (itself often put forward as a model of public–private partnership (Fogarty and Christie, 1990)) and includes a well-developed commitment to social regeneration (SERC, n.d.). In a sense, however, this positive expression helps to illustrate the extent of the changes and the ways in which they have influenced interpretations of 'welfare' as well as interpretations of 'enterprise' and economic regeneration. Sheffield's strategy is organised around a 'vision' and has five main themes that come together to provide objectives, described as the 'Vision Becomes Reality objectives' because when they have been achieved the 'vision' will indeed have become reality. Sheffield is to become: a natural centre for business and industry; a new decision centre; an international centre for sport, leisure and tourism; an international centre for teaching, learning, research and technology; and a 'city of life'.

It will be clear simply from reading the overall titles given to these themes that the first two are explicitly oriented towards business: the first affirms the desire to sustain and expand existing manufacturing, commercial and service industries and to attract new employers; the second builds on this to make claims to a share of office development and particularly the headquarters of national and international businesses. The second two, in practice, have a similar orientation since aiming to become an international centre for leisure and sport reflects ambitions to change the image of Sheffield (and the quality of life it has to offer) as much as any ambition to improve locally provided services. The stress on teaching, research and technology also reflects the selling of the city as one in which innovation and enterprise will flourish. In other words, the city's leisure and educational policies are seen as part of the selling of the city and an essential element of business infrastructure rather than being seen as something provided for residents (the idea of providing anything for anybody is by now – of course – in any case almost universally derided within the new orthodoxy as a symbol of Fordist paternalism to be avoided at all costs). The final theme is more explicitly aimed towards social regeneration, looking to create 'a positive environment for the health, benefit and enjoyment of all Sheffield people'. But even this positive expression is prefaced by the desire to 'foster a vibrant and dynamic city' (SERC, n.d.: 21) which implies a continued concern with image that owes more to business than to the needs of residents. Where the argument about social regeneration is developed further, again stress is placed on the need to link economic regeneration and social regeneration, with the implication that the latter is dependent on the former, even if the obstacles which make it difficult for one to lead to the other still need to be overcome.

But not all aspects of the local welfare state lend themselves quite so easily to direct business involvement and influence. The linkages may be rather more subtle, suggesting changes in the dominant common sense or what is taken-for-granted as much as any direct business involvement. It is this that helps to make the 'agenda' more pervasive and unchallengeable. Bennett and Krebs (1991) argue strongly that one of the tasks of local government is to become more 'business-like' in order to ensure that more effective collaboration with business is possible on a range of issues. In this they are merely echoing the more widespread common sense of the 1980s which contrasts the perceived inefficiency of the public sector – and particularly welfare bureaucracies – with the perceived efficiency of the private (business) sector. This has, of course, found its clearest expression in the privatisation policies of recent Conservative governments, but it has also influenced organisational changes in what is left of the public sector.

Business models have increasingly been appropriated within local government for the organisation of its own activities – from strategic policy-making and mission statements, down to the issuing of contracts and the monitoring of service provision. In the 1960s the language of management was utilised to justify expansion (Friend and Jessop, 1969), but this time it is being taken up in the context of contraction. The influence of popular management texts has been widely noted, and, perhaps unsurprisingly, Tom Peters' notion of 'Thriving on Chaos' seems to have struck chords with some senior managers (Smith, 1989) while Moss Kanter's identification of post-entrepreneurial styles of management offers still more possibilities (Moss Kanter, 1989) pointing to the extent to which they may be able to find increased 'freedom within boundaries' as an alternative to strict bureaucratic hierarchies (Hoggett, 1991b: 250). At least some public-sector managers seem to be drawing on these approaches to escape from the neo-Taylorist implications of the reforms of the early 1980s with their rather narrower stress on targets and performance measurement (which are considered by Pollitt (1990)). Local government's own writers on management have not been far behind in reinterpreting the new approaches for public-sector consumption (Brooke, 1989; Clarke and Stewart, 1990; Hambleton and Hoggett, 1990; Stewart and Walsh, 1989). Major consultancy organisations such as Price Waterhouse (now with the help of the one-time leader of Islington Council) and Coopers and Lybrand have played an increasing role in providing advice on management and organisational restructuring, as carriers of blueprints from the private sector.[1]

These changes have been reinforced by a more subtle form of shift in agenda, as actors within the state have begun (despite frequent hand-wringing about the importance of maintaining professional standards) to take on a rather different understanding of their role. Strategic managers have begun to make claims to higher status. They have increasingly moved away from the notion of local welfare state as self-sufficient provider to that of local government as 'enabler' which – in principle at least – allows them to have a much greater influence as well as giving them a status closer to that of senior managers in large private-sector organisations rather than the more traditional welfare-state role model of senior civil servants. However illusory their hopes may turn out to be in the harsh light of the 1990s, they present themselves as being at the centre of complex networks of influence. They alone, it is argued (Brooke, 1989; LGTB, 1987; Stewart, 1989), have the potential to embody the overall interests of their areas (and 'communities') and so to manage the contributions of a range of agencies and interests to achieve the best possible welfare outcomes. They are the defenders of 'quality assurance'. Senior managers in local government (and chief executives, in particular) are now able to claim a powerful role with a higher status than that of the welfare professionals they have had to manage so frustratingly since the 1960s.

The link between these changes and the business agenda is made easier by the way in which managerialism has become the evangelism of the new age, linking private and public sectors, and helping to erode the older hierarchies of welfarism, while replacing them with new and apparently equally unchallengeable hierarchies. Pollitt highlights the power of managerialism as an ideology because of the way in which it emphasises the importance of managers in all organisations, whether in the public or private sectors (Pollitt, 1990). It links the public and private sectors in ways that help to give local government managers external and personal legitimacy in the new climate of welfare. Clarke and Newman note the evangelical tone of the new management literature, and echoes of this are apparent in all the 'visions' and 'strategies' which are proliferating throughout local government (Clarke and Newman, 1993). This can probably be illustrated well enough with the help of just one example. The vision of Buckinghamshire's Social Services Department is: 'To be the best and give of our best'. And its Mission is:

> to enable people who are in need because of disability or vulnerability to achieve, maintain or restore a defined level of social independence or quality of life. It does this by identifying and assessing needs, and by making the best use of available resources to provide access to appropriate individualised services.

As usual these broad statements make no reference to actual resources and – above all – no reference to the difficulties of providing individualised services of a high standard when available resources are significantly (and increasingly) constrained. In the longer term it is difficult to avoid the conclusion that 'needs' will only be identified if the resources to meet them are available.

Within local government, stress is increasingly placed on the need to change existing organisational cultures and the move to managerialism has become a key element in the reshaping of welfare, challenging the service professionals. As Newman and Clarke note:

Management is the necessary corollary of the dismantling of the familiar structures of bureau-professionalism. Managers are those who 'understand' markets; who can extract the untapped potential from the 'human resources'; who are sensitised to the 'needs of the customer'; who can deliver 'results' and who can be relied on to 'do the right thing'.

(Newman and Clarke, 1994)

In this process central government has played a rather more subtle part than is normally credited to 'Thatcherism' and the new right. The Audit Commission set up in 1983 to explore and monitor the 'economy, efficiency, and effectiveness' of local government and the health service has succeeded in carving out a relatively independent role for itself, feeding into both detailed discussion of particular service areas and more general discussion of local government organisation. While it may not have had the effect originally intended, which seems principally to have been to reduce costs in the name of 'value for money', it has certainly helped to reinforce moves towards managerialism by suggesting that generic expertise in accountancy and management is powerful enough to question (welfare) professional practice across the board. Although largely funded directly by central government, as a representative of local authority employers, the Local Government Management Board (formed later in the decade) seems to have taken on a similar role, seeing itself – to use its own slogan – as 'promoting better practice' by encouraging substantial organisational change and managerial 'innovation'. Again it is assumed that the new management has messages which cut across old professional boundaries, like the Audit Commission, however the Board is not commenting from the outside but is itself part of the national local government system (Walker, 1992).

THE CHANGING WORLD OF SOCIAL SERVICES

So far, the focus of this chapter has been on the local welfare state as a whole, but looking more specifically at the experience of the personal social services is helpful in highlighting some of the main directions of change. The personal social services became a core part of the local welfare state in the 1960s and 1970s, receiving departmental status in the wake of the Seebohm and Kilbrandon reports. Social workers were expected to work directly with 'clients' and the departments were expected to provide services and support to them. But within the 'enabling' authority, the role of social services departments is expected to be a rather different one. They are now seen to be responsible for managing rather than providing welfare or – to use the language which has increasingly been adopted – care services. Legislation and government guidelines on community care now talk of care managers, rather than social workers. The Griffiths report argues strongly for more management training in qualifying and in-service training for social workers to cope with these changed responsibilities (Griffiths, 1988). Social work – which has effectively been defined as a 'bureau-profession' through employment within social services departments – becomes redefined as 'a provision in its own right, to be commissioned by the care manager, although the role of care manager may well encompass a degree of counselling and support' (Audit Commission, 1992: 27).

The key skills are increasingly identified as those of assessment, of managing a range of different providers (preparing plans for individual cases) and of being able to engage in inter-agency working. The assumption seems to be that outside a strictly limited area in which specialist expertise may still be required (for example working with child abuse (Pietroni, 1991)) the bulk of social services work can be dealt with under the supervision of care managers by relatively 'unskilled', low-paid and part-time labour or through 'informal' arrangements (usually by mothers, sisters or daughters). In this expression of the managerial revolution, managing includes the 'human resource management' of a much more complex 'labour force', much of which is no longer directly employed by the agencies formally responsible for managing it. The traditional bureau-professionalism of social work is significantly undermined, not least because the 'bureau' on which it depends is substantially fragmented. It becomes much more difficult to defend a generic set of professional skills when the new arrangements implicitly suggest that some of them are little more than common sense. While a recognition of the importance of informal care may raise the status of those providing it, it also effectively undermines the professional status of those previously defined as experts (see Cochrane (1993) for a more extensive discussion of these issues). The rise of care management can be seen as a means of undermining social work as a profession by constructing an alternative professional discourse.

These legislative changes are the end product of debates which have gone on through the 1980s, at local and national levels, within policy networks and professional communities as well as in party politics. As Hudson (1990) stresses in his discussion of the community care legislation, they are not simply the product of a 'new right' policy agenda. There is not a high degree of party political controversy surrounding the legislation itself. Nor – except in terms of the individual responses of social workers having to deal with the changes in local authorities – has there been any significant professionally based resistance. On the contrary, most professional commentary has been concerned to identify the positive (or 'progressive') points of the legislation and to focus on how it may be used most effectively, or to complain about financial resources allocated to its implementation. This may or may not be an appropriate response to the legislation but it certainly illustrates one of the ways in which managerialism works as an acid with which chains of welfare professionalism may be dissolved, to the extent that welfare professionals themselves seem unable to present an alternative vision.

Although local authority social services departments are formally given a leading role both in the fields of community care (in the National Health Service and Community Care Act, 1990) and child protection (in the Children Act, 1989), in practice the legislation helps to fragment responsibility between agencies, only bringing it together in forms of collaboration and joint working. In community care this has been particularly focused on collaboration between the local authorities and health authorities, but, of course, other agencies have also been involved, from voluntary bodies to the private sector, for example through direct negotiation over residential care with private-sector homes. Even the police have begun to make claims to social-work expertise and they have, of course, begun to play an increasingly important part in child protection investigations, particularly where they involve the interviewing of children on video (Brake and Hale, 1992: ch 4; Home Office and Department of Health, 1992). In the field of child protection the growing stress on inter-agency cooperation changes the position of social services departments in rather a different way, since it implies that no one agency has the necessary expertise in the area and that the ability to negotiate with others to produce consistent child-protection plans is more important than any specific expertise. In both cases managerial rather than professional skills become more highly valued. A recent survey of existing research evidence on the gains of collaborative working in child protection points out that the results are equivocal (Hallett and Birchall, 1992: 97). But – of course – that's not necessarily the point of the changes.

The parallel changes taking place in the health service with their increasingly complex divisions of responsibility between fund-holding general practitioners, health authorities (including family health service authorities), hospital and community health service trusts and purchasing agencies have begun more clearly to break down traditional local government dominance within the local welfare state. The division of responsibility between personal social services and health services has become increasingly unclear and this has been encouraged by the community care reforms, even if the lead role is formally allocated to local government agencies. Joint planning and consultation through Community

Care Plans are now the norm as networks of collaboration and negotiation are constructed to reinforce the position of strategic managers in the different agencies (Allen, 1991). At a more basic level, the assessment role formally given to 'care managers' and frequently assumed to be that of social services departments is also claimed by health professionals. General practitioners are, for example, often given a key role in the assessment process within community care (Buckinghamshire Health Plan, 1992: para. 79).

Perhaps the most interesting shift is the way in which health authorities, rather than local authorities, have begun to take new initiatives, building on responsibilities for primary health care to develop wider programmes. Emphasis is increasingly placed on primary health care and holistic approaches, rather than hospital-based (or secondary) care. The new emphasis (encouraged by government documents such as Home Office and Department of Health (1992)) insists that ordinary life rather than medical intervention is the key to health. This suggests that health authorities are likely to have an increasing interest in areas previously defined as local government responsibilities: an increased interest in primary care and health promotion, for example, may encourage a focus on housing, on community facilities, on child care and on education. The new health services orthodoxy using the language of 'empowerment' presents itself as setting out to elicit views and gain input from local service users through forums of different sorts (Buckinghamshire Health Plan, 1992: paras 81–2). Health authorities have already begun to draw other agencies into a processes of 'locality planning'. In North Staffordshire and Newcastle, for example, neighbourhood forums have been set up involving professionals (from the statutory and non-statutory sectors), community representatives and local residents. The aims of these forums have been to feed into health authority (general manager) decision-making, to allocate small amounts of resource at local level and to bring different agencies together. The forums have opened up some aspects of decision-making to wider discussion, and seem to have been welcomed at local level, although levels of community involvement remain modest (Gott and Warren, 1990).

In one sense welfare provision has become more integrated, potentially managed more effectively through a network with strategic managers at the core (or in multiple cores linked through forms of inter-agency working, in which the dominant partner may vary over time). But this has also been accompanied by an increasing institutional fragmentation, characterised by the growth of a multiplicity of providers of one sort or another – from housing associations to health service trusts, from locally managed and grant-maintained schools to training and enterprise councils, from not-for-profit welfare agencies providing residential care to enterprise agencies. State expenditure is increasingly being channelled back to the private sector or to state-based private-sector-like agencies through contracting out. Although this was originally most obvious for activities such as street cleaning, refuse disposal and housing maintenance, it is inexorably spreading into other areas such as residential care, casualised social-work services and even architectural services.

STRATEGY AND 'EMPOWERMENT'

Within the changing system the key decisions about resources are taken by the strategists, the budget setters and the representatives of major interests. The fragmentation of the local welfare state, because it leads in turn to a greater emphasis on networks linking and cross-cutting different parts of the public, voluntary and private sectors, helps to confirm these shifts. It moves key decision-making into increasingly enclosed arenas, such as the joint committees bequeathed by the abolition of the metropolitan counties and the inter-agency bodies demanded by child protection work, even while parents are expected to 'participate' in child protection conferences. There is a proliferation of strategic committees and strategic plans, for health care, for community care, and for housing. Professionals and managers involved in these networks are likely to become increasingly concerned with finding technical solutions to the difficulties of operating in a world with no clear hierarchy in ways which make accountability still more difficult to identify (Alexander, 1991).

Alongside these moves, however, there is also a growing rhetoric of 'empowerment'. The new arrangements emphasise the role of the strategists, who seem to operate outside traditional forms of political control, particularly electoral accountability. But they also point to the need to more actively involve users, consumers and communities. In a sense, of course, by doing so they further undermine notions of accountability through the electoral system on which existing forms of local government have been based. Again the example of 'Sheffield 2000' is interesting here. Stress is placed on notions of 'community empowerment' which is intended to ensure that decision-makers listen, but also effectively shifts responsibility to them and makes it easier (for business and local government) to license particular groups by stressing the extent to which they require financial support. The discussion of collaborative work in 'Sheffield 2000' indicates that:

> Communities and the voluntary sector need to make links with businesses and other enabling organisations to work in collaboration. The voluntary sector needs to be clear about its role and its limitations

to enable effective participation. An initial and pervasive difficulty is the imbalance of power between participants, particularly when community groups work with large and powerful organisations. Powerful agencies will therefore need to resource their less powerful partners for effective participation.

It is easy and probably right to be cynical about the claims made for 'empowerment', particularly when the terms on which it is to be encouraged are substantially limited by decisions (and strategies) already made elsewhere. The warning that those being 'empowered' need to be aware of resource limitations is usually either stated explicitly or taken for granted as part of the new common sense. But the rhetoric may foster the growth of rather different sets of political movements, too. Fragmentation may even encourage the growth of more challenging politics by breaking the atmosphere which suggests that users of welfare services should be grateful for everything they receive. The introduction of the poll tax provides an example of the way in which some reforms may have unexpected consequences. It was originally intended to 'empower' local tax payers by building an alliance between a central government opposed to wasteful spending and local residents opposed to paying higher rates of tax. Although in practice important questions about the funding of the local welfare state were raised through the politics of the poll tax, the questions were directed towards central rather than local government. Equally important, it encouraged the development of locally (often neighbourhood) based political movements which played an important part in forcing the government to retreat (Bagguley, this volume).

Attempts to have licensed 'empowerment' in other areas may have similar consequences, since it is unclear that user groups will accept the secondary, 'responsible' part they are expected to play. The evidence so far is, at least, equivocal. While moving responsibility for service provision to voluntary organisations relying on state funding may save money, it may also result in fierce resistance when cuts are proposed, particularly if the voluntary organisations have – as the rhetoric suggests they should – been successful in putting down roots in the communities of which they are a part. If they have been successful, they are unlikely to accept the legitimacy of decisions taken by politicians and managers who emphasise strategic issues. In some cases, too, the 'empowerment' may encourage the growth of independent organisations not solely reliant on state funding and prepared, therefore, to present alternatives which may be embarrassing to their sponsors. Organisations such as Women's Aid, for example, continue to operate as a critique of more official responses to the problem of domestic violence. Even opening up the possibility of assessing 'need' within the community-care legislation may backfire, if those whose 'needs' are being assessed fail to accept a passive role and seek to play a part in identifying their own 'needs'. They may even refuse to acknowledge that resource limitations are important in this process.

CONCLUSION: THEORIES AND PRACTICES

Although many of the arguments of this chapter are consistent with some versions of post-Fordist theorising, it will be apparent that no explicit attempt has been made to refer back to those theories. In large part this reflects a concern that they are too often used to avoid a more direct engagement with the analysis of processes of restructuring. There are too many versions of Fordism and post-Fordism to allow any confidence in utilising the theories: every time one is criticised the hydra-headed beast seems ready to produce another offspring with the same name, but a different content. It is difficult to avoid the suspicion that instead of providing useful guidance in the analysis of the changes which – undoubtedly – are taking place, the theories either provide an excuse for not looking more closely at them or actively obscure the nature of those changes by imposing some pre-ordained direction on them (see Cochrane (1991: 285–90) for a further discussion of these concerns in the context of local government). This chapter has had rather different ambitions.

Before constructing a fully developed theoretical analysis of the changes which have taken place, it is necessary to be rather clearer about what has been happening. With the help of such a focus it should be possible to develop what might be called 'middle-level concepts' to assist us in understanding those changes and locating them more effectively within broader theoretical approaches. This chapter, therefore, has set itself the theoretically rather modest – if by no means straightforward – task of identifying some of the main features of change within the UK's local government system, as well as suggesting some ways of analysing the processes underlying them.

So, what are the middle-level concepts that are likely to be helpful in analysing the changes which are taking place? It is clearly necessary to move beyond straightforward notions of local government. Elected local government is only part of the wider network of relations which currently constitutes the local welfare state. But some notions originally developed for other purposes are useful in characterising and exploring the new world.

There has sometimes been a tendency to represent the (old) British welfare state as a monolithic and hierarchical structure, a bureaucratically organised delivery system linking Whitehall to the individual welfare 'client'. Recently, however, it has been argued that it might more accurately be understood as a mixed economy of welfare, since care in the domestic sphere has always been the major (unrecognised) foundation of welfare, alongside state and voluntary sector provision and a continuing private sector. The nature of that mixed economy, however, has been changing over time (Clarke and Langan, 1993) and the changes are particularly clear at local level. Focusing on the local welfare state helps to clarify the extent to which the mix varies between places. The notion of welfare regimes originally developed by Esping-Andersen (1990) to deal with differences between national systems is helpful in understanding the nature of these differences, particularly if it is used to highlight the necessary linkages between national and local levels, while allowing a substantial degree of autonomy at local level. There is substantial scope for difference between places even within an overarching national welfare regime and that scope may be increasing.

At local level it may also be helpful to build on notions of urban regime (particularly if they are not narrowly restricted to cities). These urban (or local) regimes may be defined as 'the informal arrangements by which public bodies and private interests function together in order to be able to make and carry out governing decisions' (Stone, 1989: 6). Focusing on urban regimes makes it possible to explore the precise balance between key interests at local level (including tensions between different sections of the business 'community'), although there may be a danger of slipping into a form of pluralism in which a series of interests is identified and it appears that each of them has much the same chance of influencing outcomes. Here the notion of a 'business agenda' is helpful in indicating how politics may be shaped by business interests, without necessarily implying an active participation by business groups. It highlights the importance of continuing linkages between economic and political restructuring. It is part of the process that helps to confirm the local welfare state's position as part of a wider capitalist state.

Elsewhere I have used the term 'local corporatism' to categorise the new world, but that may imply too tight a set of arrangements organised through a set of rather formal public–private structures. It is important to recognise the more amorphous and all pervasive features of the new arrangements instead, since they run through a range of institutions and relations, shaping a new common sense without necessarily implying a more centralised set of structures at local or national level. The new arrangements are clearly structured within the context of a changing capitalism and clearly, too, they reinforce the power of some at the expense of others. Above all, they clearly distinguish between the managers and the managed, promising the end of traditional forms of politics and promise the end of conflicts over the allocation of resources. It may be, however, that the managed are not prepared to play according to the rules of the game, and that in practice new opportunities for locally based political movements open up in the 1990s.

ACKNOWLEDGEMENTS

This chapter owes a great deal to discussions with others, although many of them will probably not recognise what I have done with their ideas. I would like explicitly to acknowledge the contribution of John Clarke, who introduced me to many of the debates about public-sector management, and Amanda Farr, who has taught me about some of the difficulties of surviving in the new world.

NOTE

1 It is difficult not to see parallels with the role played by consultants in the late 1960s and early 1970s (and charted, for example, by Cockburn (1977: ch. 1)). The proposals may change dramatically, but the message remains the same: if you want to know how to manage, the private sector knows best.

8 Planning for and against the divided city

A case study of the north east of England

David Byrne

INTRODUCTION

This chapter is written with a considerable degree of scepticism about the general tenor of identifications of a division between 'Fordist' and 'post-Fordist' social forms. Not only do I agree entirely with Rustin's corrective to the deterministic functionalist element in regulation theory, when he argued for:

> the primacy of the actions and strategies of classes in explanation of changes in the political economy of capitalism. 'Post-Fordism' is better seen as one ideal-typical model or strategy of production and regulation to present with others in a complex historical ensemble, than as a valid totalizing description of an emerging social formation here and now.
>
> (Rustin, 1989: 61)

But the field I am dealing with – the organisation of the production and consumption of the built environment – is one in which Fordist production methods themselves have made only very limited headway and the production process is still essentially dependent on skilled workers (Ball, 1983). Moreover, and more importantly, the examples I will use for illustration are old industrial cities with a historical specialisation in Department I goods,[1] where Fordist production methods in manufacturing were associated specifically with immigrant Department II branch plants,[2] attracted by planning policies directed at industrial diversification. In other words Middlesbrough[3] is post-something, but it is difficult to argue that it, or the rest of the urban north east, were ever really Fordist.

Indeed it makes a great deal more sense to conduct this discussion in terms of 'post-Keynesian' planning: in terms of regulation theory's identification of the method of regulation characteristic of the post-war period up to the early 1970s, rather than of the mode of accumulation. I am going to deal with a situation in which there certainly has been a transformation of planning policies from a set which can be clearly identified as Keynesian:

> The essential characteristic of this 'Keynesian' regulation relationship was the inclusion, obtained by the social democratic (or similar) parties, of the workers, organized into trade unions in the process of state administrative decisions, and a stable legitimation of the socio-political relationships, supported by growth, consumption and a class conflict institutionalized in a reformist way.
>
> (Esser and Hirsch, 1989: 421)

into something where the consent of workers is not obtained, and their representatives have frequently been incorporated into decision-making processes which are flatly antagonistic to the working class and the poor. This is a *strategy*; motivated by a combination of ideological commitment to free markets, and the interests of that fraction of capital which combines speculative finance and realty development.

This is rather more important than I originally thought it was. My original emphasis was going to be on the way in which post-Keynesian, market-asserting 'catalytic' planning promoted social division, both by attacking land uses which were crucial in maintaining traditional production and hence an organised working class, *and* by systematically segregating the affluent consumers from the deprived poor, the so-called 'underclass', through the use of exclusivity as a planning principle. These were certainly the intentions of such policies. However, the reality is that this strategy has backfired very badly indeed. In 1987 David Harvey argued that:

> Heightened inter-urban competition produces socially wasteful investments that contribute to rather than ameliorate the over-accumulation problem that lay behind the transition to flexible accumulation in the first place ... Put simply, how many successful convention centres, sports stadia, Disney Worlds, and harbour schemes can there be? ... Over-investment in everything from shopping-malls to cultural facilities makes the values embedded in urban space highly vulnerable to devaluation. Down-town revivals built upon burgeoning employment in financial and real-estate services where people daily process loans and real-estate deals for other people employed in financial services, depends upon a huge expansion of personal, corporate and governmental debt. If that turns sour . . . .
>
> (Harvey, 1987: 265)

He summed his argument up thus:

> Flexible accumulation, in short, is associated with a highly fragile pattern of urban investment as well as increasing social and spatial polarization of urban class antagonisms.
>
> (Harvey, 1987: 278)

He certainly got that right. The advocates of exclusive consumer capitalism may have thought it could live with the permanently dispossessed. It cannot live with dispossession coupled with financial collapse. What we have after more than ten years of post-Keynesian urban planning (dating this from the 1980 Planning and Land Act in the UK), is a situation where 'reclaimed' brown-field sites on formerly 'derelict' land seem to have *negative* value, and social division is so acute that we have created a serious *non-ethnically based* problem of urban disorder.

This chapter is about planning in old, clapped-out, industrial cities. These are really rather important. Nearly half of the population of the UK actually lives in such places, and they were and are the traditional location of the core industrial proletariat – the universal class with transformational capacity. *All* of the urban agglomerations of Eastern Europe have reached this stage in double-quick time. *Most* of the so-called 'world cities' seem to have much of their population living under conditions of 'clapped-out industrialism'.[4] London Docklands' history suggests that catalytic market-orientated planning has created no more value there than in industrial dumps like Sunderland.

It will proceed by outlining the transition from pre-Keynesian development to Keynesian planning in the North East, and then go on to review the content of Keynesian planning and argue that the planning strategies of that period, and particularly in the second half of it which can be described as the phase of 'modernisation', were crucial in making flexible accumulation strategies possible. The chapter will then give an account of the turn to 'postmodernisation' in relation to the socio-spatial context left by modernisation's impact. It will conclude by asking what political strategies are appropriate for planning, given the wreckage of modernisation, as subsequently vandalised by postmodernisation, in a cultural context of hegemonic social democracy (while it lasts).

FROM BOOM TO SLUMP AND OUT OF IT – THE ORIGINS AND CONTENT OF KEYNESIAN PLANNING

The first thing to realize about Keynesian planning strategies, as developed in Britain's special area programmes in the 1930s, was that they were strategies for areas which between 1850 and 1920 had been key areas of industrial production and had been very prosperous indeed. There was a real difference between the UK's inter-war unemployment and that of its competitors. First, the UK's lasted longer because of secular intervention directed at maintaining the city-imperial link – the economic consequences of Mr Churchill. Second, the worst-affected zones were not those of redundant plantation or settler agriculture, but those of Department I production – the power-houses and armouries of the Age of Empire. However, those power-houses in their years of prosperity, and particularly in the period of very rapid population growth from 1910 to 1920, had been characterised by a situation in which productive capacity outstripped reproductive capacity. In other words when the post-World War I slump hit, they had enormous social deficits.

Thus inter-war planning, which came in alongside simple continued development in the form of the very large growth in suburban owner-occupation based on the high real wages of the securely employed in the 1930s, always had two linked projects. One was meso-economic in terms of the diversification of the industrial base, which necessarily meant the importation of branch plants, many of which employed women, which produced Department II goods and which were Fordist in form. The other was macro-economic public works. The public works deficit (housing, road transport and sewerage) identified in the 1930s provided the social and infrastructual planning agenda of the North until about 1975.

It would be a serious mistake to think that all industrial development post-1920 was Fordist. Two major north-eastern industries which date from this period – Teesside chemicals and Tyneside heavy electrical engineering – were firmly in Department I and were pre-Fordist. In terms of labour process the first was a mixture of manufacture (construction, which was ongoing, and maintenance) and machino-facture (which could be converted into Fordism). The second was firmly manufacture. It would also be a mistake to think that planning ignored these pre-Fordist elements. Although the concern did not really develop until the 1960s, the Department of Economic Affairs and then Department of Trade and Industry regional policy and reorganisation policy, was very much addressed to the traditional sectors, and especially to the needs of steel and chemicals on Teesside. Indeed it seems hard to fit 1960s and 1970s regional policy into a Fordist-Keynesian frame because much of the Department I subsidised investment was job-destroying through capital intensification (Hudson, 1989).

However, the focus of this chapter is on the reproductive sphere. Here it is useful to follow Carney and Townsend (1977) and make a distinction between planning policies concerned with social justice and those concerned with modifying the productive base. The distinction is heuristic, because modernisation was always justified in terms of job creation or job defence, and full employment was a crucial social goal. However, in the years from 1945 to 1960 when the first phase of general land-use planning was developed and implemented, the continuation of full employment in the traditional sectors, coupled with the relative ease of attracting female employees by Department II plants in conditions of general labour shortage, meant that the planning emphasis was on social needs.

That emphasis was largely on housing and, between 1945 and 1957, on the provision of very good-quality council housing on overspill estates. Typical of the plans of this period are those prepared by the Max Lock group for Hartlepool and Middlesbrough which led to the development of East Middlesbrough, as their Tyneside and Wearside equivalents led to the development of the massive 1940s and 1950s overspill estates.[5] This can be characterised as the period of 'left-Keynesianism' because the mechanism of provision was planned and the mode was public.

After 1957 when Conservative governments controlled the national state, the system shifted to right-Keynesianism with the public sector confined (for most of the period) to providing new housing for the poor, and the provision of mass good housing handed over to developer-builders (who closely resembled Davis' (1990) west-side Keynesian developers in Los Angeles) – usually operating at one remove from political power given Labour's hegemony (not always absolute in this period) in the urban north.

In the first of these periods land values were not of great significance. Betterment levies etc. were intended to confiscate development gains, and most urban development proceeded on very cheap peripheral sites. In the second period there was a change, with the value of peripheral housing sites becoming much more important to developer-builders who made much of their return by changing 'white' (agricultural) land's planning designation, although in the north east this was probably always less important than simple profits on the construction process. What was very important was the 1960s reconstruction of urban centres as shopping precincts, with developers utilising the compulsory development powers of local authorities in partnership arrangements and the advantages offered by slum clearance and radial road development. This was the period of instrumental corruption (recall Poulson and Andy Cunningham for example) and clever legal use of position by traditional elites in a wholly traditional way – an era of the manipulated city.

To a considerable extent developments recapitulated those of the 1930s with the important difference that now almost everybody was aboard the consumption gravy train. Unparalleled levels of employment (given the new female employment) generated very high household incomes and mass consumption. Revealingly throughout this period new house prices in the north maintained a traditional 3:1 ratio to skilled workers' earnings in contrast to the 5:1 reached at the height of the property boom in the late 1980s. This was a corporatist era with the general development of mass universalist social services. Housing was the big exception, in the second right-Keynesian phase, but the quality distinctions between council housing and owner-occupied housing were small (with the very significant exception of the 'mass housing' – see Dunleavy (1981) – built for some slum-cleared people after 1960).

What cannot be ignored is the enormous planning success in social terms of these two eras in combination. Inadequate housing and over-crowding were virtually eliminated from the region. Towards the end of the period the level of good provision was such that in a context of population loss throughout migration, it has subsequently been possible to demolish much of the worst of the 1960s and 1970s mass housing. This is the significant difference between old industrial conurbations, of which Tyne, Wear and Teesside are extreme examples, and 'world cities' where continuing growth pressure prevented such gains; hence the growth of bed and breakfast accommodation and homelessness in London. Other major social infrastructural gains were made in education and health-service provision.

At a key date in this process Robson (1969: 132) observed of Sunderland, that:

> The development of local authority housing both in peripheral areas and in central redevelopment areas, together with the general increase in the role of central and local town planning, the spread of affluence and its concomitant eroding of social differentials, or at least the increase in social and geographical mobility that this has brought with it, and the very fact of the great decrease in rates of urban growth: all have led increasingly to shortcomings in the classical models, and to their limited usefulness in the modern setting.

It is important to recognise the actual scale of urban reconstruction. The population of all three of the north east's conurbations is now somewhat smaller than it was in 1921 but the actual built-up area has increased dramatically – by nine times for the County of Tyne and Wear (not including adjacent shire county suburbs). Some of this increase occurred in the inter-war years, but the bulk of it is from post-1945 building. This geographical change is not trivial. As Lever observed for Glasgow: 'This outward expansion of the conurbation has permitted much greater social polarization within the built up area' (Lever, 1991: 987).

If we look at the origins of this real polarisation, we find it firmly located within the modernisation phase. This raises the interesting question of at what level we should seek an explanation of such changes. My argument is that they result from an interaction between (1) the global level of restructuring, (2) specific national policies of UK governments, and (3) the local form of suburbanization in specific places. This local element requires some elaboration.

Land is not mobile, but nothing in capitalism is more mobile than money. However, if money is related to land it has to be done in specific places where the specificity of the place is an important determinant of potential profitability. The production of the built environment is intrinsically placed.

This means that the production of the built environment, and the consequent ordering of urban space, is an intrinsically local process. Cox and Mair (1989) point out that urban capital, and the urban bourgeoisie, are necessarily local, precisely because the forms of the use made of space (originally of course the interaction of the forms of space with the use made of it) are the determinant of site values (which in the long run have to be understood as capitalised rents).

The importance of consideration of these local development capitals and associated bourgeoisies is that they play a role in the restructuring of places, and especially of larger towns, which is at least in part separate from the impacts of transnational productive capital. This is essentially local, intra-locale, but it is restructuring none the less and it is intimately associated with planning operations.

The relationship between finance capital and local urban bourgeois interests and personnel is fascinating and complex. It is by no means necessarily antagonistic. As has already been implicitly suggested, the local urban bourgeoisie are very often the agents of much larger-scale finance capital interests in urban development processes. In the USA, of course, finance capital remains to a considerable, albeit diminishing extent, locally organised. The UK clearing banks were organised nationally during the First World War and building societies have moved in the same direction. Nonetheless it is interesting to note the role of regional directors in clearing banks and regional interests in building societies. These groups preserve local connections and local interests. The general absence of attention paid to the sociology of these aspects of economic life is again characteristic of the direction of gaze of the discipline.

It must be emphasised here that I am not contending that capitalist restructuring on a world scale is irrelevant to the nature of social polarisation in old industrial cities – quite the contrary. What I am saying is that a form of urban development – right-Keynesian – in the preceding period of modernisation, which was not itself a necessary product of 'Fordist' relations but rather reflected a UK interaction between national and local politics and planning, set the matrix on which the consequences of restructuring of industrial employment have been written. This is a general phenomenon in all the major UK conurbations outside London, and is not a London phenomenon precisely because of the local impact of restrictive planning policies by suburban authorities which prevented major overspill development in the pre-Greater London Council (GLC) days.

When this was happening it was not socially divisive, although the production of mass housing for the slum-cleared was. However, the slum-cleared still had jobs and were part of the working class. What mattered was the way deindustrialisation had differential impacts on the urban forms produced by modernisation.

In planning terms, modernisation's last gasp was structure planning. In the northern region this had a very direct relationship with the reformists' modernisation-orientated corporatist programmes contained within George Brown's National Plan. There is a direct link from the Northern Economic Planning Council to the Northern Regional Strategy (NRST) of 1977, which was commonly taken as the regional frame into which structure plans were set. The NRST itself included a crucial change in objectives. In its first version a strong regional economy was identified as one which could achieve full employment. By the final version this was lost, but the strategy still emphasised industrial development, prioritising growth in the indigenous structure but remaining committed to branch plant attraction.

The structure plans of this period show a marked emphasis on industrial projects. Teesside's which derived from the 1960s *Teesplan*, had more of a commitment to capital-intensified industry, and Teesside has always suffered from a relative lack of industrial diversification in comparison with the rest of the industrial north. Tyne and Wear's asserted social objectives, at least in *Choosing the Strategy*:

> The strategy has two principal aims: to help increase the number and range of jobs in the County, and to help direct the greatest benefits to the most deprived sections of the community.
>
> (Tyne and Wear County Council, 1978: 1)

Although subsequently *The Report of Survey* pointed out that in legal terms: 'The Structure Plan is a land-use plan, not an instrument of social planning' (Tyne and Wear County Council, 1979: 15, para. 2.1), the actual content of the structure plan did translate the strategic objectives into land-use terms by prioritising industrial land retention, and in particular the retention of unique deep-water sites, and seeking to control overspill development, particularly in the retail sector. Issues of land competition were less apparent on Teesside where the local topography and industrial history made much derelict industrial land available, although in Stockton a crucial site was designated for industrial development, with the usual diversification objective.

The significance of the structure plan is that, until the formal adoption of Unitary Development Plans in Tyne and Wear, and of revised structure plans in the shire counties, they provided the strategic framework into which land-use decisions should be set. However, almost from the beginning of these modernising projects, they have been eroded by postmodernising initiatives which have effectively sterilised their potential.

POSTMODERNISATION AFTER 1980

The first mechanism which was used to subvert the modernising social reform objectives of the structure plans was the designation of enterprise zones. The general net effect of these was to concentrate a good deal of development into particular places within industrial conurbations, notably on Team Valley South in Gateshead where much of it would have gone anyway. The postmodernising 'land value' market-led element was the redesignation of industrial sites for non-industrial uses. Much of this, although annoying and awkward in that it reduced the availability of large industrial sites in Tyne and Wear, was not 'heavily symbolic'. Certainly the use of Team Valley land for non-industrial uses was a major retreat from tradition.

However, the great symbol was the development of the Metro Centre near Gateshead. This was a radical departure from the structure plan's commitment to not allowing large retail malls outside traditional shopping centres. It happened on a site originally included in the enterprise zone specifically for industrial development, attracted massive subsidy, and created a post-industrial icon of the new north east and a postmodern mouthpiece in the form of John Hall, its developer. Most of the employment is part-time. Most of the employees are female and are returners from the domestic sphere. The money came from the pre-modern Church Commissioners. The proposal was enthusiastically supported by Gateshead Metropolitan Borough Council (MBC) in the best spirit of urban competition as a way of stealing commercial rateable value from Newcastle. The introduction of Unified Business Rates has meant that the enjoyment of ill-gotten gains has been strictly temporary.

The Metro Centre fits easily into a modern/postmodern dichotomy because its (interior) form is so bizarrely traditionalist modern in that it mimics mid-nineteenth-century market halls and arcades made possible by the use of cast-iron load-bearing members. It is harder to fit something which belongs so firmly in the sphere of circulation into the Fordist/post-Fordist frame. True, some of the clothes shops are post-Fordist, given the direction of the clothing industry, but for every £1 spent in a Benetton clone there will be £10 spent in Marks and Sparks, whose producers in the north east are firmly Fordist, as are the far-Eastern producers of cheap electronic goods (at least in terms of labour process). However, the ideological emphasis on service solutions to deindustrialisation is very important.

An enterprise zone initiative which fits more clearly into the Fordist/post-Fordist frame is the massive development of 'business parks' with 'B1' type facilities. B1 planning use designations were not required in enterprise zones and were readily obtainable outside them, but these 'producer service' facilities do fit well with production systems organised around flexible specialisation by providing a spatial base for the elements which are contracted in. Again the actual architectural form is generally postmodern, with a distinct preference for oriental pavilions.

Enterprise zones were contradictory. Their original ideological justification as expressed by Peter Hall and modified by Heseltine was post-Fordist to the extent than it emphasised the removal of planning restrictions in order to allow for a flourishing of the entrepreneurial spirit. The emphasis was on industrial production. They have facilitated this to perhaps a greater extent that interim investigation revealed. Certainly there is now rather a lot of manufacturing on Team Valley South and much of it is non-union in a previously union dominated space. However, that is explained by mass unemployment, without the need for any special spatial referent, and the production processes for disposable nappies etc. are low-wage Fordist. There is an important spatial element in the Metro Centre. This is a non-public (in terms of legal rights of access) public space. This legal status has been used to exclude very mild proposed leaflet distributing campaigns by the local Trades Councils aimed at union recruitment of non-unionised workforces, although there are unionised workforces in Metro Centre in some of the larger establishments.

The enterprise zones were explicitly founded on a rejection of directive or indicative planning, in favour of 'market freedom' although the real land market was absolutely transformed by massive state subsidies outside the testing for displacement and dead-weight effects which is applied to general regional assistance. These subsidies were available to service as well as manufacturing developments. The post-industrial trend is clear as is the explicit rejection of local political determination, although local political collaboration was easily achieved.

Indeed a major function of enterprise zones seems to have been the re-education of local authorities. Districts have generally (especially in Tyne and Wear with the significant exception of North Tyneside) sought to promote developments which generally accord with the orientation of the enterprise/service ideology. Examples include the development of the Asda super-store at Boldon in South Tyneside, and the same authority's support for the 'Hebburn Village' project on part of the site of the Hebburn shipyard. The latter was the first example of the transformation of industrial land whose 'derelict' status was highly debatable, into a residential zone. The scene was set for the entry of the Urban Development Corporations (UDCs). The two north eastern UDCs were established in the second wave in 1986. They acquired local planning powers over large parts of the estuarine Tyne, Wear and Tees. It is important to emphasise that these planning powers were local: in other words under the existing legal framework the structure plans remained the strategic guideline. On Teesside the County Council operated as a guardian of structure plan objectives, although it has been over-ruled, even when supported by district councils, as with the UDCs redesignation of a key Stockton site for retail rather than industrial uses. In Tyne and Wear the County Council had been abolished in 1985, leaving districts with varying views as defenders of the original strategy.

Conflict on Teesside has been about style and the direction of resource application, rather than (with the Stockton exception) about specific sites. In Tyne and Wear things have been more complex. In his evidence to the House of Commons Select Committee on employment the Chief Executive of Tyne and Wear Development Corporation (TWDC) identified the problem, as he saw it, of:

> derelict factories, warehouses, shipyards, slipways and dry docks along both rivers . . . which are unlikely ever to be used again for their original purpose.
>
> (House of Commons, 1987–8)

This statement was made just as Sunderland Shipbuilders, the nationalized operators of the most modern yards in Europe, were facing the situation which led to their closure. In practice TWDC has set its face against marine industrial development of the Tyne and Wear. In particular it has promoted residential, leisure and service uses on two key sites: 'Royal Quays' (Whitehill Point and Albert Edward Dock at North Shields reserved under the structure plan for port/marine related uses) and 'St Peter's Riverside' (the industrial north bank of the Wear downstream of the Monkwearmouth bridges and operating shipyards/docks at the time of the structure plan). In both cases it has done so against the objections of local marine industry. TWDC has pursued a policy of active deindustrialisation. North Tyne Council has resisted this. In Sunderland despite the opposition of the local MPs, the council has endorsed the general 'post-industrial' strategy. I have written elsewhere about North Tyneside (Byrne, 1993). Sunderland deserves attention here.

Not only does the unfortunate City of Sunderland have to contend with the operations of TWDC, it is also the location of Nissan, and is just about to experience the self-inflicted wounds of its own successful bid for City Challenge. The story of Nissan is partially told in Garrahan and Stewart (1992). The relevance of Nissan to the themes of this volume is that, as Garrahan and Stewart point out, there is not much that is post-Fordist about what goes on inside it. The relevance to the theme of this chapter is the way in which much of the peripheral industrial land in Washington New Town (far more than is needed for its own operations) has been handed to Nissan who, in effect, now controls industrial development in that locale (Garrahan and Stewart, 1992: 24).

However, Nissan is not about post-Fordism. The shenanigans of TWDC and City Challenge are. To understand these we need to examine both the rhetoric and the reality of the kind of planning they represent. The crucial phrase is 'catalytic planning'. I first encountered this expression in the evidence given by TWDC in connection with its compulsory purchase of sites on the East Quayside in Newcastle. The idea is that in derelict inner-city areas there is no real market in land because the private sector cannot see how developments can ever be profitable. The task of planning is to subsidise 'flagship' schemes that will transform the development possibilities in such locales. These schemes will act as a catalyst, stimulating market activity where none previously existed. This goes rather farther than Peter Hall's assertion that in the 'City of Enterprise' it is the task of planning 'to facilitate the most rapid feasible recycling of derelict urban industrial or commercial land to higher and better uses' (Hall, 1988: 354).

Catalytic planning is intended to do more than facilitate market operations. The objective is to create markets where none would naturally exist. This has turned out to be an expensive process. It is very difficult to accurately assess the actual real public cost of UDC schemes. In addition to underwriting all land reclamation costs, and thereby producing 'brown-field' sites, there has been a mixture of direct contributions, tax subsidies through enterprise zone status, infrastructural expenditure, and transfer of long-term servicing costs to local authorities. Despite all this the attractiveness of most sites to the private sector has been minimal. In Sunderland, apart from some limited B1 development at Hylton Riverside, much of the actual development is by other public bodies, including housing associations with 'assured tenancies' (and that means rents which only make sense for the wholly benefit-dependent), and in particular on the crucial Manor Quay site, a new campus of the University of Sunderland, originally described as a 'Business School'.

Manor Quay is very important to any efforts at reviving marine manufacturing in Sunderland because it is a downriver fitting-out berth which can be used for work that cannot be done in the upriver surviving Pallion yard. The University of Sunderland Business School is justified in terms of the service development of the Sunderland economy. Thus, just as the post big-bang boom is finally collapsing in the world city of London, taking Canary Wharf with it, plans are being implemented for business service-led growth in Sunderland. It could only get dafter, and it did.

Peter Ambrose (1985) described UDCs as a way of taking land into care from recalcitrant local authorities. Sunderland's successful bid for City Challenge looks more like the parent leaving the baby on the orphanage steps at midnight. First, and very unusually (compared, for example with Middlesbrough where elected representatives and community groups dominate management bodies) in the Sunderland City Challenge area, effective control is handed over to a combination of the private sector and the nominated state. The proposal cedes real planning powers over the area inhabited by the 37,000 'citizens' of north Sunderland to 'Community North'. This will be managed by a twenty-member committee made up of three city council representatives (one of whom will be the Chief Executive), three from the Riverside North Business group, one from the Chamber of Commerce, three from schools, colleges and the University of Sunderland, two from the Police, two from 'Public Agencies' (TEC, UDC and Health bodies), and six community representatives. The crucial smaller executive board of six will comprise the City's Chief Executive (not an elected member!), two business representatives, two from the community sector, and one from the quangos. As the bid stated, it calls for a 'dramatic change in culture, not least within the council'.

Abandoning democratic responsibility is indeed a change in culture. The actual proposals are a mix of mundane (but nonetheless important) schemes for housing improvement, transport and community services, coupled with the usual collection of postmodern schlock – viz. a Glass City theme attraction, a new Bridge Shopping Centre, the Concord Centre incorporating a new ground for Sunderland FC, and the new University Campus. It is a vivid illustration of the accuracy of Thornley's analysis of 'Thatcherism and the erosion of the planning system'.

> This system [of UDCs] operates with very clear objectives. The aim is to generate market confidence in the area through stimulating those activities for which there is a market demand and providing their infrastructural needs. The acceptance of UDCs by Local Authorities because of their expected economic benefit implies also accepting a shift in the objectives and priorities of the planning system. It could be said that UDCs cover only a small geographical area and hence are not all that important. However, the impact could extend over a larger area.

The ability of the Local Authority in which the UDC falls, to plan strategically for its area is severely handicapped as a large number of potential sites are removed from its control.

(Montgomery and Thornley, 1990: 40)

Indeed things go farther. Sunderland seems to show that the 'ideological impact' of UDCs goes beyond Thornley's suggestion that authorities elsewhere will be forced to change their relationships with developers in order to compete with UDC areas. It seems that UDCs buy the souls of those who cooperate with them.

On a practical level it is impossible for those former GLC and Metropolitan County authorities whose territories contain UDCs to plan without taking account of them. Lewis has pointed out that:

The DOE has decided that local authorities should not draw up unitary development plans (UDPs) for UDC areas, but rather that unitary development plans should adopt the strategies of the UDCs. Moreover, local authorities are required to take into account in their UDPs the impact of UDCs outside the UDC's area. In effect then UDCs become the plan-making authorities for their areas – and have a right to influence planning matters well outside their areas.

(N. Lewis, 1992: 53)

Sunderland's draft UDP became available in December 1992. Much of the content is non-contentious, although it takes all UDC proposals as given. What is contentious is the general sensibility of the document. On the first page there is a list of contextual statements including assertions of:

the upturn in the industrial future of Sunderland, reflected in the grant of City status and the attractions of major Japanese industrial investment[6] ... the role of the UDC and Enterprise Zone initiatives which enhance the City's potential for development ... the trend towards local authority/ private sector partnerships to secure the implementation of major projects, together with structural changes in the roles and responsibilities of publicly elected authorities ... [and finally] ... a society looking for additional outlets for its leisure time and increasing prosperity.

(*Sunderland Unitary Development Plan* –
Draft for Consultation, 1992: 1, para. 1.3)

The tragedy about all of this is that it is directed at a market which does not exist. Ambrose (1985) identified UDC style strategies as offering opportunities for private developers to overcome the resistance of socialist local authorities to market systems. At the time that looked right, but it is not the case now. I have to say that I never thought there was any real money in urban development in peripheral ex-industrial cities (Byrne, 1987) and subsequent developments seem to have proved me right. It cannot be said loudly and often enough that there is no market demand for any of this nonsense. Preliminary figures from the 1991 census show that north-eastern urban populations are falling so fast that UDP estimates of housing need are widely over the mark. In any event there is ample peripheral green-field land, which is what the market wants. In Middlesbrough there is a £20,000 differential between the prices of new three-bedroomed semis on green-field and brown-field sites. Retailing is in a major slump and there are no signs of it emerging. I would not want my money invested (although my pension fund probably is) in 'fun water' or 'glass cities' in the lean and miserable 1990s. Those who are buying UDC land are being given money to do so, or are other publicly-funded bodies (including the joint (Teesside and Durham) University College, Stockton (UCS) – on the Teesdale site in Stockton).

So what sense can we make of postmodernisation planning? It was clearly intended to substitute market-led private sector orientated procedures for anything resembling either democratic or participatory planning (the two are not necessarily the same – a point to be returned to in the conclusion). The overt aim seemed to be to put an ideological gloss on a rapacious pursuit of profit. The reality seems to be that the gloss – the rejection of planning and universalism, was more important than the actual profit potential. It has all gone badly wrong.

The actual impact of these things on the ground is not yet great. In principle they are divisive and exclusionary. Tyneside has private yuppie space with a wall around it in the 'exclusive' St Peter's Basin in Low Walker, but, as with much of Docklands, very few people seem to live there. The intention was to underpin and serve a divided society – to establish citadels of the rich in confrontation with the ghetto poor, with that poor admitted as service personnel and otherwise excluded by cost. It has not happened because the service-led, market-orientated world it was directed at has gone belly up. It seems as if this is more than just a downward turn in short-term cycles. This looks like a real long-term collapse. So where do we go from here?

CONCLUSION

If we return to the general Fordist/post-Fordist debate, we find that this review of planning developments suggests that one aspect of the arguments of proponents of 'new times' may be absolutely misconceived. In general those who propose this idea and develop political programmes in relation to it, seem to have been seduced by a kind of Marxist political economy for and on behalf of capitalism and capitalists. Although not explicitly part of the 'post-Fordist' game-show, Gorz (1982) is typical of the general line. Essentially capitalism (and hence by implication capitalists) have got it all sorted out. They have found a way of defeating the industrial proletariat and proceeding with the continued growth of the system. The usual refuges for those who come to this conclusion are either in cultural journalism or dark-green, fundamentalist ecology.

When we look at efforts at flexible accumulation through the use of postmodernisation planning in relation to urban land, the situation looks rather different. Far from the triumphant progression of a new capitalist logic, we see a disintegrating system which seems to be giving the world financial system a bad dose of gangrene, and there is no easy way to cut off the offending limb. The failure of Canary Wharf is of course the best example of this tendency, but the collapse of property values is very general. Recent parliamentary answers obtained by Steve Byers, the MP for Wallsend, show that all UDCs have written down the book value of their land holdings very substantially and these book values in any event are largely notional because there is no present or foreseeable market activity. Further, this is a world phenomenon. Everywhere, urban real-estate values are collapsing. The system of overaccumulation/overconsumption which underpinned them has broken down.

This chapter has used the urban north east as illustrative material. It is always best to work with what one knows, and I was very much guided by Rustin's (1989) remark to the effect that one characteristic of the post-Fordist position was its lack of empirical foundation. The urban north east is interesting precisely because it shows the effects of a very rapid oscillation from fully Keynesian planning – these places have been as planned as anywhere in the post-war West – to externally imposed non-planning. Despite the real need to recognise the genuine gains of the Keynesian period(s), any attempt to develop a new planning process has to pay close attention to the defects of approaches then.

This chapter has emphasised the objectives of planning rather than the processes by which planning has been carried out. It is now time to turn to processes. Planning in the Keynesian era was elitist and corporatist. The elites were not professionals – the bureaucratic evangelists – but rather representatives of powerful social groups, including the development industry. The innovations in consultation practice introduced after the Skeffington Report, and implemented in relation to the formulation of structure plans and consequent local plans, were an attempt to redress a real sense of grievance on the part of communities who felt that plans had been imposed upon them. It is noticeable that postmodern planning has abandoned all this with its emphasis on speedy executive action based upon glossy 'executive summaries'.

Of course planning in a democratic society should be democratic. Land-use planning is in fact a very powerful tool of democratic government because it is impossible for the owners of land to export it or otherwise withdraw it from social use. Indeed a good start to the whole exercise would be the reintroduction of 100 per cent betterment levies to confiscate all development gains, along with a Community Land Act with teeth which would ultimately transfer all development land into public ownership. However, democratic representatives can also be an elite. What is required in process terms is some combination of democratic determination with participatory formulation of planning objectives and details, which would be an operation within civil society as much as within the state.

It is worth considering just what the actual objectives of a planning system might be. One consensual social objective would certainly be full employment. Planning to this end would have two components – productive and reproductive. Productive planning in the short-term would involve a rejigging of regional competitiveness from the sphere of circulation to the sphere of production. In other words competitive advantage would be sought through the development of support systems for advanced manufacturing rather than through the subsidising of circulation. If the resources wasted by the two north-eastern UDCs had instead been spent on civil research and Design in energy engineering and on genuine skills training, the employment potential would be very great. This of course presupposes the operation of a regionally determined meso-economic medium-term industrial strategy, and that would require a major reformulation of the machinery of government and administration in the UK.

On the reproductive side there is an important contrast with the Keynesian era. There is a general agreement that throughout the Keynesian era, capitalism had a shortage of capital goods, and that one of the factors in bringing that era to a close was the elimination of that shortage. It is true that during the Keynesian era there was an absolute shortage of social capital goods, of houses, hospitals, schools, sewers, and decent urban transport systems (although in the last case, it was the development of car-based suburbanization which led to the active destruction of very adequate intensive urban transit systems). The north-eastern example shows that much of this social capital deficit has now been filled. This means that land-use-based strategies of job creation through construction are less appropriate than they used to be. The implication is that we need a kind of left post-industrialism with intensive human services in the public sector substituting for socially orientated construction, in any job creation programme.

If we look at the actual balance of social forces in post-industrial cities, we can actually quite easily identify a social bloc which would support such programmes. Given the terminal decline of the housing-based credit boom, which Saunders (1990) and others thought would underpin a whole new pattern of social cleavages, the present situation is one in which the working class and its reserve armies have an immediate interest in any planning system which maximizes employment. So indeed do the 'middle classes', that vital status category combining lower-level service-class personnel with the elite of the industrial working class. Only the rich, the beneficiaries of post-Keynesian strategies in general, would be net losers because they would both be taxed and lose control of land.

A concluding note – in a discussion of a planning system which requires the production of 'ecological impact statements' for all large-scale projects, there has been no discussion of ecological issues. This is partly because all the ecological impact statements produced by the post-modernisers that I have ever read have generally been a combination of vacuousness and lies. However, the main reason for this neglect is that the ecological programme, other than as a prettifying postmodern gloss, has not yet entered the planning process. Ecological sentiment has. Many of the major environmentally damaging projects of the 1960s and 1970s, justified at the time in terms of job creation and therefore uncriticizeable in a labourist region, would not get away so lightly now when real unemployment is massively greater. The energy engineering cited as a possible regional speciality has an ecological orientation in that it would emphasise the use of renewable marine energy sources. However, ecology was not a Keynesian concern and has not been a post-Keynesian concern. It could very well be a post-post-Keynesian theme.

NOTES

1 That part of the economy which produces the means of production: factories producing machinery or mining for raw materials, for example.
2 That part of the economy which produced consumer goods: food, clothing and so on.
3 The University of Teesside, the venue of the conference from which the present volume derives, is located in the centre of Middlesbrough in Cleveland, in the north east of England.
4 See Davis (1990) where Los Angeles begins to look strangely like Teesside. Culturally, perhaps not so surprising when one considers that the futuristic LA of *Blade Runner* was produced by Ridley Scott who once attended Hartlepool Art School.
5 Such as Leam Lane, Longbenton, Marsden, Biddick Hall, Red House, Thorney Close, Collingwood, Marden etc.
6 But perhaps not reflected in the proposed closure of Monkwearmouth Colliery, Sunderland's largest remaining traditional industrial employer.

9 Public services and local economic regeneration in a post-Fordist economy

Mike Geddes

LOCAL PUBLIC SERVICES AND ECONOMIC GROWTH IN THE POST-WAR PERIOD

It may be argued that two views have dominated thinking about local public services over the post-war period, and neither of them have emphasised economic objectives. Social democratic thinking has been rooted in the notion of a mixed economy in which the private sector is seen as the productive economy and the public sector is seen as economically unproductive and capable only on distributional concerns. The economic role of the state is concentrated at the level of national government, where functions such as macro-economic management and planning, and the control of nationalised industries, were located. Public services at the local level were seen as primarily concerned with the delivery of social and welfare provision. Clearly local public services do have an economic role in this perspective – services such as education and transport are important to the productive economy. But this role is not emphasised or fully utilised, and it is interesting to note that in specific instances such as new and expanded towns, where the economic role of local public services was crucial, control was removed from the local to the central government level (Turok, 1990).

Over the last decade this perspective has been strongly challenged by the neo-liberal perspectives of the new right. The new right challenged the social democratic assumption of a mutually supportive relationship between a productive private economy and a redistributive welfare state, arguing that the public sector was parasitic on, and a drain upon, the private sector. Many of those arguing from social democratic perspectives have found difficulty in countering the view that social and distributional concerns must be subordinated to the imperatives of economic regeneration and competition.

Regulation theory[1] offers us an opportunity to escape from this *cul de sac*, by suggesting that stable, long-term economic growth is dependent upon the effective integration of production, distribution, exchange and consumption, and therefore upon the role of the state and not just the market. During the post-war boom, Keynesian domestic demand management and the growth of the social wage through the expansion of the welfare state played a major role in the steady expansion of consumption which provided the market for Fordist mass production and the climate of confidence in which regular and long-term productive investment was feasible. Public services were, therefore, not merely the social benefit permitted by economic growth, but a key element in the institution and stabilisation of a regime of growth.

The stability of Fordist growth was of course not permanent. During the 1960s and especially the 1970s the productivity gains associated with Fordist production methods became increasingly limited, and profitability fell, undermining the scope for wage rises and government policy to maintain domestic demand (Glyn, 1992). Firms began to turn from the domestic market to exports as the propulsive sector, and the economy, became increasingly internationalised as firms sought both to gain economies of scale and to secure positions in external markets. A second phase of the crisis then developed from the later 1970s, associated with monetarist and austerity measures by national governments designed to strengthen the competitiveness of national capital by reducing wage costs and social expenditure rather than by maintaining domestic demand. This led to the stagnation of demand with the internationalisation of the recession.

It is easy to see how in this context public expenditure and public services have come to be regarded as a luxury dependent upon, rather than contributing to, economic growth. Such perceptions are also fuelled by the fact that many public sector activities proved relatively impervious to the productivity gains achieved by Fordist production methods in key sectors of the private economy. Thus while many public services copied elements of standardised mass production from the private sector, including limitations to product diversity and consumer/user choice, they tended to benefit less from the rising capital intensity which flowline production permitted in the private sector. Moreover, public services reflected in their orientation the specific features of the post-war political compromise. The tripartite corporatism of the post-war period, recognising the interests of a predominantly white male unionised industrial workforce, led to a welfare state posited on the notion of a family wage, and indeed to the control of public services at the local level by similar local tripartite coalitions in many localities. As changes in both production and consumption made the pattern of economic and social interests more diversified, and as rising standards of expectations were engendered by economic growth, the limitations of standardised Fordist public service provision became more and more apparent to a range of groups of users, from professionals to women to ethnic groups. At the same time, the successful extension of strong trade union organisation from the private into the public sector enhanced the ability of producer interests to defend the status quo when under threat.

In Britain, the limits to the permanence of Fordist growth became apparent relatively early, emphasising what has been called the 'flawed Fordism' of the British economy (Jessop, 1989a; this volume). The domestic post-war settlement in Britain was one which reflected the dominance of the international interests of the financial sector rather than manufacturing, but which was also a short-termist political settlement, rather than one oriented to long-term modernisation of production. This created a political commitment to full employment and a level of welfare state provision which was not adequately underpinned by policies and institutional change to modernise the economy effectively. Initially in the post-war period a balance of production and consumption was sustained by the UK's initial advantage over its war-damaged European competitors, but the relatively rapid re-emergence of balance of payments problems demonstrated the failure to secure a stable domestic balance. The point is not that high levels of public expenditure and public services are antagonistic to economic growth – rather that a successful long-term strategy for public services must be integrated with a strategy for economic modernisation. In particular, it is notable that Britain's 'flawed Fordism' offered very little opportunity for government at local and regional level to contribute actively to objectives of economic growth and modernisation. The highly centralised nature of the British state has prevented the emergence of any effective tier of regional government able to develop and implement modernisation strategies at the sub-national level. Such regional policies as have been pursued have remained under the control of central government and have been primarily oriented towards the redistribution of investment and economic growth rather than modernisation. Even the Wilson government's attempt to introduce a national and regional indicative planning system failed to confront the economic forces and institutional obstacles militating against an effective modernisation strategy. Local government, from the time of the post-war settlement, has been largely denied any substantial and proactive economic role. Criticisms that local government is not equipped to deal with economic issues must therefore be laid primarily at the door of successive central governments that have restricted local government to a powerless 'sites and premises' role in the local economy.[2]

THE NEO-LIBERAL STRATEGY FOR ECONOMIC REGENERATION AND ITS IMPLICATIONS AT LOCAL LEVEL

The neo-liberal strategy for economic regeneration that has been adopted during the 1980s is promoting a market-guided transition to a post-Fordist economy (Jessop, 1989a: 24–5). For the private sector, this has involved deregulation, liberalisation, and a restructured legal and political framework to provide a passive but supportive context for market forces. For the public sector, it has involved a mixture of privatisation, liberalisation and the introduction of commercial criteria into the residual state sector (Flynn, 1990). Economic policy has undergone a major shift from demand management to supply-side policies, and the Keynesian commitment to full employment has been abandoned as not merely unfeasible but inimical to labour-market efficiency and flexibility.

Neo-liberal policy has largely not resisted, and indeed has often actively promoted, the decline of traditional industries and the restructuring of those still deemed potentially competitive (e.g. steel and cars respectively) (Jessop, 1989a: 38). At the same time, new sectors have been supported, either actively and directly, or through indirect or hidden forms of intervention. Likewise successive Conservative governments have done very little to counter-balance the geographical implications of these patterns of industrial change, particularly as the re-emergence of the north-south divide in the 1980s was not inconsistent with a 'two nations' political strategy.[3] In the context of overall high levels of unemployment, neo-liberal industrial policy has therefore been associated with the collapse of many local economies previously dependent on older industries, and with the need for major restructuring in areas as diverse as the 'sunrise industry' regions, central cities and docklands.

Policies for the 'regeneration' of particular local economies where private sector interest is strong, and more generally for the local implementation of neo-liberal supply-side policies, have therefore been an important feature of the 1980s. Indeed, the role of local-level initiatives, and of local public services in relation to economic regeneration has become a more important issue than for some considerable time. This is both because of the development of a specifically local element in neo-liberal economic strategy, and because of attempts to promote alternative policies at the local level.

Neo-liberal local economic policies exhibit a number of key features. The focus of intervention has been on supply-side policies, particularly in relation to the labour and property markets, from TECs to UDCs and enterprise zones (Boddy, 1992; Campbell, 1990b; Healey, 1991). The institutional framework for local policy has sidelined elected local government in favour of executive agencies controlled by central government. Within such agencies, and within local government, there has been an emphasis on both the direct involvement of the representatives of business and a broader orientation towards the objectives of business. Entrepreneurship has replaced employment as a primary policy goal (Stoker, 1990). Local-level planning has become more market- and private-sector-led.

The emergence of neo-liberal local economic policy has major implications for local public services. The twin processes of the displacement of elected local government within the local political arena, and the enhanced role of local private sector interests, has created strong pressures for the (re)orientation of local public expenditure and services towards the needs and priorities of business. This trend takes both direct and obvious forms (public transport systems servicing 'office cities' and commuters rather than local communities; libraries diverting resources to business information services) and more subtle ones, as definitions of economic growth and regeneration are increasingly reduced to the sectional interest of business. Such a trend is apparent, for example, in the reorientation of training programmes. Local economic policy has long been oriented towards business. But the neo-liberal policies of the last decade mean that the role of local public services in relation to economic regeneration has been shifted away from the broader social distribution of the benefits of economic growth, towards the promotion of forms of economic growth which are often socially divisive in their effects.

Neo-liberalism has also subordinated social welfare provision more closely to supply-side economic policy, for example through the explicit linkage of welfare policies to labour-market flexibility. In this respect, local public services are finding themselves administering an increasingly minimalist safety-net welfare system supporting those marginalised in the labour market by divisive local economic policies, rather than providing a general foundation of support for the whole population.

During the 1980s then, Conservative governments developed an approach to local economic regeneration – labelled by some as privatism (Barnekov *et al.*, 1989) – which emphasised more strongly the dominant role of the private sector. The public sector has been cast as the junior partner, the role of public services more tightly tied to that of enabler and facilitator of private profit. The perception that local government should be 'getting closer to business' is now widespread.

There has however been considerable criticism of this approach to local economic regeneration. Major arguments have been that it is undemocratic, that it fails to work except in specific and limited circumstances, and that it has proved extremely expensive in value for money terms (Centre for Local

Economic Strategies, 1990). Thus evaluations of the activities of the London Docklands Development Corporation and the associated enterprise zone show that the ratio between public expenditure and job creation has been extremely high, while the emphasis on market mechanisms has prevented the integrated planning of development and infrastructure, such as public transport (Docklands Consultative Committee, 1990).

ALTERNATIVES TO NEO-LIBERALISM

The neo-liberal approach to local economic regeneration was not unchallenged. In the first half of the 1980s, there was a significant movement by a number of Labour-led local authorities to develop their own local economic strategies in response to recession and deindustrialisation. Often grouped under the concept of 'restructuring for labour', these strategies sought to reassert a much more significant role for the public sector in local economic regeneration, in terms of local democratic planning of the economy; employment rather than property-led strategy; indigenous development rather than inward investment; and a focus on the needs and skills of workforces and local communities (Benington, 1986). Particularly in areas where private-sector employment was being decimated by recession, this involved a concern with the role of mainstream public services in the economy, in terms of investment, employment and purchasing power.

These strategies sought to make local economic regeneration a major arena in which neo-liberalism could be contested by a radical advance beyond the limits of conventional Keynesian and social-democratic policy. Whereas the market strategy seeks to roll back the frontiers of Keynesian economic interventionism, the intention of the 'restructuring for labour' strategy was to 'reclaim production' through a more active economic role for the state at local level in restructuring the production process. It is useful to distinguish two strands of thinking underlying this approach. One, drawing critically on previous policy models such as the National Enterprise Board of the 1970s, stressed the need for macro-economic planning by the state in a mixed economy, contending that state planning and 'strategic intervention' is the route to the modernisation of the British economy (particularly the manufacturing sector). We can call this strand 'left Fordism'. The second strand, left post-Fordism, by contrast abandons the Keynesian conception of macroeconomic state planning and control, arguing rather that post-Fordist production and consumption patterns require selective and specific state interventions, often implemented at the regional and local level, to modify the market and the labour market and to invest in capital in support of labour in specific sectors and firms (Geddes, 1988).

The practical influence of the 'restructuring for labour' approach was largely ended by the abolition of the GLC and the metropolitan counties, along with the general attack on and erosion of local government resources and powers. The left local economic strategies of the early 1980s – some of which consciously perceived for themselves a role of 'prefiguring' policy initiatives by national government – remain important however in demonstrating that alternatives to neo-liberal policies do indeed exist.

Today, the length and depth of the current recession in Britain makes it even more clear that the neo-liberal strategy for economic revival is seriously flawed, while European integration is promoting closer scrutiny of the different strategies of other EC countries. At least two major criticisms may be levelled at the way neo-liberal strategy has been implemented in Britain in the 1980s. First, as in the post-war period, short-term political considerations have tended to dominate those concerned with the long-term modernisation of the productive economy. Investment has been skewed towards distribution, finance and property, the sectors most closely linked to the consumption boom. Second, the antipathy to economic intervention, public expenditure and public services of neo-liberalism has a number of negative consequences. The internationalisation of the economy has been promoted at the expense of both government economic leverage and the reconsolidation of a substantial and strong industrial base. Neo-liberal labour-market and R&D policies have not created a modern, skilled, core labour force, and the UK is increasingly becoming a low-wage, cheap labour location within the European economy. Many aspects of public services have been dismantled or neglected rather than restructured to meet changing needs. While the 'Lawson boom' of the mid-1980s produced some rapid growth, this was sectorally, socially and geographically unevenly distributed, and short-lived. The failure of consumption to revive since then indicates that neo-liberal policy has not been able to engineer the stable equilibrium of production and consumption on which investment and long-term growth depends.

THE POST-FORDIST ECONOMY

If neo-liberalism is unlikely to lay the basis for a stable new regime of economic growth (or to ensure Britain's participation in it on favourable terms), what alternatives exist? Any economic strategy today confronts an economy which is different in very significant ways from the Fordist economy. In talking of a post-Fordist economy we are referring not to any predetermined pattern of economic activity which is somehow automatically coming into being, but to a process of transition arising from the limitations of the Fordist pattern of growth, of which the outcome is, in important respects, uncertain and subject to political and policy influence.

The crisis of Fordist growth has both necessitated and stimulated the search for new production methods, products and markets. In particular, the relative inflexibility of Fordist forms of organisation of production, production methods and products has led to an emphasis on flexibility in various forms. New information technology has permitted movement away from the hierarchical and vertically-integrated organisation of production towards more decentralised forms of sub-contracting and networks, while retaining and indeed strengthening centralised control over strategy and profit. New technology is also associated with an advance from dedicated to flexible machinery, making more flexible mass production and small-batch production more profitable, and enabling firms to create and cater more effectively for more diversified and discriminating markets. These trends, along with the scope for innovation and experiment in a period of major economic restructuring, and the desire by big firms to increase flexibility and offload risk, have increased the opportunities for some smaller firms, particularly those which are highly capitalised and have invested in research and development and modern technologies. New products and new materials have diversified the structure of production.

The role of information technology, the need for continuous innovation, and the competitive emphasis on quality and consumer responsiveness has led to a growth in the so-called knowledge industries as a major growth sector, along with both producer and consumer services, the latter catering particularly for demand from the affluent sectors of an increasingly polarised labour market. Capital has also required new flexibility from labour, and the context of high unemployment has aided the negotiation or imposition of major changes in the nature of work, ranging from teamworking and multiskilling to the increase in poorly paid and part-time work, major shifts in the gender composition of the labour force, and in wage flexibility.

These changes have been quite complex. To take the issue of women's employment, there appear to have been three interacting trends, of integration, differentiation and polarisation. Women have become more fully integrated into the formal labour market, but at the same time differentiation of work by gender has intensified in some areas and the position of different groups of women in the work hierarchy has become more polarised, all within an increasingly unequal labour market. These trends have been promoted by neo-liberal government policies, but also have their origin in long-term shifts in women's relationship to the wage and household economy (Humphries and Rubery, 1992).

These trends are associated with the recommodification of parts of the public sector, both to enlarge the sphere of private profit and to raise productivity by increasing competition. The boundary between the public and private sectors has become more flexible, and measures to promote competition and flexibility have been introduced within the public sector itself.

It remains very unclear however how far a stable regime of economic growth can emerge, especially in the UK, on the basis of post-Fordist 'flexibility', particularly in the context of a neo-liberal policy framework. Whereas the Fordist boom depended on the extension of mass consumption as the corollary of expanding mass production, and the integration of supply-side and demand-side policy, post-Fordist 'flexibility' has so far meant an emphasis on so-called 'lean production' of which the inevitable corollary has been high unemployment, and the restriction of new consumption norms to the privileged 'have-lots'. Lean production means lean consumption. Neo-liberal strategy has accentuated the emergence of low-wage sectors of the economy and the development of a 'two nations' pattern of consumption. Within Europe, most of the UK is becoming increasingly marginalised in relation to the so-called 'golden triangle' at the core of the European Community. There is little evidence that new markets, for example in eastern Europe, will provide a serious basis for expanding consumption, at any rate for some time, and indeed at the moment such areas are more likely to serve as platforms for cheap labour production. While state expenditure levels are kept high by the costs of high unemployment, there remain major problems of increasing productivity levels in many public services.

What are the implications of this analysis for the role of public services in the economy? They are, first, that the achievement of stable 'post-Fordist' economic growth requires a new and more productive role for public services in the economy. A return to the old perspective, in which only the private sector was associated with economic growth and the productive economy, while the public sector was seen as unproductive, is neither desirable nor, maybe, possible. An important requirement for sustained economic growth in the emerging post-Fordist era is an economically productive public sector. This does not mean a public sector which abandons its commitment to meeting social need, nor a residual public sector operating on quasi-market principles as a pale shadow of the private sector. Indeed, the neo-liberal approach fails to create a productive public sector because of its antipathy to an interventionist economic role for the state. Defining a 'productive' role for the public sector is not an easy task, but the next section approaches this issue by examining a number of dimensions to the possible role of public services in economic regeneration at the local level.

PUBLIC SERVICES AND LOCAL ECONOMIC REGENERATION: THEMES AND ISSUES

We can begin to discuss the development of a productive economic role for public services at the local level by considering several themes which link post-Fordist economic trends to policies for local economic regeneration: new industrial districts; lean production; information technology; labour-market flexibility; public-sector productivity; a Europe of the regions?; and environmental issues.

New industrial districts

An important concept behind some of the 'new left' local economic strategies of the early 1980s, and one that has continued to attract attention and support since, is that of the industrial district. It is argued that important tendencies in the post-Fordist economy, in particular the enhanced possibility of small-batch or more customised production, the deconcentration of production to small firms and smaller units of big firms and the way in which information technology enables production to be geographically decentralised, have recreated the conditions in which linked local or regional agglomerations of small and medium-sized enterprises are becoming an important growth element in the economy. Examples often referred to include Silicon Valley in California, the 'Third Italy' in Emilia-Romagna, and Baden-Württemberg (Murray, 1991a). Further, some research suggests that the local/regional state and public services often play a key role in such industrial districts through the development of a coherent strategy for stimulating cooperation between firms. Local public services may be involved in the promotion of technological innovation, in the provision of business and marketing information, and in providing training and retraining, as well as more conventional infrastructural and land provision and policies (Cooke, 1990a; Cooke and Imrie, 1989). Proponents of this approach to local economic regeneration also suggest that – especially with a strong local state role – the industrial district model, as well as offering locally coherent business growth, can provide good, skilled and rewarding employment. In other words, in the terms of our earlier discussion of state policy alternatives to neo-liberalism, successful industrial districts demonstrate how neo-corporatist state policies at local/regional level can promote post-Fordist economic growth, through the coordination of local economic interests, involving varying degrees and forms of state economic intervention. Thus Murray, an enthusiastic advocate, argues that

as the Italian and German cases have shown, local and regional government comes to play a central productive role in diffused industrialisation, in the fostering of networks and the provision of common services.

(Murray, 1991a: 22)

There is, however, lively debate about this perspective and its policy implications. How autonomous are these small and medium enterprises from the large production or marketing multinationals to which they are often related? How stable, therefore, are the industrial-district economies? Do they increasingly depend on growing income inequalities, and on the servicing of luxury consumer markets? Do they depend on specific cultural conditions, and thus how general and how generalisable is the industrial-district phenomenon? Certainly, even the advocates of this approach recognise that, if the industrial district phenomenon extends to Britain, it does so mostly in sectoral and spatial contexts – such as financial and business services in central London – which tend to reinforce rather than reduce social and geographical economic inequality. The few attempts by local government to promote local industrial networks in the UK have not always been a success (Totterdill, 1992). One conclusion may well be that both the long tradition of exclusion of local government from policy concerns of economic growth, and the neo-liberal policies of the 1980s, militate against such efforts. The internationalised character of the British economy and the dominance of financial rather than manufacturing interests are also important. The question must therefore be whether more active public policies – not merely of course at the local level – could create the conditions for dynamic local industrial networks. In the current British context this would inevitably be a long-term process of enhancing the economic development role and capacity of local public agencies, especially local government, but it may be argued that such a policy is consistent with important aspects of the post-Fordist economy.

Lean production

The industrial district concept stresses – indeed frequently overstresses – the role of small and medium-sized enterprises (SMEs) in the post-Fordist economy. By contrast, terms such as Japanisation, just-in-time production and lean production are associated with the changes – towards more flexible manufacturing systems, diversified products and employment flexibility – taking place in big firms, especially in sectors like the motor industry which were previously most closely associated with Fordist production methods.

Neo-liberal economic policy has strongly encouraged such trends, both actively through labour-market deregulation for example, and through passive support for the internationalisation of the economy. The encouragement of Japanese car assemblers to locate in Britain, for example, has both directly introduced new standards of productivity into the motor industry in Britain and at the same time sharpened the competitive pressures on existing firms to emulate them.[4]

The neo-liberal approach to industrial restructuring has major implications both for the firms involved, and for the local economies in which they are located. Whilst investment subsidies may well have encouraged the retention of some uncompetitive capacity, the neo-liberal approach is likely to lead to other forms of inefficiency. Thus leading UK aerospace firms have recently been pressing for changes to government policy which might enable them to retain productive capacity (including, crucially, a skilled workforce seen as human capital) during periods of depressed demand, arguing that the beneficiaries of the market approach will be foreign competitors. The losers will include not only those made unemployed and the exchequer through the costs of unemployment, but also the firms themselves. Numerous studies have now demonstrated that savings from plant closures at the level of the plant itself are often outweighed by the costs to the wider economy (Geddes, 1991).

At the level of the local economy, the restructuring associated with the transition to a 'lean' post-Fordist economy means the closure of plants in some areas, the rundown and rationalisation of others, but growth and new development in others. This process places major demands on local public services. The changing demands of big firms on small and medium firms constituting their supplier networks – for new products, or just-in-time delivery systems – generate new patterns of linkage in the local or regional economy, which require the support of local public services. Moreover, there is considerable evidence that many smaller firms need the active support of local economic development services if they are able to meet the requirements of 'lean production' systems. In areas of growth, incoming industry requires new investment in infrastructure, transport, education and training. In areas of decline, public services are a key element in local supply-side policies directed to the establishment of a new economic base (Geddes *et al.*, 1992). As we have noted, neo-liberal policies for local economic restructuring have frequently failed to enable local public services to undertake these roles effectively. In areas like London Docklands, public services have not been effectively resourced, planned and coordinated to support economic growth. Where local public services have been marshalled to support local regeneration, the narrow interests of business have often dominated those of others in the local community. In such a context, the process of local economic regeneration is inevitably conflictual. Workforces and local communities will tend to defend existing jobs, even while recognising that they are not viable or are far from ideal, if there is little or nothing else on offer. There is likely to be active or passive opposition to new development which does not meet local needs. If this happens, necessary processes of innovation and change in the local economy are much more difficult to achieve.

The alternative is to build on examples of positive and forward-looking strategies for the management of local economic change, in which local public services are deployed in advance of plant closures or rundowns to retain and reorient skills, and to reshape the economy (Davenport *et al.*, 1990). This means a more pluralist and democratic approach to local economic regeneration than that promoted by private-sector-led 'partnerships' and growth coalitions. One of the main features of lean production systems in sectors such as the car industry has been the emphasis on the involvement of the workforce through teamworking, quality circles and so on. A similar approach to local economic regeneration would be based on the concept of the local economy as a 'quality circle', within which the objective would be to involve the wider local community in the achievement of economic growth, as is said to have happened in the Third Italy, for example. This would involve a much more active role for local public services in raising standards of productivity in the local economy – through upskilling and reskilling training programmes, efficient and flexible transport links between firms and between home and work, etc. Of course, the corollary of teamworking in the private sector is that the lean production it promotes means unemployment in the local economy, and flexibility at work has meant a growing divide between core and marginalised sections of the labour force. Neo-liberal policies have accentuated such tendencies. In contrast, teamworking at the level of the local economy must be based much more broadly on the whole local labour force. Our argument is that such an approach is consistent not just with the need to spread the benefits of post-Fordist growth more broadly, but with the reestablishment of the British economy as a high-wage, high-productivity sector of the global economy, and the extension of the consumption basis for sustained post-Fordist growth beyond its current limits.

Information technology

The previous section argued that local public services have an important role to play in the restructuring of local economies around older and established industries. In this section we turn to the new industrial sectors which are closely associated with a post-Fordist economy. Such sectors include the telecommunications sector and the so-called 'knowledge' industries. At the moment we will take telecommunications as an example. Telecommunications – the movement of information by electronic means – is playing a pervasive role in local economic restructuring. The telecoms sector itself is growing rapidly and is likely to become the world's largest industry by the year 2000. But the relevance of telecoms to local economic regeneration extends well beyond the direct impact of the sector itself. All economic sectors and local areas are being radically affected by the application of new telecoms technologies in production, distribution, consumption and administration. Telecoms are the generic technology of post-Fordist restructuring, and are being applied right across the economy in search of productivity and competitiveness, bringing speed, cheapness and flexibility to information flows within and between firms, between firms and their customers and so on (Graham, 1991).

This technological change is being managed in very different ways across the industrialised world. In much of western Europe the traditional public monopoly of services and infrastructures is still largely intact, despite recent efforts by the European Commission to develop a single liberalised market for telecoms. These public monopolies remain driven by more than the profit motive, recognising issues of urban regional and local development. In the UK (and the US) neo-liberal strategy has promoted privatisation, deregulation and competition, leading to a strong concentration of investment in the main cities and business corridors. The development of the telecoms sector has therefore been a major factor behind the social and geographical polarisation of post-Fordist growth in the UK. In localities such as London Docklands the installation of advanced infrastructure has underpinned the attempt to attract investment from the City. But in other areas, ranging from regional conurbations to rural areas, local economic regeneration increasingly suffers from the absence of modern telecoms facilities.

There are, however, some initiatives in the UK and more abroad which show how a proactive public service role in telecoms development can overcome the polarisation and limited spread of development associated with the neo-liberal model. In Scotland, the Highlands and Islands Development Board has invested £16 million in telecoms infrastructure. In Manchester, the HOST initiative is an attempt to spread the benefits of cheap information technology to all social groups and industrial sectors within the city that the City council feels have been excluded so far due to the commercialised nature of the UK telecoms regime (Graham, 1991). Such initiatives require a reorientation of traditional local economic development perspectives, such as the ability to perceive the local economy in terms of information flows not just flows of goods and people.

They involve the development of a key sector of local public services to promote the wider social and geographical extension of post-Fordist growth.

As Hepworth (1992) notes, local government is already one of the most significant parts of the 'information economy'. It is one of the biggest and most rapidly growing sectoral markets for IT, and, after government and the media, probably the biggest provider of information services to businesses and households. This information is currently still mostly provided as a 'public good', and is one of the major ways in which local government promotes local economic development, as well as supporting its own role as a provider of local public services. Current financial pressures to 'make a business of information' could however undermine these objectives. What is needed is not the privatisation of local information services, but the extension of the role of IT as a local public service both promoting economic innovation and promoting the access to information of poorer sections of the community.

Labour-market flexibility

The labour-market implications of post-Fordism constitute perhaps the most serious obstacle not just to the distribution of economic growth but to the achievement of long-term stable growth. At the current stage of economic restructuring, the achievement of productivity gains through lean production has resulted in massive job losses in existing industrial sectors which have not been balanced by growth in new ones. Within employment, flexible forms of corporate and intercorporate structure, and more flexible production technology have been associated with the expansion of marginal – part-time, insecure, poorly paid – forms of both formal and informal employment. By and large, labour-market flexibility has been flexibility for capital at the expense of labour. The current recession shows that even those who have done well in employment terms in the 1980s cannot count their jobs and incomes secure. But this labour-market flexibility for individual firms has been bought at a high price for the economy as a whole, in the form of the limited consumption power of those excluded from or marginalised in the labour market, and the social security costs of high unemployment. Despite the increasing internationalisation of the economy, the strength of the national market remains an important factor for many sectors and firms.

It would appear that all major industrialised countries have pursued labour-market policies designed to promote flexibility and to eradicate rigidities associated with the previous pattern of growth. However, it is equally clear that there is more than one model of how to do so. In Japan, for example, labour flexibility, at any rate in core sectors of the labour market, is achieved through a strong commitment to continuous training and lifetime employment. In the UK, neo-liberal strategy has focused on labour-market deregulation, through the elimination of legal and institutional restrictions on the 'free' operation of the labour market. The British model is distinguished by its focus on low-skill training, and on support for the unemployed, in some contrast to other major industrial economies.

Many labour-market policies are primarily implemented at the local level and constitute a key element in any local economic regeneration strategy. But the emphasis in Britain on low-skill training, combined with the control of training programmes either by a central state quango, in the shape of the MSC/Training Agency, or now by local business in the shape of the TECs, has militated against the integration of training and local labour-market policy into wider local economic regeneration strategies. Instead of having a central role in training and local labour-market policy, the policy role of elected local government has been marginalised.

Local labour-market policies must give particular emphasis to those social groups marginalised within, or excluded from, the local labour market. While local policies will be inhibited without a policy shift at national level, local strategies have a key role in combatting local spatial concentrations of labour-market disadvantages, in inner cities or on peripheral estates (Duffy, 1992).

If women are to occupy more than a second-class place in post-Fordist employment, there need to be policy initiatives at local as well as other levels, based on adequate analysis of the labour-market position of women, which address the issues of women's employment, skills and training in a comprehensive manner (Duffy and Geddes, 1990).

The argument is that public policy must be used to combat the tendencies within post-Fordism towards a polarised labour market. Neo-liberal policies, which accentuate such tendencies, are not merely socially divisive but limit the level of demand in the economy. Alternative policies, which can draw on the experience of other advanced industrial countries, need to involve the coordination of training with other public services at the local level, and would require more widely defined powers of competence for local government in the economic sphere (Campbell, 1990b; Local Government Information Unit, 1991).

Public-sector productivity

In many local economies, particularly where manufacturing has been decimated over the past decade, public-sector institutions such as the local authority or the health authority are the largest or among the largest employers, and the public sector as a whole bulks very large in the local economy. This is despite the squeeze on public expenditure and the effects of privatisation. Yet local economic regeneration strategies usually have startlingly little to say about the role of the public sector itself in the local economy. There are some notable exceptions to this. In the early 1980s a few local authorities such as Sheffield began to examine the contribution of local government expenditure, investment, purchasing and employment to the local economy. The Local Jobs Plans prepared in the context of the 1987 election campaign looked at the role of local public expenditure, on construction for example, in boosting the local economy and creating jobs.

Yet it is clear that an integrated approach to the public sector at the local level could play a major role in local economic regeneration strategies. This is demonstrated by the studies which have been carried out by the South East Economic Development Strategy (SEEDS) group of local authorities. SEEDS has worked with trade unions and user groups to produce alternative strategies for sectors such as transport, health, energy, telecommunications and postal services aimed at improving the employment contribution and the quality of service of the industry in question. Examples such as this demonstrate the case for a more decentralised and locally coordinated approach to the management of nationalised public services which is very much in tune with post-Fordist economic trends towards the replacement of hierarchical, vertically integrated structures by more flexible ones.

Superficially, this may seem to bear a close resemblance to the way in which neo-liberal policies in Britain have broken up integrated public services such as the health service and now the railways. Superficially, the objectives of efficiency and service quality are the same. But in the neo-liberal approach the search for quality and efficiency within the public sector has been dominated and distorted by the overriding objectives of cost-reduction and privatisation. The contract culture has encouraged local public-sector initiative only within the constraints of tight central managerial control over expenditure. The aim has been largely negative, to residualise the public sector, rather than a positive attempt to increase its productivity (Geddes, 1991). A productivity-based approach means the effective use of limited resources in relation not only to quality of service and of employment but in relation to the contribution of the public sector to the economy as a whole. The difficulty of either achieving productivity gains or meeting more sophisticated consumer needs in the public sector was one of the elements of the crisis of the Fordist phase of economic growth. More flexible forms of organisation of production potentially provide new opportunities to both improve public service quality and increase productivity. Our argument is that the promotion of innovation in public services, and the integration of their social and economic roles, requires coordinated planning at the local level.

Urban infrastructure is a case in point. Progressively during the twentieth century the creation of nationalised public utilities has taken infrastructure decisions away from the local level, and in the last decade there has been a massive privatisation of infrastructure agencies. Yet, as Marvin (1992) shows, key economic issues for the 1990s are the provision of coherent infrastructure support to new urban development, and the renovation of old urban infrastructure systems, as well as the social question of good access to infrastructure networks by poorer people. Failures such as the delays in providing public transport to even such key developments as Canary Wharf are indicative of the limitations of a neo-liberal approach to infrastructure. There is a clear need for integrated, local public strategies for infrastructure investment, and a rolling back of the privatisations of the 1980s.

Local public services in a Europe of the regions?

In Britain in the 1980s the struggle over the future of local public services was waged largely between national and local levels of government. However as we move from a Fordist to a post-Fordist economy the spatial parameters within which the future of local public services is being determined are changing quite rapidly. In particular the development of supranational state structures at the European level, and of a regional tier of government in all major EC states except the UK, are likely to influence the role of public services at the local level. The reasons for these changes are closely bound up with the economic transition from Fordism. On the one hand, the crisis of Fordism was a crisis of the nation-state's ability to regulate the economy. With the increasing internationalisation of the economy, the ability of nation-states to maintain domestic demand and to safeguard a coherent 'national economy' became both more difficult and less necessary to industry. The creation of the single European market and the movement towards economic and monetary union are the result. But, while the post-Fordist economy is thus associated with a shift in scale to the European level as the basis for global competition, it is also associated with the increased prominence of the regional level. The industrial districts phenomenon, to take a prominent example, represents a new regional pattern of linkages and coherence in at any rate some elements of the modern economy.

These trends are changing the context of local economic regeneration strategy in two ways. First, the perception of the importance of regional linkages within the contemporary economy is promoting the view that the region, rather than the local area, is the critical sub-national level for economic regeneration policy (Brunskill, 1990). Second, local and regional authorities are increasingly looking to Brussels as a sympathetic context and source of funds for local economic regeneration policies. The two trends combine in the concept of a 'Europe of the regions' as an escape from the rigidities of the central–local government relationship, especially perhaps in the UK where the neo-liberal policy context has been so negative to local autonomy (Murray, 1991a).

However without denying the new flexibility which a Europe of the regions might bring, it is important to continue to reassert the significance of the specifically local level of governance in relation to economic regeneration and the role of public services, and to preserve a critical perspective on the Europeanisation and regionalisation of government. There are a number of reasons for this. In the first place, while the European Community may offer new funds for local economic regeneration (such as the RECHAR funds for coalfield communities), and avenues of access for local and regional authorities, it is clear that dominant EC economic and competition policies are largely neo-liberal and free market, even while Commission institutions may engage in a more neo-corporatist consultation with a plurality of interest groups. The EC Structural Funds are wholly inadequate in size to counter the socio-economic disparities which economic integration and restructuring are producing. Moreover EC competition and deregulation policies constitute a major threat to public services such as railways and telecoms.

If the European Community is to offer a more positive context than this, it will require a thoroughgoing democratisation of its structures. In part, the case for stronger regional government is linked to this perspective, in that it is argued that regional authorities will have the political clout to influence European (and national) policy formation. The problem lies, though, in the relationship between such powerful regional authorities and the more truly local level, which is likely to remain the level at which most people can most directly influence policy issues. This issue is often glossed over by an easy assertion that regional authorities will 'coordinate' local needs, and facilitate a 'bottom-up' approach to economic regeneration. Yet much of the evidence points to the fact that regional agencies, especially where they are not directly politically controlled, serve more as a downward transmission belt for higher-level policies. At the minimum, the principle of subsidiarity needs to be very firmly entrenched if local public services are to play an active and innovative role in local economic regeneration, and if the local state is to achieve the economic role in post-Fordism which it has lacked under Fordism, rather than become the local dumping place for those excluded and marginalised by post-Fordist flexibility.

Environmental issues

Last but not least there is the issue of the environmental and ecological implications of current patterns of economic growth. There is increasingly widespread recognition of the unsustainable nature of the forms of economic growth which characterised the post-war boom. Environmental issues have also raised serious reservations about the effectiveness of neo-liberal policies, in both the short- and long-term. However the need for environmental sustainability also poses serious challenges to some of the conventional arguments for public services, couched as these often are in an uncritical model of growth and productivism.

There are indications that a 'greener' capitalism may be an increasingly important element of the post-Fordist economy, promoted both by environmentally conscious consumers and firms seeking to benefit from environmentalism in different ways. However the development of green 'niche markets' and limited forms of environmental regulation represent only very partial steps towards a sustainable economy, and on this basis ecological constraints and problems are likely to continue to worsen.

A more fully sustainable economy would require much more substantial changes to production and consumption patterns and processes. Stronger sustainability would require much more systemic forms of state regulation, and a new role for public planning at all levels, including the local level, in managing the difficult transition to sustainable patterns of development. There is also a strong link between greater social and economic equality and the achievement of sustainability, as the existence of major inequalities makes it much easier for environmental problems and costs to be offloaded onto poorer people and places (Geddes, 1993).

CONCLUSION

There is much evidence to suggest that the achievement of stable economic growth requires the regulation of the economy to link the expansion of consumption with that of production. Such regulation involves a major role for the state and the public sector, but in Britain in the post-war period state functions of economic planning and regulation were concentrated at national level while the local state was primarily concerned with welfare and collective consumption. Moreover it proved very difficult to achieve commensurate productivity gains in the public sector to match those in the private sector. The result was a form of local public-service provision which came to appear unproductive in several senses – in its orientation to 'social' not 'economic' goals, in relation to conventional measures of productivity, and also in relation to increasingly diverse and sophisticated patterns of need. Post-Fordist economic trends however offer both new challenges and new opportunities for local public services. On the one hand, there have been strong pressures to recommodify areas of public provision, to apply 'market' criteria within the state sector, and to relegate public services to a residual role catering for those marginalised in the labour market. However there are also important elements of economic change which are consistent with a more active economic role for the state, including the local level. The depth of the current recession, especially in Britain, provides powerful evidence that neo-liberal policies are not effectively achieving a new and positive balance between production and consumption, on which stable economic growth depends. The growth of new post-Fordist economic practices, structures and industrial sectors, and the restructuring of old sectors, require new institutional modes of regulation, including an active and innovative economic role for the public sector, both to achieve environmentally sustainable growth and to combat the strong tendencies towards a polarised society and labour market, which in turn limit consumption. If we wish to influence the outcome of the struggle over the shape of the post-Fordist world, we should be developing the case for a more active, innovative, productive and sustainable public sector, as part of broader strategic alternatives to neo-liberalism.

NOTES

1 Regulation theory is a body of literature which is concerned with the question of how capitalist development comes to be relatively stable over long periods of time, despite inbuilt tendencies to contradiction and crisis. It advances a view of the importance of institutionalised structures of regulation as the basis for sustained economic growth (Aglietta, 1979; Dunford, 1990; Jessop, this volume).

2 It is also true, of course, that until the era of high unemployment local authorities did not make use of the limited powers – such as Section 137 – that they did possess.

3 The severe impact of the current recession on southern Britain is of course much more problematic for neo-liberal strategy.

4 This policy contrasts sharply, of course, with the industrial and regional policies of the Fordist period which promoted industrial restructuring, not through the intensification of competition but through investment subsidies, especially for fixed capital.

Part III

Flexibility, consumption and the future of welfare

10 Flexibility in higher education

Michael Rustin

INTRODUCTION

Virtually everyone in British higher education must be aware of the current pressure to transform curricula and teaching methods in order to achieve what is usually called 'greater flexibility'.[1] Among the measures being promoted in order to further this goal are modularisation, the conversion of traditional academic terms and years into semesters, systems for credit accumulation and transfer, the encouragement of distance-learning techniques, and the pursuit of greater national and international mobility for students.

These changes are taking place within a university system which has been subjected by government to a process of marketisation parallel to those that have been imposed on other public and welfare services. Of course, the higher education system has always to some degree functioned as a market, in that students have been free to apply to colleges of their choice, and colleges have been free to select among applicants according to criteria determined, above a stipulated minimum level of qualification, by themselves. There has also always been competition between institutions for research funding, and for status and the private funding that goes with it. But these competitive disciplines have recently been increased, by an insistence that the proportion of privately-obtained funding become larger, by the introduction of 'corporate status' and a major role for 'independent governors' in the ex-polytechnics, by the ending of the 'binary division' which insulated the older universities from some aspects of competition from the former polytechnics and institutes of higher education, and by the imposition of more stringent forms of audit and quality inspection on all forms of higher education. So far as it is possible, the higher education system is being constrained to depend on funding provided by students themselves, and on contracts provided by businesses and other external agencies, rather than on funding provided by the state. Where the state continues to provide funding for higher education it does so on condition of more stringent competition between institutions, the introduction of management methods derived from business, and a regulatory system that seeks to link resource allocation to measures of quality. These developments have many similarities to the restructuring being effected within the school, health and personal social service systems. In all these, the thrust is to make providers operate as far as possible as entrepreneurs in quasi-markets, subject to new forms of regulation intended to make competition more effective.

What does this have to do with the theories of Fordism and post-Fordism? The model of the 'Fordist welfare state' only applied to a limited degree to the highly elitist and selective higher education system in Britain, which is only now beginning to achieve an authentically 'mass' character as the proportion of the 18-year-old age group entering it nears one-third. The institutions which have provided the template of higher education in Britain emphatically employ pre-Fordist models of individualised or at worst (or is it best?) batch production, not 'mass production'. If 'Fordist' methods of 'mass' higher education have had a look-in, it is only during the past twenty years, and especially perhaps in the unique combination of open entry and specialised division of productive labour which characterises the operations of the Open University. To some extent 'Fordism' is only coming to higher education now, as higher student numbers and declining budgets force institutions to take economies of scale and 'mass' forms of curriculum delivery more seriously. In the sphere of higher education, it is the law of combined and uneven development that prevails, with Fordist, pre-Fordist, and post-Fordist modes of educational production all coexisting within the same system, and with none guaranteed, in these particular conditions of production, a decisive comparative advantage.

Yet if the British higher education system is by no means Fordist in its general formation, it has certainly aroused in the present government the antagonisms similar to those generated by other forms of 'Fordist' welfare. Essentially, these amount to an antipathy to the power of the professional establishments installed in relative power by the consensus politics of the Fordist era, and to a desire to subject this system, like others, to the disciplines of markets. If the move to 'post-Fordism' is explained in part as the strategic response by the business class and its political advocates to the powerful 'resistances' to capital established towards the end of the Great Boom,[2] then the restructuring of higher education is consistent with this broader pattern.

'Flexibility' has become the idealised model through which the changes demanded of higher education by government have been interpreted and theorised within it. The doctrine of enhanced flexibility is fast becoming a dominant ideology, even though one might think that a 'neo-Fordist' reprogramming of educational production to deal with increased numbers and reduced funding is in practical terms a more imperative and likely response from the majority system. A similar paradox can be seen in other areas of the welfare system. Whilst the ideology and rhetoric speaks of consumer rights and entitlements, the managerial imperative is to ensure faster and more reliable throughput (in hospitals) or the normalisation of standard objectives (classroom practice reconstructed around compulsory testing). Curiously, the most *advanced* aspects of these systems, those corresponding most closely to a post-Fordist, organic division of labour (for example, integrated, group-based teaching methods in primary schools, individual records of achievement) are in some cases those most out of favour with the political right who have had so large an influence on the reforms of the public sector. The problem is that whilst the market-oriented right may in theory favour individualised relations of production, they care rather more about social indiscipline and the restraint of public spending. So if 'Fordist' solutions are the only ones compatible with these objectives, they will be used, though not described as such. The same, of course, is true in manufacturing where the sourcing of cheap inputs from suppliers is concerned.

Still, 'post-Fordism' is in the main an ideology of technocrats, professionals and new-style managers, the service class of the new socio-technical system, not of its ultimate proprietors. It describes how new systems might after all make things better both for producers and consumers, and might compensate for the losses of the defeated class-compromise, by providing new benefits formulated in terms of 'difference'. It is not, therefore, surprising that with its embodiment in higher education, the ideal of 'flexibility' appeals to the new academic managers who now find themselves empowered there. Nor is it surprising that it has some wider resonances, to lower-level staff in these organisations and even, by attribution anyway, to the students who might find more differentiated curriculum niches within a more open university system. The whole point of the 'post-Fordist' model is that it identifies and makes the most of the positive aspects of late-industrial, information-based forms of production. There is no reason to suppose that such positive aspects do not exist, even if there is a nastier side to these transformations too.

It is an irony of virtually all the current reforms of the public sector that the more difficult it becomes to maintain, let alone improve standards (following relative or absolute reductions in resources), the more the government demands that standards be attended to and monitored. This must be in part a straightforward diversionary ploy to shift attention away from the material sources of the problems in maintaining performance and onto the failings of under-performers (there will always be some) who can thus be made to carry the can. The school-teaching profession, whose outputs in terms of exam performance actually seem to get better by the year, has been a particularly gross victim of this process. In order to keep these incorrigible resisters in their place, it has been necessary to denounce the measures (standards of exam marking, the GCSE assessments themselves) which might otherwise suggest that the schools are continuing to do remarkably well in very discouraging circumstances (such as many of their pupils having no jobs to go to).

But for managers within the public sector who, like anyone else, want to believe in the value of what they do, and for whom measures of profitability will hardly do as measures of self-worth (for one thing, these systems still do not generate much profit, for another, the cultural system defines well-being in different terms), the issue of 'quality' strikes a positive chord.[3] Good quality is uncontroversial, and can be used to give an idealistic aspect to a restructuring process which may not be precisely driven by this goal, but may in this way be put in its most favourable light.

One key dimension of the 'post-Fordism' debate is the changed relation to space and time of these supposed new forms of production. The surmounting of locational and temporal constraints – fixed sites of production and consumption, rigid demarcations of time, and the social resistances encoded within them (solidarity in the workplace, shopfloor control of the working day, property rights in a job extending over time) is one of the objectives of 'post-Fordist' modes of production. Time- and space-transcending technologies, especially enhanced forms of communication of goods, persons and information are rightly deemed to be key preconditions of flexible systems of production and distribution. What I want to do in this chapter is to explore how far more flexible relations to time and space, in imagination or practice, figure as central issues in the reform of higher education. In so far as they do, in concepts of modularisation, customised and distance learning, credit accumulation and transfer, and the use of information technology, I shall explore some of the positive potentials and dangers of these trends.

TIME–SPACE CONSTRAINTS IN HIGHER EDUCATION

Higher education, like most organised activities, has been traditionally conducted in settings firmly bounded in time and space. Universities are usually sited in definite places. The more ancient they are, and the higher their status, the more elaborately their space has been marked out, by boundary and ceremonial entrance-way (the Oxford and Cambridge college quadrangle with its gateway and lodge at the entrance, or the bounded campuses of the great redbrick universities of a later generation like Leeds or Birmingham).

Interior spaces, in the traditional model, were also treated in a ceremonious way, with lecture room, tutor's study, dining hall, chapel, green sward, buttery bar, each marked out and symbolically elaborated in its place. More modern and utilitarian institutions were obliged to pare down this ceremonial element. In many of these it was possible to indicate distinctions of function and ritual importance only in a few selected sites awarded special status – main entrance halls, panelled board rooms, offices of senior management members, or major lecture theatres with their lecterns. Or the signs of ritual importance were kept for special occasions – for instance in the layout of a lecture room as an examination hall where the layout is intended to awe as well as to inhibit plagiarism.

Time-boundedness has been equally rigid, especially in Britain where traditional models of higher education have suffered less structural modernisation than those of many other advanced countries. There is an academic year, structured differently from the calendar year.[4] 'Degree courses' are conventionally followed by cohorts of students, expected to start and finish at the same times. Beginnings are marked by 'inductions', endings by 'finals' and degree ceremonies (the latter requiring appropriate ritual spaces of a large size, even if these have to be borrowed – or rather rented – by some architecturally deprived institutions from other sectors able to offer a higher style, such as the Barbican Centre in London). Once again, the higher the prestige of the higher education institution, the stronger and more idiosyncratic the framing of its time-boundaries. Oxford and Cambridge give their terms names little used any longer outside – Michaelmas, Hilary, Trinity – it is assumed that members can locate the weeks by their sequence in the term – fourth or fifth week – without having to bother with a normal calendar. By contrast, newer and less prestigious institutions find it more difficult to 'colonise' time for their own cultural purposes, and complain that they are condemned to be merely 'nine to five' (or taking account of the equal opportunities claims of child care even 'ten to three' institutions). They find it harder to promote extra-curricular activities on any scale. But in nearly all of British higher education the obligatory progression from term to term and from year to year, and the difficulty of doing anything out of its proper sequence, has hitherto been very marked.

These time- and space-boundaries within which educational curricula were arranged supported strong definitions of bounded cultural space, within which a 'subject' or a 'course' or a 'research programme' could be developed and protected. The distinctive qualities and integrity of a 'subject' or degree course – generalised as the ideal of excellence – was the principal object of value. This sphere was constituted, as Bernstein (1975) proposed, by forms of classification (curriculum) and framing (pedagogy or teaching method). These were essentially controlled and policed by hierarchies or collegialities of academics (in some combination of these two organisational principles) and were not amenable to pressures to change from outside. Indeed, immunity from such pressures ('academic freedom') became a moral or ideological principle, and 'tenure' an institutional means of protecting its practice. Clearly the elaborated structures of subject knowledge and of esteemed educational programmes,[5] which characterise British university education, have been sustained by this strong insulation. Newer institutions have set about trying to create their own distinctive structures on this model, there being many examples one could cite of relative success from new universities and former polytechnics alike. One can say that the downside of the successes of these bounded areas of specialism has been a good deal of institutional conservatism in regard to new areas and methods of work.

Universities have functioned as 'containers' of cultural power, just as, to use Giddens's (1981) term, cities have been the containers of broader kinds of economic and military power during the period of development of 'modern' societies. The precondition for universities fulfilling their function as generators and conservers of knowledge, and as transmitters of an elite culture, has been this degree of temporal and spatial boundedness, making possible relations of 'co-presencing' between role-players within these systems and regulating communications with the outside world such that they took place mainly at the invitation of the existing cultural power-holders. Hardy's novel *Jude the Obscure* is one of the most powerful representations of what this exclusiveness signified to those who were not allowed access to these centres of culture. The erosion and compression of these time–space boundaries is a phenomenon of the intellectual as well as of the economic and political spheres. The ideology of 'flexibility' in higher education is at the leading edge of this transformation of hitherto closed and bounded systems into more open ones.

In the major phase of post-war higher-education expansion, the post-Robbins boom from the 1960s to the 1980s, the necessity of the time–space containment of the educational process was not put in question. The intention of this phase of educational policy was to enlarge the institutional base of higher education, not to transform it into an open system. When the late-lamented Council for National Academic Awards (CNAA) took on its task of substantially extending the scope of higher education, to a number of new providing institutions greater than those already established as universities, it made the existing conventions of spatial and especially temporal boundedness into its implicit ground-rules, which it implemented in the form of criteria for the validation of new courses. These criteria were summed up in the terms 'coherence' and 'progression', respectively the synchronic and diachronic dimensions of academic language-codes. Providers of new courses were usually asked to justify their programmes in these terms. That is, the concurrently provided elements of a course were expected to be in some kind of meaningful relationship to one another. And, with rather greater emphasis, the consecutive elements of a programme were expected to follow upon one another in a developmental sequence, such that the earlier parts of the programme were necessary preconditions for gaining access to and coping with the later.

The development of 'modular' courses (i.e. 'unitised' programmes whose components were not necessarily linked in either fixed combinations or sequences) forced these implicit rules and criteria out into the open, since these ideas of coherence now had to be defended against a rival educational concept. In the compromise forms of modular curricula, which emerged from the opposed extremes of 'cafeteria' and fully prescribed menus, these 'coherence' requirements came to be defined as 'pre-requisites' and 'co-requisites' of particular course modules. The assumption within this new discourse was that it was these kinds of compulsory connections that needed to be explicitly justified, whilst the default assumption was that discrete units of study should be made as accessible as possible, with the fewest necessary restrictions.

Temporal and spatial boundedness were also required by CNAA so far as the regulation of entry into and progression through the educational process was concerned. Students had to be selected by established procedure and entry criteria as the first step of the process. How this was to be done was usually a key issue in validation. Some assessment was made of the quality of physical facilities, libraries, laboratories and so forth, though concerns here were almost exclusively with utilitarian rather than symbolic dimensions of learning-spaces. HMI, with their different school-derived methodology of classroom observation, did however take greater note of appearances, connecting environmental quality with the learning experience at least at the level of educational housekeeping.

But these bounded structures were enforced by mechanisms more powerful even than CNAA. The provision of student grants for the normal three or four years duration of a course, the higher grant for students living away from home, and capital funding for student halls of residence have had the effect of defining higher education as an activity that in Britain normally takes place within a clearly marked-out time-slot, and in a location removed from the students' normal family residence. To this day, of course, the student populations of many of the pre-binary-line universities remain largely made up of immediately post-school-age students who have purposely chosen a university which requires them to live during term-time away from their parental home. Up to a half of them may live in purpose-built halls of residence or colleges, and the majority of the rest in rented houses or lodgings.

The continental European and American patterns of higher education have broken with these traditional structures to a greater degree than has Britain, largely because they have been more responsive to the demand for popular access and have admitted a larger proportion of their 18-plus populations to higher education. But here too, the more elite the educational institution, the stronger its temporal and spatial boundaries. The continental pattern of allowing more people to enter higher education, but enforcing strict rules of progression through high failure and drop-out rates, does not dispense with a rigid temporal sequence but rather builds into it a more stringent form of continuous selection by examination. Where in the 'sponsored' system of Britain (Turner, 1961) the university takes a great deal of responsibility for progression, and sets out to minimise 'wastage', the continental and American 'contest' models place more of this responsibility on the individual. Similarly, the convention usual in France and Italy that students will remain in their parental home and study at their local university imposes a different form of spatial boundedness than that of the British residential university, but ties the student firmly to a customary location nevertheless.

In Britain, these forms of temporal and spatial boundedness made possible the construction and defence of a 'virtual space' of academic autonomy. That is, a 'cultural space' in which the university was able to define what a 'subject', a 'curriculum', an academic culture and way of life were, without too much regard for the more mundane realities of business or industrial life. David Lodge's novel *Nice Work* (and in respect of a more peripheral sector, his later *Paradise News*) has amusingly depicted some of the continuing differences between these cultures in England today. What the university offered was available to the outside world on the university's terms, in the university's space, or, virtually, not at all. In France and Italy, on the other hand, universities have been subject to more bureaucratic regulation by the state. Their professional workers have been classified as public servants, and access by students has been made available as an entitlement of citizenship.

The British convention seemed to cede to the university a significant form of cultural power over the shaping and reproduction of social elites.

But until the 1960s the system was so small and selective, and the top elites of politics, the civil service, the professions of medicine and law, science, and metropolitan business were so closely enmeshed with the peak universities, and with the public schools that preceded them in the careers of most elite members, that this produced little apparent tension. The British upper class was in fact able to delegate its socialising functions to the leading schools and universities with confidence in the values these institutions would instil, with only the occasional nasty surprise. The incidence of communist sympathies and treachery in Cambridge circles in the 1930s and 1940s perhaps had its extreme fascination because of the way these events disrupted an otherwise seemingly homogeneous surface of conformity.

Whilst the universities educated only a small elite proportion of the population, and whilst the links with establishment positions were so close, this autonomy did not produce too many divergences or conflicts of institutional purpose. In the various phases of expansion of higher education, the model was extended, on a progressively cut-down basis, to more institutions, though with appropriate compromises with the newer elites or sub-elites who were being thereby accorded a share of cultural 'voice' and therefore power. The great provincial universities gave greater weight to science and engineering, in synchrony with their local economies.[6]

The redbrick universities adopted more rational-bureaucratic modes of organisation – departmental rather than collegial in character. The University of London operated in the English-speaking colonies and ex-colonies, and until the early 1970s in Britain also, in the (praiseworthy) mode of a higher educational missionary institution, inducting the inexperienced into good university practices. The 'new universities' of the 1960s in many cases attempted to reinvent 'Oxbridge' on a more contemporary basis, in some cases explicitly seeking to define a new 'cultural centre' – or nexus of key intellectual concerns – that would be distinct from both Oxbridge traditionalism and utilitarian redbrick subject specialisation. But their predominant locations in small cathedral and county towns rather than industrial centres indicated clearly that these institutions should be centres of high-quality cultural capital, not of routine educational transmission. The outcome of the 1992 UFC research quality assessment exercise suggests that a number of them have succeeded in meeting these aspirations. For these elite purposes more rather than less cultivated kinds of physical environment are deemed to be appropriate.

The polytechnics, when they were established in the early 1970s, were encouraged to develop a 'vocational' orientation which was in keeping with the objective of extending higher education to potential recruits to lower positions in the hierarchy of occupations. Their intended and indeed actual clientele were not for the most part future members of the topmost occupational elites, but aspirants to lower levels of professional, semi-professional, or managerial employment. Their predominantly urban-centre locations reflected this assumption, as did the usual failure to provide spatial facilities which might confer on them any special cultural status. Recruits to traditional universities were expected to live away from home, and to want or need the broader spin-off benefits of a cultivated university environment, in either a traditional or more modernist form.[7] Recruits to the polytechnics were conceived more on the model of students at the local 'tech' (institutions from which most of the polytechnics had in fact evolved). Like the public housing, factory and office architecture which were their contemporaries, the polytechnic buildings of the 1970s thus symbolised a bleak democratic vision. This was of a higher education for the many, in local surroundings not different from or better than citizens would expect to encounter in the rest of their lives, in institutions governed (at least nominally) by the local authorities who were also responsible for most of the other services of 'welfare Fordism', in particular the comprehensive schools and public housing.

But whilst the architecture might symbolise a cheapening and loss of cultural density as 'higher education' was more widely diffused, its organising conception remained traditional in the terms we have set out of spatial, temporal and cultural boundedness. As usual in Britain, the dominant class-inspired model proved difficult to challenge, and the path that was followed was not to rethink this model in democratic terms, but instead to diffuse and extend it at manageable cost. The key determinants of this system remained the three-year degree course, the prescribed minimum A-level qualification, and the mandatory student grant giving both incentive and support to complete 'the course' within the allotted period. Also preserved within this enlarged system was the guild-status of the academics, whose new recruits were initially to be supervised in taking up their new roles by more experienced university mentors, first within the University of London External Degree system and subsequently through the indirect and progressively more delegated rule of the CNAA.

But whilst the binary system immediately acquired a two-class character, like the tripartite secondary system before it, there was soon more similarity than dissimilarity in the values and interests that underpinned the two sectors. 'Vocationalist' aims were only partially fulfilled. More commonly, institutions developed whichever educational programmes would best attract students. Courses in humanities and social sciences, bearers and transmitters of cultural values and all-round competencies rather than of technical knowledge, grew fastest, together with business studies programmes whose technical skill content was also usually not high. The tutelary role of the existing universities in establishing the new institutions, the prior elite educational formation of most teachers in the polytechnics and colleges, and absence of an alternative model, pulled the new sector into the gravitational field of the old. Some of the radical advocates of a more community-based form of post-school education, such as John Pratt and Tyrrell Burgess (1974) attacked what they defined at an early stage as 'academic drift'; the tendency of new institutions to betray their original mission of vocationally relevant, open-access education.

But even as this development was gaining in momentum, in the 1960s, its contradictory potentials were becoming evident. The events of 1968 disrupted the assumption among policy-makers worldwide that higher education could simply be allowed to grow to meet available student and employer demand, without any unwelcome consequences other than those of increased costs. It became evident that congruence between the ethos and goals of these expanding academic institutions and those being set by politicians for the wider society could no longer be assumed. The cultural specificity of the university that was seen as harmless and even beneficial when it revolved around scholarship and attachment to antiquities of various kinds became dangerous when its forms of knowledge became more socially relevant and critical. A student population which seemed to be becoming indistinguishable in its lifestyle from the broader youth culture began to seem downright menacing to established cultural and moral standards. A powerful backlash against the idea of mass higher education began.

THE MARKETISATION OF HIGHER EDUCATION

In Britain the first response to this new perception was the imposition of more stringent regulation of the higher education system by government. Quinquennial grants to universities became annual grants; numbers of students studying different subject-areas were allocated by quota with the object of reducing the proportion of those exposed to values indifferent or antithetical to the 'enterprise culture' – for example to sociology rather than to technology and science. Government insisted on large-scale cost reductions and efficiency-savings, and the 'public sector' (i.e. the former polytechnics and colleges), which was prepared to provide this, was favoured at the expense of the university sector which clung as long as it could to its traditional 'academic standards'. The demand that institutions should raise a larger proportion of their budget from the private sector, or from full-cost (or greater-than-cost) overseas recruitment were other measures designed to break down the institutional autonomy of the higher education system, which of course had always depended largely on the willingness of the state to fund it. The introduction in the Education Reform Act of 1988 of 'corporate status' for public-sector institutions, and the requirement that their governing bodies be composed of a majority of 'independent' members ('independent' being a synonym for a background in business) were among the many measures intended to break down the insulation of the academy from the other dominant institutions of the society.

The first phase of this programme created almost continuous confrontation between the higher-education system and government, similar to that which the Thatcher government found itself engaged with in its relations with the school and health systems and their professional employees in its early attempts to bring them to order. Just as in other areas of the welfare sector, what has happened is that an initial period of head-on conflict with the 'vested interests' of unions and professionals has been followed by the development of a new market-oriented model, carefully designed to appeal to consumers (to whom it offers the reality or appearance of enhanced choice) and to the more managerial and entrepreneurial kinds of professional, to whom it offers greater autonomy, rewards, and power. General practitioners, hospital trust managers, head teachers, and senior academics are alike in being offered more control over budgets, greater freedom of initiative in their new quasi-markets, and performance-related pay. The subtle intention has been to seduce an important sub-class of salaried, public-service professionals into an identification, both material and ideological, with the market and with the enterprise culture.

There are similarities between the development of 'post-Fordist' strategies in the industrial and welfare sectors, and in the higher educational system. Economic constraints, whether driven by market forces or by the government's own defunding strategies, forces a more 'commercial' and competitive orientation on institutional managers. Resistance by traditional 'interests' (whether trade union or professional or, as in the NHS, the schools, and universities a combination of both) is defined as obstructive and conservative, and becomes a target of attack. Established forms of trade union and professional self-defence are undermined, and more individualised contracts are imposed in place of collectivised ones. 'Management grades' are more firmly defined, and their incumbents put under pressure to identify with these roles against the main grades of academic staff, with whom they may have formerly felt linked in a form of professional, collegial or trade union solidarity. Ideological support for the new enterprise regime is sought from business appointees to governing bodies. Material incentives have been given through new contractual arrangements and salary increases for top managers, the imposing of which was the very first significant action of many of the new corporate polytechnic governing bodies. Subsequently, performance-related pay and performance appraisal have been imposed as obligations on the new institutions, on pain of forfeiting a significant percentage of their funding.

The demand for continuing 'efficiency gains' in educational delivery has forced managers to aim for significant cost reductions. The demand that institutions should raise more of their budgets from the private sector has forced a market-orientation upon them, both in regard to teaching programmes, recruitment (especially from overseas) and research and consultancy. The increase in the 'fee' dimension of funding made marginal 'fee only' recruitment possible, and provided a poisoned market incentive for institutions to compete with one another to reduce unit costs. This incentive is now being curtailed, by the reduction of recoupable fees for students taking 'classroom' rather than 'laboratory-based' subjects. The reduction of the size of student grants, and their partial replacement by repayable loans, has required students to weigh the costs and benefits of their time spent at university more carefully, and provided them with incentives to choose more cost-effective courses, and more marketable qualifications. The abolition of the binary line is intended to break a cartel, to expose the university sector to competition from proven lower-cost producers. Both pull factors (the incentives of growth) and push factors (more stringent measures of quality, defunding of the inferior) are being deployed to cajole institutions into playing by the new rules. Whereas in the first phase of public-sector reforms, the government mainly battered these institutions (abolishing Quinquennial grants, increasing overseas student fees to reduce 'subsidies', fixing subject-quotas, making the most of the excesses of the educational philosophy of the 'sixties' to discredit colleges or departments) the latter phase has been dominated by a strategy of 'restructuring', of providing incentives and sanctions intended to make institutions go with the flow.

This strategy appears likely to be successful because of its appeal to the interests of key sections of both producers and consumers. Public-sector managers have been given many inducements to identify with the new system. Even ideologically it is possible to interpret the new marketised environment as one which enhances educational opportunities and breaks down restrictive barriers of status between the new institutions and the old. But also significant, in both the business sector of industry, commerce and finance, and the welfare sectors of education, housing and health, has been a populist appeal to 'consumer' interests against the more paternalist and massified conceptions of the Fordist era. Financial services have been packaged for the ordinary citizen; goods are produced in more diversified and customised varieties; parents, patients, rail-passengers (or customers as they are now styled) and now students, are made the objects of promises of greater choice and consideration.

These populist appeals are not without their force in a higher-education system distinguished in Britain by its profound traditions of elitism. The 'modernisation' and 'flexibilisation' of higher education is taking place in the context of a promise of a large expansion of access, amounting (at least until the recent government rethink) to a more-than-doubling of the age-participation rate. The cost of the insulation of universities from the wider society has been a very narrow and exclusive conception of who was deemed fit to receive higher education. These segregated locations, and the transitional life-spaces or moratoria that went on inside them, and the high cultural entry fee were all very well for those inside, but were a means of exclusion from the university for the great majority. Unlike the NHS or the comprehensive school, the higher-education system was never intended to be a universal system. This Conservative government's goal has been to make it more responsive to the market and to the imperatives of business and its ideology, as well as more accessible to the public, but the latter goal exceeds the former in its probable long-term consequences. Some of the current changes in higher education which are defined as greater 'flexibility and access' mobilise an idealism of the left as well as of the competition- and market-oriented right. The successful transformation of the system depends in fact on this multiple process of conversion, working on several dimensions of material reward, power and ideology.

THE IDEA OF 'FLEXIBILITY'

The ideology of 'flexibility' is a potent and subtle instrument of this design. It is a strategic response to these multiple pressures on the system, as 'post-Fordist' modes of production are a response to similar pressures and opportunities in the sphere of commodity production. Resistances can be overcome, new technologies can be exploited, new markets can be found, through an ideology and practice of 'flexibility' in all forms of production and exchange. The solution is all the more effective because it does not present itself as overtly ideological, and because it mobilises (like many other Thatcherite conceptions) radical as well as conservative sympathies.

'Flexibility' in higher education implies that the constraints of space and time which have hitherto limited access to and experience of the university should be lessened or removed. Modularisation and unitisation of programmes theoretically allow students, now redefined as autonomous interest-maximising consumers, to compile programmes at the locations and in the time-slots they prefer, rather than by compelling them to conform to the spatial and temporal organisation convenient to the university. The development of 'distance-learning techniques' promises to facilitate the physical dislocation of higher education from the university's own territory, and make it possible for students to study whenever and wherever they want. The Open University has already shown the great potential of such methods, both to widen access to the hitherto excluded, and to reduce the unit costs of provision. Universities are encouraged to take their programmes outdoors, and to offer them on the premises and to the customised requirements of outside agencies, such as firms. The development of 'two-year degrees', using time and space more intensively, offers to remove an important temporal constraint of the traditional university curriculum.

Europeanisation has its role in all this. The European Community's nominal objective that 10 per cent of EC students should undertake part of their studies in another member country would be a dramatic form of globalisation if it occurred, and in support of this objective the EC is a strong advocate of the standardisation and transferability of qualifications (Commission of the European Community, 1991).

Information technology, or anyway the most optimistic scenarios about its potential, is part of this dream of a higher education emancipated from the constraints of time and space. Libraries become redefined as information centres, accessing learning materials via computer terminals linked in real time to the outside world rather than via the older storage system of books on shelves. Curriculum materials are imagined to be provided on computer file, or on video-cassette, enabling students to access teaching at any time they choose. Electronic mail systems give academics a sense of membership of an international academic community, and schemes are hatched up for ERASMUS students to work together from their locations in different countries via computer link-ups. So far, information technology in higher education has probably been used more to enhance traditional methods (better preparation of materials, large-screen presentations, the teaching of computing itself) than to transform them. Putting a computer on an academic's desk may be a way of getting him or her to spend more rather than less time in the university, and two secretaries with IT equipment may do the work of four with typewriters. Nevertheless, the potential for doing things more quickly, for transmitting information more widely, and for connecting with networks of computer-users not bounded in the traditional ways, is obvious. There may be some subtle changes of identity involved in individuals' becoming related as IT users to information systems and networks, rather than to the more collectivised routines of traditional pedagogy.

Flexibility and modularisation undermine and attack the 'virtual spaces' of the academic subject and course as well as the temporal and spatial constraints on their delivery. The idea is not just that students should be more free to move physically and organise their time more flexibly, but that they should also have more discretion over what they study. The idea of 'credit accumulation and transfer' – of standard-size course modules carrying equivalent credits – allows not only freedom of movement between institutions, or different rates of progression within them, but also, in principle, infinite freedom of combination of units, subject only to specific pre-requisites and criteria of academic levels. This framework undermines the power of the academic controllers – in effect the leasehold proprietors – of traditional single-subject courses, since it denies academics the power to insist that students only gain access to their programmes if they follow the entire curriculum in the prescribed forms. One of the attractions of 'flexibility' and 'modularisation' for new academic managers is precisely that it does undercut or circumvent the power of the subject departments and their hierarchies. It, in effect, attacks their monopoly of supply of 'psychology' or 'sociology' to students and to the institution of which they are a part.

Flexible 'unitised' systems require uniform procedures – for admissions, for timetabling over the year, week and day, for assessment, and for generating information and marketing publicity. Whilst allowing greater freedom of choice to the individual student, flexible and unitised systems of instruction paradoxically require a much higher level of integration and coordination at the level of the institution, to guarantee access and transfer, and to ensure that the benefits of economies of scale are achieved. There is incentive and pressure also to achieve this integration across institutional boundaries, through credit accumulation and transfer arrangements, and by the 'franchising' of university courses, or at least the lower level of these, to satellite colleges in their student catchment areas, which may sometimes be worldwide as well as local. This may be viewed as an equivalent of 'peripheral Fordism' (Lipietz 1987) in the university sector. This coordination and integration necessitates better organisation and management, and is again attractive to those identified with the development of roles as professional academic managers rather than as traditional academics. The disciplines of cost-effectiveness empower managers over academics in the universities, in the same way that they threaten to subordinate medical consultants to managers in the NHS.

The foundation model of traditional university education was a 'pre-Fordist' form of studio- or craft-apprenticeship to individual tutors, in which most of the real work was done on a one-to-one or small-group basis, and attendance at lectures was deemed optional. 'Fordism'– or the routinised large-scale production of graduates – was begun with the departmentally organised courses of London University and the redbrick universities. Pedagogy in the newer institutions was rationally organised, 'courses' being systematically taught through obligatory lectures and seminars designed to transmit knowledge. In the later phases of expansionary higher education in Britain in the 1970s and 1980s, institutions were driven to attempt this form of transmission on a larger scale, in effect aiming to combine increased student numbers and thus economies of scale with conventional subject-oriented assumptions about curriculum and pedagogy. The dominant model remained that of a standard specialist curriculum, often organised as a compulsory core with discretionary options, delivered in prescribed segments, and assessed by fairly inflexible means. At first the newly appointed teachers borrowed the curricula and teaching methods of the dominant producers – for example, the sociologists of London University – and set themselves up in production much as an assembly plant might produce Ford cars in Mexico from specifications laid down in Detroit. Degree courses in Law, Sociology or Psychology with annual intakes of 100 or 150 represented (by small-scale British standards) a 'Fordist' solution to the problems of producing students with reduced unit costs. Although curricula and teaching methods evolved in the new sector in some distinctive directions as greater experience and autonomy was acquired, the fundamental pattern did not usually change very much.

This system of educational production depended on economies of scale to meet the requirements of cost-reduction of the 1980s. For courses which could enlarge their intakes from 50 to 100 or 150, this could be achieved. But there were many subject-areas where such expansion was not feasible, and such programmes tied up substantial resources of every kind. An organisational system which seemed to work for a number of programmes in high demand was quite dysfunctional for programmes which could no longer attract students, and offered their course teams little opportunity for escape.[8] It was also difficult for institutions to take full advantage of potential economies of scale, in a system which was far from being a perfect market. Student numbers were regulated by subject-area quotas, and even when the government stopped discriminating explicitly against social sciences in apportioning these, there were usually still limits on how many students it was feasible to recruit in the most popular areas.

A form of 'flexible specialisation' by modularisation seems a good solution to this problem, from the perspective of those institutions – usually the former polytechnics – most committed to expansion and to achieving economies of scale. Modularisation offers the possibility of providing many new subject-combinations, simply by separating the components of existing programmes. This is a much quicker and more efficient route to subject-innovation than the traditional one of starting a new specialist degree course with its long lead-time of development and validation. Subjects that might not recruit enough students for a whole degree course, might nevertheless attract students for some optional units, or be offered in joint-honours combinations with other subjects. This form of flexibility is beneficial to areas both in rising and falling demand. It can provide a relatively soft landing, with a longer decommissioning time for subjects in decline, but also a gradual take-off from small beginnings for subjects on the rise. Since within a modular programme a subject can be offered in any number of units, from a minimum of one to a maximum which exceeds the menu of a full degree programme, it is possible to develop new subjects from a very small base, allowing them to rise (or fall) as their own initiative and market-response makes possible. New subject-area 'niches' have opened up, for subjects offered first in combination with others, but then with the chance of growing into full-scale degree programmes. This offers huge advantages both of market-responsiveness and of producer-initiative to institutions which adopt this design principle. 'Flexibility' is consistent with the interests of managers, wanting above all efficient use of resources, and of educational innovators, who find in this more open unitised structure the space to initiate new programmes with minimum impediments.

Greater flexibility in the organisation of time has its attractions to educators as well as to resource managers. The established 'mass' system with its conventional assumptions about contact-time and progression by annual cohort is being driven into severe strain and dysfunction by worsening staff–student ratios. With smaller relative staff resources, either teaching staff conditions of work are rendered intolerable, or students are placed in such large groups that the whole meaning of the learning experience is degraded. There seems no choice but to give students more responsibility for the learning process, and to redefine teaching away from the model of mass-production pedagogy, towards a more facilitative student-controlled model.

To make this possible without devaluation of the meaning of education seems to require shifting attention from the quantity of instruction to its quality. Attention must be directed to what actually happens when student meets teacher, even if this only occurs during six class-contact hours per week. It becomes necessary to attend both to the efficient large-scale delivery of standard curriculum materials, and to the purpose and effectiveness of individual- or small-group interactions between lecturers and students. Methods of large-scale delivery include providing high-quality printed materials, distance-learning techniques, and open-access resource facilities; all these using new information technologies more effectively.[9] Many of these particular methodologies – often excellent in their own way – have been pioneered by the Open University, whose course books have in many fields long been market-leaders.

The purpose of small-group contact in these new conditions will above all be to motivate students, and provide them with both the techniques and the interest to learn. Avoiding an anonymous, nomadic institutional environment, and providing some sense of settled spatial and intellectual location, seems likely to be the precondition for making effective use of 'mass-learning' techniques.[10] The Open University has always recognised the importance of its annual summer schools in providing high-intensity learning experiences for students, but this seems an insufficient form of provision for the average undergraduate under twenty-five years old. There is, however, probably scope for making use of graduate teaching assistants, on the American university model, to provide a context for learning at the necessary level of personal contact but at tolerable cost to institutions.

A key dimension to take into consideration in planning effective forms of learning is the emotional dimension of the learning experience. Where learning is intended to take place at any deep level, it involves the need to reconsider existing beliefs and identities, and to take the risk of being found inadequate as learning proceeds and is assessed. Sustaining this burden usually requires relationships of trust to be established with teachers or other students.[11] For this reason, high quality forms of individual attention by teachers to students are likely to remain functional for all forms of education, and cannot be sensibly regarded as a 'luxury' to be dispensed with on economic grounds. Nor are 'counsellors' and psychotherapists an alternative to providing good quality contact in the learning relationship itself, as comprehensive schools found at an early stage when they tried to compensate for the absence of a structured learning environment by providing 'safety-nets'. Safety-nets will be necessary, but they are not substitutes for relationships in which students feel that they are known and kept in mind from one week to the next (Salzberger-Wittenberg *et al.*, 1983).

Semesterisation can also provide positive opportunities in these present circumstances of declining unit costs. This restructuring of academic time may allow the curriculum to be sub-divided into component units which can be studied sequentially rather than in the conventional concurrent form. It may be more effective to study fewer subjects intensively, – even one at a time – than a combination of several subjects concurrently over a longer time period. This may make possible a greater concentration of students' attention, and thus a more effective use of both teachers' and students' time. Some of the apparent economies of neo-Fordist educational production – production lines of concurrent courses, each allotted two hours per week – may have been false economies, because of the gap between what was intended as 'transmission' and what was received or made use of by the students. Paradoxically, a return to a 'studio' or 'craft-apprenticeship' model for a carefully-selected portion of the student's learning experience might turn out to be more efficient, cost-effective and enjoyable for all concerned.

Piore and Sabel (1984) argued in *The Second Industrial Divide* that hyper-Fordism might be a less effective response to competitive pressure than a climate of 'cooperative competition' between small-scale producers highly sensitive to difference and complementarity. A 'flexible curriculum', with more mobile groups of 'subject producers', relating themselves to fluid markets, and with students conceived as 'intelligent learners' encouraged to work both as individuals and as small-group cooperatives, might be a viable form of production in the university environment too.

COMPARISON WITH BROADCASTING

One main reason for the adoption of 'post-Fordist' strategies by firms has been the enhanced bargaining power of workers operating under 'Fordist' conditions of high demand, and within integrated production processes which gave a high measure of control to workforces. Government acting on behalf of the market, as well as corporations, has sought to break up these resistances in many different sectors. One case analogous to that of the universities is public-service broadcasting. Here the government was faced with a situation of a duopoly of providers, one a public service and the other a regulated private network, each relatively insulated from competition, and nurturing distinctive ideologies and value-systems by no means entirely synonymous with the present government's. In-house monopolies of production also led to relatively high costs, to which exposure to competition by independent producers, on the Channel Four model, was an initial solution. In this sphere, the remedies to this monopoly power have been sought in marketisation, enhanced competition, deregulation, and the overcoming of the boundaries imposed by time and space. Technical developments play a part here that they have scarcely yet done in the mainstream of higher-education, in that satellite broadcasting (and also cable, once there is the initial investment) has made it technically possible to provide a multiplicity of channels and has removed the technical advantages of the existing limited-channels system. Thus the licensing of satellite channels, the auctioning of existing terrestrial programmes, the dilution of requirements of 'quality', and the enforced exposure of local producers to the competition of international media corporations, have the intention and effect of overwhelming the local monopolistic producers' control of their previously relatively captive audiences.

This analogy might suggest that a step that might in future be taken to erode the monopoly of higher education providers is the wider deregulation of provision. 'Independent producers' might be permitted to offer courses, perhaps through a system of competitive bidding for franchises, or corporations made of up senior academics might be invited to take part in 'management buyouts' of their institutions or parts of them, in order to increase competitive provision within the system. There is some parallel with the actual funding of research, where independent and quasi-independent research agencies have always had a large role.

Reforms in the spheres of both broadcasting and higher education appeal to similar concepts of popular consumer sovereignty. Television programmes that can be freely subscribed to through numerous competing channels are analogous to educational programmes that can be studied in units that are of variable size, and are available at variable times, and in various locations (or no location in particular). Power could thus be transferred from the monopolistic take-it-or-leave-it provider, to the educational consumer, who will only take as much of it as he or she wants at that moment, and who will be attentive to better market deals wherever they become available. Of course there is a possible element of enhanced consumer freedom in this conception.

Thus in broadcasting, the licensing of satellite channels, the auctioning of existing terrestrial programmes, the dilution of requirements of 'quality', and the exposure of local producers to the competition of international media corporations, have the intention and effect of overwhelming the local monopolistic producers' control of their captive audiences. The broadcasting 'space' represented by channels and wavebands, and by the rules governing who has access to it and under what quality constraints, constitutes a cultural space which helps to define a distinctive lifeworld for its audiences. Alan Bennett has recently argued that British public-service broadcasting is perhaps the most important unifying element in the national culture, and has drawn attention to the paradox whereby a government supposedly committed to extolling British nationality (in its secondary education curriculum for example) should appear to be pulling out the cultural roots of the nation in this way. But of course it is problematic to decide who does and who should control this cultural space.

THE PROBLEMS WITH FLEXIBILITY

These marketised models are being developed in opposition to the former monopolistic, producer-dominated systems of production, whether of welfare, education or culture. They appeal to the idea of consumer choice, competitive efficiency, and speed of adaptation to new needs and demands. They posit a rational, well-informed consumer who will be able by his or her individual choices to safeguard whatever values were worth defending within these former Fordist structures of 'mass citizenship', and indeed will be able thereby to enforce better quality in each sphere.

The problem is that in each of these sectors, 'value' has depended on the existence of occupational communities, and on the traditions and consensuses evolved by 'corporations' who were able to establish their own notions of value. They were to a degree able to impose their values on the wider society, by defining what counted as a 'university education', by developing a set of standards and aspirations for public health care, or by developing ideals of 'public-service broadcasting' in both its earlier paternalistic Reithian version and in its later more pluralistic forms, for example during Sir Hugh Greene's reign as Director General of the BBC, or within the partially marketised (but also subsidised) pattern of Channel Four. Standards of any kind appear to depend on the existence of discrete and bounded communities which can nurture and sustain them. Competitive pressure can select between different goods and services, and between different norms regulating their production (between high-quality, high-cost customised forms of production, and lower-quality, lower-cost forms, for example, whether in fashions, motor cars, or books). But competitive pressure, like the Darwinian struggle for survival, selects between options, it does not itself generate them. It seems that in all spheres of production, from the factory that makes machines to the theatre that makes plays, the quality of outputs depends not only on the competition which selects between goods, but also on the existence of 'cultures of production' from which they are generated in the first place. Unless there are such cultures (which are found in family businesses, professions, and large corporations) where members become committed intrinsically to the nature and quality of what they produce, there will be few quality products which markets can select between. It is the excessive attention to markets, as a form of competitive discipline, in contrast to a contempt for the conditions of production itself, which explains in large part the gross failure of the Thatcherite economic experiment in Britain, and that of Reagan and Bush in the United States.

It therefore seems unlikely that a fully marketised system of broadcasting would retain the conception of standards across a wide range of programme-genres that has been developed within the cultures of the public-service corporations. Nor does a National Health Service fully exposed to market competition seem likely to be able to defend an ethos of universal standards of health, where this conflicts sharply with considerations of profitability. In the case of higher education, there is the danger that 'flexibility' will undermine not only the self-serving powers of academic corporations (which might be in part desirable) but the very idea of a high-quality educational experience. The distinctive values of these various sectors are embedded in 'callings', in occupational communities which to some extent are able to define the terms of their own activity. In other words, differences are nurtured within 'containers' which have a capacity to retain their contents and encourage their germination and fruition.

'Individual choice' will be most meaningful when there are a variety of options of quality from which choices can be made. It *can* be constrained or negated by monopoly power and exclusion of alternatives. This is the problem to which market theorists are most sensitive. But it can also be negated by a process of banalisation and homogenisation of everything, so that whilst consumers can choose freely between the goods available, all the goods available are really the same goods. This is the risk inherent in globalisation and in the apparently infinite flexibility of choice it implies. The frictional resistance to change and movement imposed by limits of time and space allowed cultural differences to develop, in the same way that the isolation of species on remote islands allowed evolutionary variation. A 'global' architecture based on standard techniques (a debased version of the 'International Style') and a 'modular' ideology of construction has needed to be corrected by a proper regard for local space and distinctive tradition, in order to produce spatial environments which retain a cultural identity.[12]

The problem with the globalisation of markets, and the abolition of local or temporal constraints on access to them, is that it also erodes the density and specificity of the 'virtual spaces' which develop within defined locations and behind their protective barriers. It is because of the insulation and autonomy of institutions such as the BBC, or universities, that they are able to develop over time a distinctive set of capabilities. The competencies necessary to high-quality output require lengthy socialisation, prolonged learning processes, subscription to common values, and the experience of intra-institutional competition. In short, these are products of prolonged and intensive discursive relationships, involving a commitment to traditions, to long-term development, and to qualities which are specific to particular institutions. Another way of putting this is to say that high-level performance often depends on a deep-level identification with an institution and with professional colleagues. Such identification and the loyalty and commitment it engenders is nurtured by face-to-face relationships (relations of 'co-presencing') over lengthy periods of time. The best teaching and learning relationships also often have this character, depending on trust, personal recognition, and implicit commitment to sustain the strain and difficulty of real learning and growth.[13]

The specialists in the general functioning of marketised systems – accountants, marketing specialists, human resource managers and the like – usually understand the universalistic dimensions of these systems better than they do their specifics. Organisations that have hitherto socialised their members into distinctive producer cultures – those of broadcasters, teachers, doctors, academics, or even footballers – will degenerate if they lose this 'producer power'. They will then only be able to offer to consumers a synthetic replica of 'choice' between specious alternatives. It must also be noted that in an egalitarian society in which profit counts for so much the intrinsic values of each marketised calling will always be under severe pressure.

For the universities, therefore, there is a difficult balance to be struck. On the one hand, there is the need to defend the innate values of education and scholarship, and the relations of 'co-presencing', time-boundedness (intellectual tradition) and spatial containment on which these depend. On the other hand, education needs to be open to more people, for a larger part of the life span, and in ways that are more subject to individuals' control. There may be a new model of 'flexible specialisation' in higher education, of freely chosen, customised, but nevertheless craft-produced, educational programmes, emerging in the current conditions of uncertainty. This needs to be neither a 'mass' form of education of common curricula and routinised delivery (the national secondary school curriculum translated to higher education), nor a supermarket in which no meaningful quality of intellectual interaction survives.

ACKNOWLEDGEMENTS

I would like to acknowledge the stimulating comments I have received on earlier versions of this article from Philip Arestis, Robin Blackburn and Alan White. I am indebted to Denis Cattell, Tim Butler and many others at the University of East London for many hours of discussion of the implications of modular schemes and their implementation.

NOTES

1 Flexibility of provision has been much discussed in the literature on British higher education in the last few years, as the means to enhanced access, increased efficiency, broader curricula, and adaption to the needs of part-time students. See for example Bligh (1982), Cave *et al.* (1988), Pratt and Silverman (1989), Fulton (1989), Watson (1989), Johnes and Taylor (1990), Smith and Saunders (1991), Tight (1991) and Brown and Lauder (1992). Pressures to

increase student numbers whilst reducing unit costs are one explanation for the present vogue for modularisation and semesterisation. Another factor may be the wish of managements in the former polytechnic sector to be seen to be exercising to some effect the powers given to them by incorporation under the 1988 Education Reform Act, in the new managerialist culture which now pervades the public sector.

2 I developed this argument in Rustin (1989).

3 It seems, incidentally, to do this in the sphere of manufacturing also. 'Total quality management' (TQM) and the quality-oriented writings of such new wave authorities as Peters and Waterman (1982) probably gain their appeal from their purchase on the idealism and self-esteem of managers as well as from their instrumental contribution to profitability.

4 The oscillations of policy as to whether the academic or the fiscal year is to provide the main organisational time-frame is incidentally an indicator of an underlying conflict of values now being negotiated within these institutions.

5 'The Cambridge English School', or 'Oxford philosophy', or the work of renowned departments such as in one period the Sociology Department at Leicester.

6 D.H. Lawrence remembered his unhappy days at Nottingham University with the lines:

In Nottingham, that dismal town
where I went to school and college,
they've built a new university
for a new dispensation of knowledge.
Built it most grand and cakily
out of the noble loot
derived from shrewd cash chemistry
by good Sir Jesse Boot.

Nottingham's New University

7 At least some of the new university campuses were designed by recognised contemporary architects.

8 Early retirement from dying sectors became one sad recourse once imposed economies began to bite.

9 Incidentally, manufacturers of educational technology seem to be seeking a share in this market, and may even be one of the lobbies pushing effectively for its reconstruction.

10 The University of East London's design axiom for meeting this need in its new modular scheme is that 'every student shall have an academic home.' Debates about the introduction of a modular scheme at UEL have focussed on the problems of preserving a sense of intellectual place and community for students, whilst at the same time widening their freedom of subject choice. Rather than facing students with almost infinite combinations of discrete course units, the UEL scheme has given priority to enlarging the available range of joint and single honours programmes.

11 Adult students often report their debt to family members in supporting their study, but this form of support is not usually appropriate as a primary resource for late adolescents who most often need to establish some distance between themselves and their parents in order for individual development to be possible.

12 These issues have been debated by many theorists of modern and post-modern architecture. The negative consequences of a process of globalisation led by

capital, and the value of local 'resistances' to this have been outlined by Harvey (1989b). The concept of 'critical regionalism' developed by the architectural historian and critic Kenneth Frampton (1992) is also relevant to this argument.

13 However, the economic pressure for increased flexibility is working against this cohesive approach, in changing the conditions of employment of staff as in other ways. This follows the employment pattern that is developing in most public-sector spheres including broadcasting. At more junior levels, departments rely more on short-term contracts and hourly paid work, and may develop graduate assistantships on American lines, to provide more teaching at lower unit cost. At senior levels, a 'star system' of individualised contracts is beginning to develop. A quick way for departments to improve their research ratings may be to go to the transfer market. The Funding Council Research Assessment Exercise now enables the economic value of a 'rated' staff member to be precisely calculated.

11 Labour flexibility and the changing welfare state

Is there a post-Fordist model?

Steven Pinch

INTRODUCTION

Central to most post-Fordist visions of society are various concepts of flexibility. But, as many commentators have observed, these visions are often extrapolations based on limited evidence. This chapter therefore attempts to subject post-Fordist ideas to some empirical scrutiny through an examination of the extent to which the welfare state in the UK can be regarded as having become more flexible in recent years.

Ideas of flexibility are especially important in any consideration of changes in welfare states because they concern two important elements in the post-war structure of the advanced industrialised nations: first, the direct provision of public services such as health and education on a non-market basis; and second, the general commitment to policies of full employment, minimum wages and safety at work (Pfaller *et al.*, 1991). The Thatcher governments of the 1980s were the first amongst the advanced industrialised nations to renege on these second obligations by tolerating mass unemployment and undermining legislation to ensure workers' rights. These policies were intended to induce greater flexibility in the labour market, and may be envisaged as the prelude to the introduction of greater flexibility and diversity in the ways in which welfare services are provided. In this way the scale of direct public-sector provision has been reduced, and the efficiency of those elements remaining within the public domain has been increased.

It should be obvious, even from this brief outline, that 'flexibility' is a value-laden term that involves a multitude of changes in the structure of organisations and in the labour process (Pollert, 1989). The first part of the chapter will therefore consider the various interpretations given to the concept of flexibility within post-Fordist ideas. This is followed by an assessment of the extent to which functional flexibility, numerical flexibility and sub-contracting strategies have been adopted by public welfare agencies in Britain in recent years.

POST-FORDISM, FLEXIBILITY AND THE WELFARE STATE

Although he referred to neo-Fordism rather than post-Fordism (to indicate his belief that the crisis in Fordism was still in the process of resolution), the work of Aglietta is an appropriate starting point in any consideration of post-Fordist notions of flexibility. In fact, like most regulationists, he had remarkably little to say directly about welfare states. However, in one important passage he argued that Fordism 'only proves effective in the repetitive long production runs of standardised commodities. It is totally inadequate in the production of collective services' (Aglietta, 1979: 166).

His interpretation thus echoes many conservative theorists in suggesting that the inefficiency of the welfare state is an increasing drain upon capitalist economies. However, Aglietta argued that neo-Fordism may provide an interim solution:

> This involves a major revolutionization of the labour process that tends to replace the mechanical principle of fragmented labour disciplined by hierarchical direction with the informational principle of work organized in semi-autonomous groups. This is a principle of work organization capable of effecting a considerable saving of labour power in the production of effective means of collective consumption, while also transforming their use in far reaching ways. This flexibility may be the condition for a profound reshaping of the urban environment which would deploy new methods of production of collective services.
>
> (Aglietta, 1979: 167–8)

Aglietta thus argued that new technologies and managerial structures might overcome a central problem of the Fordist system – the divergence between productivity growth in manufacturing and services. New technologies would thus enable welfare services to become more efficient and enable them to be provided through private markets.

These ideas have been criticised on at least two counts: first, because they focus upon the labour process at the expense of wider regulative mechanisms; and second, because they have overtones of technological determinism. The first charge, though commonplace, loses sight of the fact that, above all, regulationists seek to understand 'the intimate relationship between the labour process and the mode of consumption that it shapes.' (Aglietta, 1979: 160). The second charge is more serious but it should be remembered that Aglietta was writing in the early seventies when the implications of the new micro-electronic technologies were even less clear than they are today. Subsequent experience has shown that changes in welfare structures such as privatisation are not the inevitable outcome of technological or economic necessity but are inherently political in character (Coombs and Green, 1989; Hambleton *et al*. 1989).

Though differing in its interpretation of the causes of recent changes in economic organisation, the theory of flexible specialisation shares a number of broad similarities with regulation theory (Hirst and Zeitlin, 1991). Both approaches argue that central to understanding the changing fortunes of Western economies are the rise and fall of particular types of regime of economic organisation. Central to both theories is the division of labour within production. Each approach conceptualises broad types of industrial production, each with a distinctive labour process: first, mass production using special-purpose machines and semi-skilled workers to produce standardised goods; and second, flexible specialisation using flexible machines and craft workers to make small batches of specialised goods. In addition, both theories argue that regulatory mechanisms are necessary to underpin different types of industrial system to ensure a match between production and consumption. Like regulation theory, flexible specialisation theory also has relatively little to say about the welfare state.

Given these similarities, it is hardly surprising that both approaches have been subject to the same types of criticism. These include charges of reliance upon insufficiently specified concepts (Wood, 1989); the use of simplistic 'binary histories' (Sayer, 1989); the oversimplification of complex historical trends (Clarke, 1988); and limited analysis of the mechanisms effecting the transition from one regime to another (Harvey, 1989a). Another criticism of post-Fordist approaches is that they present stylised descriptions of the labour process in a limited number of manufacturing sectors, thereby neglecting the labour process in service industries and the public sector – industries in which it is perhaps no mere coincidence that women form a large proportion of the workforce (Meegan, 1988). Indeed, such has been the welter of criticism directed at these ideas that there is a growing tendency amongst many writers to renounce the whole notion of post-Fordism, or at least to treat it with considerable scepticism (Gilbert *et al*., 1992).

Despite these limitations, it is possible to extract from both flexible specialisation theory and regulation theory a model of what the typical welfare organisation might look like in a post-Fordist welfare state. One of the best depictions of this structure emerges from yet another post-Fordist vision – Atkinson's (1985) model of the 'flexible firm'. This model, which appears to be loosely based upon the structure of a large Japanese company (Wood, 1989), makes a distinction between a core of functionally flexible workers who are able to change their skills and tasks in relation to changing market conditions, and a periphery made up of various types of numerically flexible workers whose numbers can be adjusted as market conditions dictate. Although less ambitious in theoretical terms than many other post-Fordist ideas, with less to say about causes of change and regulatory mechanisms, Atkinsons's model has been both controversial and influential. The controversy has arisen in part because of disputes about the applicability of the model to recent developments in Britain. At one extreme is the 'there's nothing new' interpretation of the Warwick School (Pollert, 1988; 1989; 1991), whilst at the other extreme is the celebration of recent developments by New-Wave Management theorists. Whilst most observers would no doubt fall somewhere between these two extremes, there does appear to be a growing consensus that few manufacturing firms in Britain have adopted the structure suggested by the flexible firm model (IMS, 1986; McInnes, 1987; Oliver and Williams, 1988; Pinch *et al.*, 1991; Sloan, 1989). However, it is clear that the flexible-firm model has become part of a powerful managerial ideology in Britain. Thus, Hakim (1990) argues that the model is best treated as a Weberian ideal type and, indeed, the exponents of the model make this clear themselves:

> The model is helpful, not because it describes the situation of any actual organisation, but because it contains all the main parameters of change observed in the research to date . . . The model is therefore used as an analytic tool.
>
> (IMS, 1986: 3)

The model is particularly useful in the present context because, as Pollert (1988) was amongst the first to recognise, whilst restricted in the private sector, the model is remarkably close to the structure that some would like to see adopted in the public sector. Central to this structure would be a core of permanent public-sector managers who sub-contract work to diverse agencies comprised of various types of secondary and peripheral workers. Such a structure may be envisaged as an extreme form of 'welfare pluralism' (Johnson, 1987) in which the state would continue to be a major source of finance for welfare services but its role in direct provision would be considerably reduced by greater reliance upon private-sector and voluntary agencies. This was stated explicitly in the Griffiths report on community care:

> The primary function of public services is to design and arrange the provision of care and support. There is value in a multiplicity of provision, not least from the consumer's point of view, because of the widening choice, flexibility, innovation and competition it should stimulate.
>
> (Griffiths, 1988: 5)

In a similar vein, Lash and Urry (1987) suggest that increasing social diversity will lead to a much more varied form of welfare provision within disorganised capitalism. Stoker (1989b) also argues that in a post-Fordist era local governments are having to respond to changing market conditions in a manner analogous to commercial firms. Thus, allied with the shift towards diverse and fragmented welfare agencies would be a host of other changes reflecting market and commercial influences: 'leaner and flatter' managerial structures, decentralised cost centres, devolved budgets, use of performance indicators and output measurement, localised bargaining, performance-related pay, and customer-orientated quality service (Hadley and Young, 1990; Hoggett, 1987; 1991b; Kelly, 1991; Stoker, 1990).

It is argued that within the private sector the flexible-firm model enables firms to adjust to an environment of increasing change and uncertainty with relation to markets and technology. In addition, such a structure can intensify and consolidate productivity gains (IMS, 1986). It might be assumed that peoples' welfare needs are fairly predictable compared with their diverse desires for consumer goods, and so the adoption of the flexible-firm model in the public sector context is principally a way of increasing productivity. However, advocates of 'responsive' welfare services emphasise the complexity of consumer/client needs and the diversity of ways in which these needs can be met (Hadley and Young, 1990). Furthermore, in those spheres of welfare provision where private-sector companies are able to compete with public agencies to provide services, there is also an environment of increasing uncertainty over contracts.

An important question then, is to what extent do recent changes in the welfare state in the UK represent a shift towards the flexible-firm model? This issue is bound to be clouded in a complex period of change but it is possible to put together some data and make some preliminary conclusions. Together with a wide range of social surveys, this paper also draws upon a study by the author of the economically active in the Southampton city region. This household questionnaire survey sampled the economically active across the whole range of different industrial sectors and thus enabled the sorts of changes experienced by workers in welfare institutions in the public sector to be compared with workers in industry as a whole (for further details of the research design see Pinch *et al.*, 1991; Pinch and Storey, 1992a; 1992b).

The flexible firm model may be used in two broad ways: first, to judge the extent of changes in working practices in the welfare state; and second, to judge changes in the overall structure of welfare organisations through increased sub-contracting and the like. The two approaches are of course related; for example, the low cost of a tender by a sub-contractor may be the result of employing a workforce that is more flexible than a competitor's' (Coyle, 1985). However, the two strategies do not inevitably coexist; for example, it might be possible to introduce changes to working practices within an organisation without changing its overall structure or the degree of sub-contracting. Each of these different approaches will therefore be considered in turn.

FUNCTIONAL FLEXIBILITY

Functional flexibility involves the ability of firms to adjust and deploy the skills of their employees to match the changing tasks required by changes in workload, markets or technology (IMS, 1986). Such changes usually involve workers extending the range of their skills, and may involve breaking down the barriers between different occupational groups. There has been much debate over the extent to which functional flexibility has been introduced into manufacturing industry in Britain in the 1980s. The general consensus appears to be that, despite some extensive and radical changes in a few high-profile manufacturing plants, there has been a limited degree of functional flexibility introduced into manufacturing plants in Britain. Thus, Fairbrother (1987) notes that changes have been 'hesitant and partial' rather than comprehensive. This piecemeal approach is interpreted as a reflection of managerial uncertainty and the continued importance of the unions in the organisations concerned. There has been much less work on functional flexibility in services but it is generally recognised that service organisations are less demarcated and more flexible than manufacturing organisations for a number of reasons including: the nature of the work, lower levels of unionisation, the smaller size of establishments and the high proportions of white-collar workers and women working in the sector. One survey showed that services had made fewer moves towards functional flexibility than had manufacturing (Pinch *et al.*, 1991).

Compared with the vast literature on manufacturing in the private sector, there is also relatively little work on changing practices in the public sector. A major problem in this context is that it is easier to understand how work is organised on a factory floor compared with welfare services which are highly diverse and scattered in many types of institution (Beechey and Perkins, 1987). In the Southampton survey workers were asked whether they had experienced any changes in the skills required for their job in recent years. If we combine together the percentage of workers who claimed that they needed 'more skill' or had adapted to a 'different skill' in the predominantly public 'other services' category from the Standard Industrial Classification (SIC), the percentage is just under 58 per cent – a figure which is exceeded only by the energy and extractive sectors (see

Table 11.1). The figure for 'other services' is also higher than either of the two manufacturing sectors. Such evidence suggests that public services have been subject to changes in working practices at least comparable with those elsewhere in British industry in the 1980s. A detailed examination of individual respondents showed that, as in the private sector, the majority of skill changes involved training to use new technology such as computers, copiers or electronically controlled machines. However, a significant proportion of the skill changes involved increasing the rate of work output, often as a consequence of reductions in staff numbers. Although more skill is required to work faster, intensification of work is not a form of flexibility in the strict sense. Furthermore, an inspection of the responses showed that as in industry as whole, there have been few, if any, radical job extensions in the public sector. Particular attention was paid to the responses of professionals such as teachers, doctors and social workers. With a few exceptions, these respondents indicated an intensification of existing work rather than the adoption of new tasks.

The above findings might be explained by the fact that those professionals with increased responsibility for budgeting and contracting are senior members of their professions and a relatively small proportion of the total public-sector workforce. However, it is also important to note at this point that most of our evidence about flexibility is derived from studies in the late 1980s, and there are recent indications of a gathering rate of change

Table 11.1 The relationship between sector and change in skill required of the currently employed in the Southampton city-region (column percentages).

	% workers in SIC division								
Change in skill required	*1* Energy	*2* Extract.	*3* Metal Goods	*4* Other manu.	*5* Cons.	*6* Distr.	*7* Trans.	*8* Bank.	*9* Other serv.
More skill	59.1	54.9	25.0	41.2	–	31.8	13.5	44.4	40.0
Different	18.2	11.8	6.3	11.8	38.1	11.2	37.8	3.7	17.6
No change	22.7	27.3	68.8	45.6	61.9	56.1	37.8	51.9	38.8
Less skill	–	6.0	–	1.5	–	0.9	10.8	–	3.6

Key: Energy – energy and water supply industries; Extract. – extraction of minerals, manufacture of metals, mineral products; Metal goods – metal goods, engineering and vehicles industries; Other manu. – other manufacturing industries; Cons. – construction; Distr. – distribution, hotels, catering, repairs; Trans. – transport and communication; Bank. – banking, finance, insurance, business services and leasing; Other serv. – other services.

by private companies, although this has so far had only a tentative expression in the academic literature (McGregor and Sproull, 1992).

There are also signs of an increasing rate of change in the public sector, especially in the NHS following the introduction of the internal market and trust hospitals. For example, three trusts are planning to introduce enhanced functional flexibility through the concept of 'patient focused care' (*Health Services Journal*, 1992b). This will involve small teams of health workers who care exclusively for a small group of patients. This will reduce the bewildering range of personnel that patients often have to see in hospitals but is also potentially a way of saving money. It should also lead to a blurring of professional boundaries, such as nursing and physiotherapy, as job roles are extended.

The recent growth of multiple-service or 'hotel' contracts in the NHS is also likely to encourage increased functional flexibility. Various private sector companies are active in this field including P&O Total Facilities Management, BET Contract Services and ISS Servisystem. Their combined provision of catering, cleaning and portering enables them to deploy workers between roles in a functionally flexible manner. However, most of the work by these companies is for other private-sector companies, and they complain about the heavy emphasis upon cost-saving rather than quality in NHS contracts. More important in this context, therefore, may be the direct activities of trusts. For example, Doncaster Healthcare NHS Trust has agreed to suspend competitive tendering in exchange for about 300 portering, domestic, catering and laundry staff becoming 'generic hotel service workers' (*Health Services Journal*, 1992a). The new community care arrangements also hold out the prospect of increasing functional flexibility as traditional professional rivalries may be subsumed within 'integrated care teams'.

NUMERICAL FLEXIBILITY

Numerical flexibility involves the ability of firms to adjust their labour inputs over time to meet fluctuations in output. This type of flexibility can take many forms including the use of overtime, flexi-time, new shift patterns, part-time workers, temporary workers, casual workers, or sub-contracting work to outside agencies. The many different types of numerical flexibility make it difficult to assess the significance of this approach. Nevertheless, there is a fairly clear consensus from work on the private sector about major trends.

In manufacturing, there has been declining use of part-time labour but a general increase in the use of temporary workers. In services, in contrast, there has been a considerable increase in part-time working, especially in retailing. These part-time workers are used to adjust to short-term variations in demand throughout the day or week. However, there is also evidence that part-time workers are being used to adjust to longer-term variations in demand and to replace temporary workers. But, given the reduced pay and employment rights of part-time workers, it appears that the strategy of using part-time workers is often a cost-cutting strategy as much as a flexibility strategy. The two strategies are related, since numerical flexibility can cut costs, but not inevitably so. It is important to remember in this context that the overwhelming majority of part-time workers in Britain are women. The social construction of certain types of work as part-time work for women is therefore crucial in understanding the growth of this type of work; it cannot be understood in economic terms alone (Beechey and Perkins, 1987).

In the Southampton household survey no less than 38 per cent of the 'other services' workforce were part-time, second only to 'distribution' with 39 per cent part-time workers (see Table 11.2). As Beechey and Perkins (1987) show, although the work is often very different, the reasons for employing part-time workers in the public sector are broadly the same as in the private sector. Vitally important is the need for flexibility. Many part-timers are required to do jobs at particular times of the day such as children's crossing wardens, kitchen staff or school-meals workers. In addition, part-time workers may be used to extend the range of the working day at evenings, nights and weekends. This is particularly important in the public sector because many of the services require continuous care. Part-time workers may also be used on a temporary basis to provide flexibility over longer time periods, as with the use of teachers and librarians during school or university terms (Luck, 1991).

Table 11.2 The relationship between sector and full-time and part-time employment amongst the currently employed in the Southampton city-region (column percentages).

	% workers in SIC division								
Employment status	*1 Energy*	*2 Extract.*	*3 Metal Goods*	*4 Other manu.*	*5 Cons.*	*6 Distr.*	*7 Trans.*	*8 Bank*	*9 Other serv.*
Full-time	100.0	85.7	100.0	88.2	100.0	61.0	100.0	90.0	62.2
Part-time	–	14.3	–	11.8	–	39.0	–	10.0	37.8

For Key see Table 11.1

There are, however, some major differences between the public and the private sectors. First, the use of part-time workers is long established in the public sector and predates the recent enthusiasm of retailers for part-time staff. Indeed, in some spheres of the public sector the true extent of part-time working remained hidden. In social work, for example, it was long assumed that part-time workers were unimportant, an assumption which was not supported by detailed research (Hall and Hall, 1980). Second, the public sector employs a higher proportion of part-time skilled workers such as teachers, nurses, social workers and secretaries than does the private sector. This leads to a third difference: whereas in the private sector the increase in part-time workers has often been an employer-led strategy, to reduce costs and increase flexibility, in the public sector the use of part-time workers has often been a response to the difficulty of obtaining full-time staff. This has been the case in the NHS in the Southampton area where competition from the private sector makes it difficult to obtain full-time secretaries. Similarly, the use of part-time nurses is often a response to the difficulties of getting full-time staff.

It is clear, therefore, that part-time workers *are* being used in a numerically flexible manner in welfare services. However, it is also clear that, despite the gradual increase in part-time workers, there is nothing particularly new about this process, and it predates notions of flexible specialisation. It is certainly true that, in an era of public-sector retrenchment and uncertainty about future budgets, there are clear advantages in employing part-time workers since many are exempt from employment-protection legislation and may be more easily disposed of if conditions dictate. Thus, Karan (1984) has argued that local authorities have greater flexibility in the face of financial uncertainty if they use part-time workers. For example, it has been reported that some local authorities have reduced the numbers of hours worked by their part-time school-meals staff to evade employment-protection requirements. Some local authorities including Kent, Hertfordshire, Somerset and Wirral have changed the conditions of service for part-time school meals staff by making them redundant and re-employing them to work shorter hours without the benefits of free lunches, holiday pay or retainer payments during school holidays (Webster, 1985). In addition, use of competitive tendering and sub-contracting of welfare work has in many cases led to the increased use of part-time workers, and to further managerial control over, and intensification of, such work.

Nevertheless, different sections of the public sector have responded to pressures for expenditure cuts in different ways. For example, some local authorities have laid off part-time workers while others have sought to protect full-time jobs (Webster, 1985). This diversity serves to emphasise the fact that the growth of part-time work is not simply the result of economic logic. Even if men and women's jobs both require flexibility, it is usually only the work undertaken by women that is done on a part-time basis. Thus, portering undertaken by men is required at particular times of the day but is done by shifts rather than by part-time workers. Similarly, there are alternative (albeit longer-term) policies than using part-time women workers for dealing with shortages in certain professions such as teaching and social work – like providing better pay and conditions – that would make the job more attractive to full-time workers. It is interesting to note in this context that in some cases increased use of part-time staff in the public sector can lead to greater *in*flexibility. Whereas in the past low-paid full-time ancillary staff had been prepared to work overtime to increase their wages, it has in some instances proved more difficult to persuade part-time workers to extend their working hours. The reason for this is that part-time work is often taken up by women with pressing domestic commitments, most notably child care (Cousins, 1988). However, Pulkingham (1992) notes that the restructuring of domestic ancillary services in the NHS has led to a change in the composition of part-time workers; they are now more likely to be below thirty years of age, single and non-householders.

Another type of 'non-standard' worker extensively used by public-sector welfare agencies is the temporary worker. However, in contrast to part-time workers – whose use seems to be for essentially traditional reasons – there is tentative evidence of new rationales for using temporary workers, especially in local government, health and education (McGregor and Sproull, 1992). Budget constraints and uncertainty over future funding levels in the public sector have increased the desirability of temporary workers.

The regulatory framework underpinning the labour market is crucial for determining the forms of 'non-standard working'. In the USA, for example, where there are fewer economic advantages in employing part-time workers, plus a greater supply-side push for full-time working, the construction of work is often different. Thus, sub-contracting is often undertaken by agencies who, nevertheless, employ full-time workers. In Britain, the shift towards the use of so-called peripheral types of worker is not only a flexibility strategy but also a cost-reduction strategy. This has been achieved by an intensification of work and an erosion of working benefits.

PAY, SECURITY AND JOB SATISFACTION

The flexible-firm model suggests that, in exchange for functional flexibility, 'core' workers are rewarded with 'good' jobs in terms of pay, security and working conditions. The Southampton household survey provided an opportunity for a partial assessment of these propositions by examining variations in the pay and conditions of public-sector workers and also how these compare with workers in other industrial sectors.

It is certainly true that, like the financial services sector, the public sector has a somewhat polarised employment structure with relatively high proportions of both high-paying and low-paying jobs (see Table 11.3). This pattern reflects the occupational structure of the public sector with relatively large proportions of professional and managerial workers underpinned by relatively large numbers of ancillary staff. There is, however, a much higher level of dissatisfaction with earnings in the public sector than in the financial-services sector (see Table 11.4). This cannot be explained by the higher incidence of part-time working in the public sector, for part-time workers expressed relatively high degrees of satisfaction with their pay and conditions (Pinch and Storey, 1992b); more important is the dissatisfaction amongst better-paid workers who feel that their incomes have fallen behind the private sector.

Perceptions of promotion chances are also somewhat polarised in the public sector with a relatively high proportion of workers feeling that they have a 'definite' or 'good' chance of promotion but also a relatively high proportion feeling that they have 'no chance' of promotion (see Table 11.5). Furthermore, after the highly volatile metals sector of manufacturing, the public sector has the highest proportion of workers feeling that their jobs are 'not very secure' (see Table 11.6). Cousins also found

Table 11.3 The relationship between sector and income amongst the currently employed in the Southampton city-region (column percentages).

Income per week	% of workers in SIC division								
	1 Energy	*2* Extract.	*3* Metal Goods	*4* Other manu.	*5* Cons.	*6* Distr.	*7* Trans.	*8* Bank.	*9* Other serv.
< £100	–	9.1	11.8	31.3	53.2	53.3	–	34.2	35.6
£100–£199	20.0	18.2	66.2	50.0	44.9	44.9	42.1	37.0	24.4
£200–£299	70.0	54.5	11.8	12.5	1.9	1.9	55.5	18.5	28.1
£300+	10.0	18.2	10.3	6.3	–	–	2.6	10.3	11.9

For Key see Table 11.1

Table 11.4 The relationship between sector and degree of satisfaction with earnings amongst the currently employed in the Southampton city-region (column percentages).

Degree of satisfaction	*% of workers in SIC division*								
	1 Energy	*2* Extract.	*3* Metal Goods	*4* Other manu.	*5* Cons.	*6* Distr.	*7* Trans.	*8* Bank.	*9* Other serv.
Satisfied	63.7	100.0	55.9	84.4	63.2	54.2	65.8	68.6	61.1
Neither	18.2	–	13.2	9.4	–	18.7	5.3	20.4	18.7
Dissatisfied	18.2	–	30.9	6.3	36.9	27.1	28.9	11.2	27.1

For Key see Table 11.1

strong feelings of job insecurity amongst managers on three-year contracts in the NHS (Cousins, 1988). This uncertainty, together with relatively low pay, and public denigration by politicians of the right in the 1980s, is reflected in the relatively low morale of workers at all levels in the public sector. Indeed, when considering their jobs as a whole, the public sector has the highest proportion of workers feeling dissatisfied (see Table 11.7).

Table 11.5 The relationship between sector and perceptions of promotion prospects amongst the currently employed in the Southampton city-region (column percentages).

Perceptions of chances of promotion	*% of workers in SIC division*								
	1 Energy	*2* Extract.	*3* Metal Goods	*4* Other manu.	*5* Cons.	*6* Distr.	*7* Trans.	*8* Bank.	*9* Other serv.
Definite	–	–	1.5	9.4	–	5.8	5.3	14.8	8.5
A good chance	36.4	27.3	13.2	12.5	23.8	16.3	18.4	40.7	17.7
Fifty-fifty	4.5	18.2	38.3	28.1	14.3	8.7	34.2	39.3	17.7
Low	18.2	36.4	16.2	34.4	14.3	5.8	34.2	3.7	13.4
None	40.9	18.2	30.9	15.6	47.6	63.5	7.9	1.5	42.7

For Key see Table 11.1

Table 11.6 The relationship between sector and perception of job security amongst the currently employed in the Southampton city-region (column percentages).

	% of workers in SIC division								
Perception of job security	1 Energy	2 Extract.	3 Metal Goods	4 Other manu.	5 Cons.	6 Distr.	7 Trans.	8 Bank.	9 Other serv.
Very secure	38.9	10.0	20.6	40.6	55.6	24.5	19.4	53.7	37.0
Secure	61.1	80.0	57.4	56.3	38.9	68.9	69.4	35.2	48.5
Not very secure	–	10.0	22.1	3.1	5.6	6.6	11.1	11.1	14.5

For Key see Table 11.1

These results suggest clear parallels with the polarisation of jobs in the private sector along the lines of the flexible-firm model, and are corroborated by evidence from the ESRC Social Change and Economic Life Initiative (SCELI) (Gallie, 1991). One important difference, however, is that public-sector managers do not perceive themselves as enjoying the same level of benefits as managers in the private sector. Again, it should be stressed that such data is derived from studies in the late 1980s. Developments in the early 1990s, such as increased sub-contracting in the NHS, and the additional freedoms and rewards given to managers in trust

Table 11.7 The relationship between sector and degree of satisfaction with occupation of the currently employed in the Southampton city-region (column percentages).

	% of workers in SIC division								
Attitude towards job	1 Energy	2 Extract.	3 Metal Goods	4 Other manu.	5 Cons.	6 Distr.	7 Trans.	8 Bank.	9 Other serv.
Satisfied	100.0	100.0	78.8	100.0	94.7	78.2	84.2	98.2	47.3
Neither	–	–	16.7	–	5.3	12.1	2.6	1.9	28.1
Dissatisfied	–	–	4.5	–	–	9.3	13.2	–	24.6

For Key see Table 11.1

hospitals, suggest an intensification of the process of polarisation noted above.

DISTANCING STRATEGIES

Given the limited and patchy evidence for the growth of the flexible firm from changing working practices within welfare institutions, it is arguably through changes in the overall structure of these organisations that the strongest case can be made for the development of the flexible welfare agency. The most striking of these changes has, of course, been the widespread sub-contracting or 'contracting-out' of activities – what in the private sector is also often termed 'outsourcing' or 'distancing'.

Contracting-out involves the situation where one organisation contracts with another for the provision of a good or service (Ascher, 1987). Contracting-out of activities within the public sector has taken place for some time; in the 1950s, for example, it was used by local authorities and the NHS to overcome recruitment problems in an era of labour shortages. However, the use of agencies and contractors by the public sector was on a small scale and mostly confined to the tight labour markets of the south east of England (Ascher, 1987). It was only after the election of the Conservative Administration in 1979 that contracting-out increased significantly. However, it is not only the scale of contracting-out but the way in which contracts are awarded that makes this type of activity different from previous decades. Most important has been the increased financial and managerial control exerted through performance specification and competitive tendering for contracts. Sub-contracting has also been on the increase in the private sector. The IMS study found that 71 per cent of firms in their sample had increased their degree of sub-contracting (IMS, 1986). Similarly, a survey of restructuring by forty manufacturing firms in Southampton found that between 1981 and 1987 no less than twenty-one had displayed an increase in sub-contracting (Pinch *et al.*, 1991).

However, the relationship between sub-contracting and flexibility is complex. On the one hand, it is clear from the examples given in the IMS report that sub-contracted workers are an important part of the peripheral workforce that can be used to provide numerical flexibility. For example, firms can sub-contract work out during periods of market uncertainty or during cyclical increases in demand, thereby reducing risk and the need for capital investment. On the other hand, the IMS study also claimed that distancing is seen by companies as an alternative to numerical flexibility rather than another form of it (IMS, 1986). Thus, distancing was associated by a desire amongst private-sector companies to concentrate resources in areas of corporate advantage, to find cheaper ways of undertaking non-core activities, and to reduce the formal head-count and wage bill.

It is clear, therefore, that contracting-out is as much a cost-reduction strategy as a straight flexibility strategy. This assertion is supported by the types of activities that have been contracted-out in the private sector. As in the case of many public services, these are most commonly ancillary services such as catering and cleaning. For example, in a Southampton study of forty large manufacturing companies, only three significantly increased their sub-contracting of their core production process, and eight actually reduced their degree of sub-contracting. The reasons given for the reduction of sub-contracting included the desire to increase quality through increased control over the production process (Pinch *et al.* 1991).

It has been argued that the extent to which state-funded welfare services have been contracted out is also limited (Johnson 1990). It is certainly true that an increasing number of services in health and local government are being subjected to competitive tendering, and the Secretary of State has powers to progressively increase the numbers of these services. However, in the case of local government the seven services which must be subjected to tenders – school meals, other catering, refuse collection, street cleaning, building cleaning, grounds maintenance and vehicle maintenance – are far less than the forty-one services some radicals wanted to subject to competitive tendering (Johnson 1990). More importantly, the majority of these services both in the NHS and local government are being won by in-house tenders.

The extent to which work is sub-contracted to private-sector operators rather than in-house tenders also shows wide variation between areas (Mohan, 1988; Painter, 1991a). One of the reasons for this geographical variation in contracting-out is that the process of competitive tendering is fraught with conflict. The competition between in-house tenderers and other contractors makes the process much more complex than a simple choice between a number of external contractors. On the one hand, the performance-related pay of managers is determined by their ability to make cost reductions but, on the other hand, a successful external bid requires closure of the internal department. The net outcome is that the policies adopted in particular area depend not only upon strict economic criteria but the attitudes of health authorities, district managers and local union representatives.

Of course, even when the in-house tender wins a contract there are usually important changes to the labour process, for the service will have been subjected in most cases to the discipline of market competition. Such changes can include: the introduction of labour-saving equipment; employing casual and part-time staff; leaving vacancies unfilled; amending bonus schemes; and intensification of work (Walker and Moore 1987). Furthermore, since the contract is only for a limited period there is a continual need to maintain productivity, whilst the uncertainty created often demoralises the workforce (Cousins 1987). However, the extent to which sub-contracting can achieve flexibility in the public sector is also questionable. For example, the intensification and routinisation of ancillary work means that such workers have less flexibility in their contribution to patient care (see also O'Connell Davidson (1990) for problems in the water industry). As Cochrane (1991) notes, competitive tendering seems, above all, to have been a way of imposing discipline upon highly unionised public sector workers. The extent to which competitive tendering reduces costs is also questionable, and evaluating the evidence is especially difficult because of the highly partisan character of most studies. Whilst opponents of contracting-out admit that savings have been made, they also point to the neglect of various hidden costs such as the administrative work involved in contract specification, monitoring and evaluation, together with the additional costs of redundancy and contract failure (Radical Statistics Health Group, 1987).

Once again, it is important to stress that much of this discussion is derived from developments in the late 1980s. There appear to be growing press reports of an increasing rate of outsourcing in many areas of manufacturing; and the rate of change also appears to be increasing in the public sector. This is especially the case in the NHS following the introduction of the internal market. Whereas previously competitive tendering was restricted to ancillary and support services, core health services are now competing with each other to win contracts for referrals. However, the system is a far cry from a demand-led market in which consumers have purchasing power; instead it is a 'quasi-market' in which consumers' demands are mediated by various agents.

CONCLUSIONS

This chapter has sought evidence of changes in the structure and operations of welfare agencies to balance the flood of speculation about the nature of neo-Fordist and post-Fordist welfare systems. In so doing, it has concentrated upon the changing nature of the labour process in the public sector – a much neglected topic compared with the vast literature on the labour processes in the private sector (Cousins 1987). The results suggest a complex pattern of both change and continuity.

In the case of functional flexibility, it is certainly true that throughout the 1980s changing working practices have been at least as widespread in the public sector as in the private sector. However, many of the changes in welfare services may be regarded as an intensification of working patterns, rather than a genuine extension of job descriptions of the type that has occurred in some high-profile manufacturing companies. Numerical flexibility and the use of 'non-standard' workers is also widespread in the public sector and is becoming increasingly valuable to welfare agencies in an era of increasing financial and workload uncertainty. Yet, while some of the reasons for using part-timers may have changed in recent years, there is nothing particularly new about the use of this type of worker by the public sector. This contrasts with manufacturing, where the use of part-timers is going down, and retailing, where the use of part-timers has increased rapidly. However, as in much of the private-service sector, the use of part-time workers by welfare agencies seems to be as much a cost-reduction strategy as a straight flexibility strategy. The two strategies are, of course, related, since flexibility of labour is a way of saving costs; but being more responsive to market shifts can involve additional costs, especially if it requires the use of skilled functionally flexible workers and expensive technologies. In this context it is important to remember that many peripheral workers are women and that gender is crucial to the construction of these jobs (Beechey and Perkins, 1987).

In contrast to part-time work, competitive tendering and, to a lesser extent sub-contracting of publicly funded services to the private sector, has increased considerably in the last decade, albeit at an uneven rate in different areas. However, in contrast to many private-sector companies, who have cut costs and reverted to their core interests by closing internal departments, the majority of public services put up for tender have been won by in-house bids. Furthermore, the range of services contracted out has, so far, been limited mostly to ancillary services rather than the core activities of the public sector (and in this respect the public sector pattern does follows the private sector). As with the case of part-time workers, this would seem to be a cost-cutting strategy rather than a true flexibility approach (and this is another pattern where the public and private sectors seem to accord). Indeed, in many respects sub-contracting may reduce flexibility. Furthermore, the degree to which costs have been cut by sub-contracting is subject of considerable controversy.

Where the public sector does appear to most strongly mimic the flexible-firm model as applied to the private sector is in the polarisation and segmentation of the public-sector workforce in terms of pay rewards, working conditions and promotion prospects. However, once again this seems to be the extension of a pattern that has long existed in the public sector. Furthermore, there are still differences between the public and private sectors, for it appears that, despite recent improvements in their pay and conditions, many public-sector managers feel that they lack the fringe benefits and job security of the private sector. There is also evidence that unions have managed to protect the incomes and working conditions of the lower paid in the public sector rather better than they have for similar workers in the private sector (Cousins, 1987; *The Economist*, 1992).

The above conclusions are, however, largely derived from studies in the late 1980s, and there are indications of an accelerating rate of change in the early 1990s. Thus, Hakim's (1990) survey of employers' labour strategies, based on 1987 data, found that only 5 per cent were adopting the conscious core–periphery approach, but there are indications in 1990 data of a significant increase in this percentage (McGregor and Sproull, 1992). In the public sector there is also an increasing rate of change following the introduction of the internal market in the NHS, trust hospitals, opted-out schools and the community care programme. Recent developments include increasing functional flexibility, increased use of temporary workers and increased sub-contracting. It is therefore ironic that, although the flexible-firm model was derived from the private sector, it appears to be extended in a far more explicit and conscious way in the public sector.

If, as seems likely, the pace of change continues to accelerate, this is likely to have enormous consequences for both workers and consumers of welfare services. However, current evidence would suggest that while contracting-out will increase, the state will remain a key funder and organiser of many services. Unlike the private sector, therefore, the application of the flexible-firm model to the public sector will continue to reflect quasi-markets in which consumers' needs or wants are interpreted by intermediaries. Thus, despite all the talk of choice, flexibility and quality of care, cost savings are likely to remain a driving force in such a system. However, there would seem to be limits to the amounts of money that can be derived from efficiency reviews in the welfare services (especially when services such as the NHS are already relatively cheap by international standards). Furthermore, recent history would suggest health and local-government issues are highly sensitive in political terms, and this is likely to restrict the nature of change.

The final big issue is the extent to which the flexible firm is the ideal model for the welfare state in an age when capital investment can shift between countries so rapidly. In this context it is important to note that the contracting-out of welfare tasks to both profit and non-profit bodies has been undertaken for many years in other countries – especially in the USA – and certainly dates back to the Fordist era. The recent attempts to introduce commercial logic to the public sector in Britain may therefore be seen as part of the continuing trend towards Americanisation. In an age of intense competition for capital investment there would seem to be advantages for those countries such as the US with limited welfare systems and low taxation regimes. However, although measurement problems are considerable, there appears to be only a very weak negative relationship between welfare spending and economic competitiveness (Pfaller *et al.*, 1991). Indeed, there are many doubts over whether the 'lean and efficient' welfare state will provide the appropriate conditions for what regulationists would describe as a stable 'regime of accumulation'. The failure of welfare systems to counter the widespread immiseration resulting from labour-market dualism and segmentation could be leading to insufficient demand for consumption, a disparity that was masked by the deregulation of finance in the 1980s.

Post-Fordist concepts are beginning to look like an ornate sandcastle that is rapidly being engulfed by a tide of criticism. Yet a few battered turrets – such as the flexible-firm model – still remain. If used carefully, such concepts can provide insights into the complex character of recent changes in the welfare state.

ACKNOWLEDGEMENT

This research was funded by the Economic and Social Research Council (project D0023180). I am also grateful to Nick Goodwin for providing me with the latest information on multiple-service contracts in the NHS.

12 Consumers, consumption and post-Fordism

Alan Warde

INTRODUCTION

For the British population since 1945, state-provided services have contributed a considerable proportion of the value of household consumption. In the post-war years, the welfare state distributed money, through transfer payments, and directly delivered services, like education, health care etc., in increasing amounts. Reforms in the 1980s, however, aiming to restructure the welfare state, have sought to introduce market mechanisms (or/and criteria) into many more aspects of the production, access and delivery of such services. The mode of consumption has been altered (Warde, 1992), initially by small degrees, but potentially culminating in an extensive recommodification of welfare for all but the poorest sections of society. This has been met with alarm in some quarters, but with a surprising degree of equanimity in others.

In this chapter I want to deal with two bodies of literature, both of which intimate that a transformation, usually presented as irreversible, has occurred in the character of consumption. The first has direct relevance for predicting the continued decline of state-provided welfare, because it presupposes a type of consumer who cannot possibly derive satisfaction from universally provided, collectively financed and state-allocated services. The second offers a similar prognosis, though much less directly. Building on the axiom that production and consumption are integrally meshed (as in regulation theory, for example), any resolution of the current crisis of capital accumulation will necessarily affect the nature of consumption practice. 'Post-Fordist' scenarios presently offer a weak periodisation of consumption based on deducing that consumer tastes have become aligned with the capacity for differentiated production. However, if more fully elaborated they also suggest radical implications for the operation of the state services, implying that universalist welfare provision is insupportably expensive and that it conveys the wrong signals to labour markets.

This chapter explores literature concerned to analyse changes in consumption. The first section sketches Bauman's account of the changing role of consumption in advanced societies, an example of the contention that refined orientations of individual consumers undermine the acceptability of state provision. In the second section, I identify various models of the consumer and criticise particularly conceptualisations of the 'heroic' consumer – a self-reflexive, postmodern creature whose primary orientation is towards constructing a distinctive lifestyle. The third section outlines the way that accounts of a post-Fordist economic transition have described concomitant developments in consumption practices. The fourth section contends that there is little reliable evidence to support such a view.

STATES, MARKETS AND THE CONSUMER

In his book *Freedom*, Bauman (1988) argues that reproduction of the capitalist system is effected by making individuals free to choose as consumers rather than by constraint or repression. He maintains that the consumer market 'offers freedom to people who in other areas of their life find only constraints, often experienced as oppression' (Bauman, 1988:61). Consumerism helps to create a fantasy community which includes freedom and certainty, independence and togetherness. It is primarily a way of solving the intransigent problem of creating and sustaining self-identity in modern society. People increasingly use commodities (including expert advice) to establish their individual self-identities. Bauman describes this as a competitive process, but explicitly not a zero-sum game. Competition therefore does not necessarily have a socially hierarchical outcome: 'Identities are not scarce goods' (Bauman, 1988:63). People may, therefore, be left to choose, free from regulation, without prejudice to social integration.

Of course, Bauman recognises that some people are excluded from this fantasy world on the basis of absence of resources. They are not free. They are 'the repressed', persons excluded from the category of 'the seduced'. This argument is first and most strongly developed in Bauman's (1987) *Legislators and Interpreters*. One element of the account is consumer culture and the way that increasing commodification operates systemically to establish a relationship between a majority of happy shoppers and a minority subject to state surveillance. This, effectively, restates the argument for the emerging importance of consumption cleavages (Edgell and Duke, 1991; Saunders, 1986). But it has a more harrowing twist. Whereas, for Saunders, dependence on state-allocated services resulted in poor-quality provision, for Bauman such people are deprived of liberty and self-expression.

A decade characterised by Thatcherism and the collapse of East European communism has been reflected in social theory as increasing hostility to the state. State power in all its forms is identified as the main enemy of human freedom; market processes, pluralistic because not amenable to central control, are deemed preferable in virtually all situations to allocation by public authorities. Bolstered by comparisons between the Western world and 'squalid' communist bureaucracies that politicise everything and reduce all forms of freedom (Bauman, 1988: 88), Bauman concludes that freedom is now consumer freedom. Consumer freedom satisfies individual concerns, social integration and system reproduction; though it does so without the 'consumers' in any way controlling the system.

Ironically, it used to be sociological wisdom that state intervention and regulation prevented the emergence of a set of undesirable and unjust distributive outcomes. Though passionately concerned with injustice, Bauman explicitly turns his back on state-organised solutions. Indeed, it has been the theme of a good deal of his recent sociological writing that the only solution is a form of tolerance without indifference, expressed and practiced through the medium of everyday life. Having given up on agents of progress like the proletariat, the means for securing decent human values must be sought close to home.

This is a distinctive position, including the view that there has been a long-term historical shift from a work-centred to a consumption-centred society. In so far as the old socialist utopia of self-fulfilment through non-alienating work is no longer a viable political objective, the freedom of the consumer is to be welcomed, for it is a field where most people can express themselves, without prejudice to others.

Bauman thus constructs a semi-sovereign consumer; one who makes meaningful, personal decisions in the market place and whose freedom of choice is taken as a yardstick for unfavourable comparison with the situation of the welfare client. State provision is found entirely unsatisfactory as a mechanism for distributing services to citizens. As an account of the functions of welfare, Bauman identifies a disciplinary function, controlling the minority of failed consumers.

One objection to this account would surely be that the seduced are, as a matter of fact, major, if not the principal, beneficiaries of public welfare expenditure. This begs the question of how exclusive the boundary is between the seduced and the repressed. It is necessary also to recall that states intervene in a multitude of ways to secure the operation of markets. Market sphere and state sphere interpenetrate, a key theoretical axiom of regulation approaches and a point demonstrated empirically in studies of comparative welfare systems (Esping-Andersen, 1990). Welfare expenditure enhances social legitimation through supporting a social norm of consumption and is instrumental in achieving economic stability. How the state manages welfare provision impacts upon the consumption of commodities in the market sphere and vice versa. However, if shopping is the highest mass form of human freedom, then it will be unsurprising if people prefer to obtain access to services through markets. If individual consumption is conceived in this fashion the consumer will, by definition of his or her key objectives, be averse to state-provided services. The way the consumer is conceived cannot but colour evaluations of the effectiveness and desirability of public provision. Bauman constructs 'the consumer' in one particular way. There are many others.

CONSTRUCTING THE CONSUMER

There are many models of 'the consumer' and the characteristics attributed to this actor often make an enormous difference to accounts of contemporary social change. Until recently, the consumer was primarily an abstraction of economics, but sociologists have modified the model for their own purposes.

The abstract consumer

The consumer as an abstract actor in economic theory is not easily, nor should it readily be, imported into other areas of social science. *The* consumer has very few properties:

1   the consumer chooses to buy something, but *nothing in particular*;
2   the consumer wants to buy that something *'cheap at the price'*. This in no sense means that the consumer wants to spend a small amount of money, indeed there are lots of reasons for wanting to spend lavishly. But the consumer's interest is to get a good deal;
3   whatever thing the consumer wants must be *available for sale*. It is sometimes said that everyone and everything has its price. But this is doubtful. Moreover, it may be that even though something is for sale the potential purchaser cannot find out where, or who is the current owner, or cannot get through a traffic jam to peruse the required object, or whatever. Whether one can get access to what is wanted is a constraint on the consumer. The consumer's interest is that whatever is wanted can be bought; and
4   the consumer must have (if not lots) *sufficient money* with which to purchase whatever.

These I think are the necessary conditions of existence of the abstract consumer, a nobody, rather vulgar and not a little selfish. To an important degree, 'the consumer' is merely a dignified version of the term 'shopper'. The consumer is the abstract individual required in a commodified world where money is the main instrument of economic exchange. For economics, a consumer is just somebody who buys something. Economic theory does not tell us why a consumer buys that particular thing. The concept of 'revealed preference' provides the syllogistic reasoning that passes for an economic theory of consumption; people want the things that they buy and you can tell they want them because they bought them. For certain accounting purposes this is a perfectly reasonable axiom, but it is sociologically unilluminating. The abstract individual of neo-classical economics is not the burdened, worried, haunted, embedded, memory-infested, befriended, kinsperson that stalks the social stage. There are no generalisations that one can sensibly make about the socially relevant behaviour of this consumer.

The social consumer

Sociologists, recognising the limited and one-sided nature of the abstract consumer, have tended to elaborate the model, but usually in relatively limited ways. In particular they exhibit an unfortunate tendency to imagine that all consumers can be considered to have similar orientations and that acts of purchase are guided by a narrow range of concerns. Sociological models of the consumer are various, including:

1 *the calculator*, perhaps associated with the Consumer's Association and readers of *Which?*, where purchase is inspired by careful calculation of the usefulness, appropriateness and comparative cost of particular items;
2 *the dreamer*, Campbell's (1987) modern consumer, is one who primarily is inspired by imagining the pleasure to be obtained from possession of certain commodities, but who, because the dreaming is all-important, can never be satisfied;
3 *the addict*, one who purchases compulsively, seduced by the very act of shopping, who is therefore more likely to buy on impulse without much prior thought or reference to need;
4 *the dupe*, who, according to critics of the advertising industry in the 1960s and 1970s, was inveigled by cunning media messages into buying exactly what producers happened to have available for sale; and
5 *the Joneses*, a much-maligned couple whose irritating habit of exposing newly-acquired consumer goods to neighbours presently bereft of such items caused epidemics of envy in Britain during the long boom.

For the purposes of this argument, however, I want to consider in detail another construct – the heroic consumer – versions of which are increasingly prominent among analysts of postmodern culture. Some elements of the heroic consumer can be found in Bauman's account; the hero is self-reflexive, probably narcissistic, somewhat lonely and compelled to construct a self-identity from commodities. Similar orientations can be found described as typical of the individual in late modernity in the recent writings of Giddens (1991). Once this person is also endowed with an active lifestyle project, as in one of Featherstone's (1991) instructive essays on contemporary consumption, a firmer link is established between consumer culture and postmodern attitudes. This type of consumer bears an uncanny resemblance to contemporary orthodoxies of market research and invariably inflates the degree of recent change entailed.

The heroic consumer

The concept of lifestyle has sneaked into sociological accounts of contemporary cultural change from the marketing literature. Sociological interpretations of the 'new' consumer bring with them a confusing concept of lifestyle that derives partly from classical sociology, partly from market research, partly from universalising the experience of a social minority. Some commentators reduce its utility for describing collective belonging and identity by aligning it with a picture of a heroic consumer.

The principal current sociological sense of the term is captured by Featherstone in a description of the way in which creating a lifestyle may become a conscious project. He sees a calculating hedonism developing in the twentieth century:

> Rather than unreflexively adopting a lifestyle, through tradition or habit, the new heroes of consumer culture make lifestyle a life project and display their individuality and sense of style in the particularity of the assemblage of goods, clothes, practices, experiences, appearance and bodily dispositions they design together into a lifestyle. The modern individual within consumer culture is made conscious that he speaks not only with his clothes, but with his home, furnishings, decoration, car and other activities which are to be read and classified in terms of the presence and absence of taste. The preoccupation with customising a lifestyle and a stylistic self-consciousness are not just to be found among the young and the affluent; consumer culture publicity suggests that we all have room for self-improvement and self-expression whatever our age or class of origins
>
> (Featherstone, 1991: 86)

Most people in late twentieth-century Western societies will recognise what Featherstone is describing. It is a way in which some people ('heroes') might organise their lives, as symbols drawn from consumer culture are adopted and adapted to express identity, belonging and opposition. Lifestyle is not, however, a well established sociological term and Featherstone in that article, for instance, makes no attempt to define it. What is implied is an active, individual and personal project, free from the constraints of social location, driven forward by an overriding pre-occupation with style and self-presentation.

The figurative hero is premised on the belief that sustaining self-identity is an exceedingly problematic process. This type of social consumer is born out of social theories that emphasise the intensification of symbolic communication in the contemporary world. The influence of Baudrillard is not far from the surface. The power of socially disembedded images and appearances and the hyper-reality of the world of signs become the exclusive context of consumption. In a sense, the consumer becomes chronically engaged in negotiating self-identity with mass-media messages. It is debatable how widely generalised is the behaviour that would suggest the imminent dominance of the heroic consumer.

Critique of models of the heroic consumer

Some people certainly have conscious style projects that are delimited by their collection and display of commodities. Nor can it be denied that notions of style are inherently important in our consumer culture. However, it is not clear whether this is a good description of the principal concerns that most people bring to the organisation of their lives. Most obviously, accounts of identity-led consumption projects perhaps generalise from the experience of a small fraction of the middle class. Almost all recent accounts of consumption seem to me to exaggerate the part played by establishing self-identity. Central to Bauman's view is harmless competition over the construction of self-identities. In this way, the pluralistic aspect of consumer culture is emphasised to the neglect of its hierarchical element. Status competition was once thought to be governed by a logic of hierarchy. It is a much less critical rendering that postulates difference without power, differentiation without hierarchy. Identity is isolated from distinction. Such accounts are excessively individualistic and fail to specify the effects of competition on comparative status.

Moreover, being socially acceptable seems an equally important and ineradicable objective of consumption. Accounts giving priority to self-identity tend to be weak on the mechanisms securing a sense of belonging. People belong to groups that have a collective history of consumption which constrains choice. They do not enter the department store naked. It is partly for that reason that concepts like lifestyle, style-groups, sub-cultures, etc. are invoked. But these too are often unhelpful in analysing the mechanisms and specifying the stakes involved in social differentiation. The concept of lifestyle in particular very easily lends itself to an exclusive concern with appearances. In Weber's usage, style of life indicated a position in a system of honour from which real social benefits accrued; the essence, or the basis behind style, was the usurpation or protection of social status. In many contemporary usages it is not clear what style is an expression of, and the gains and losses to different people are hidden.

In many accounts, the range of motivations considered is very limited; the purpose of style is narrow, especially when lifestyle projects become socially inert episodes in the search for self-identity. Recent literature might seem to entail that whole populations of Western societies are constantly in the throes of individual identity-crises and that the possession and display of material-objects principal means of handling these crises. The implication of this view of consumption, as a response to problems of personal identity, would suggest a considerable growth of psychiatric problems among the most affluent consumers, since they have most choice of identity. This is implausible. We are not the displaced, or disembedded, personae that these explanations of the role of the appurtenances of a lifestyle seem to suggest.

A final source of discontent with the model of the heroic consumer is that I am not one. (The role of introspection in sociological analysis is often overlooked!) As I surveyed my possessions and reviewed my shopping habits, I concluded that for me consumption was a form of *bricolage*. I have a not very coherent approach to consumption. Many of the objects that are around me have not been acquired in accordance with the image of the marketing process: they are not bought from new, but inherited or borrowed, thus owing nothing to advertising; they were not acquired simultaneously but accumulated throughout my adult days and mostly have been displayed in several different contexts; they reflect limited financial capacity and the inability to replace major items except when they cease to function adequately; and they do not constitute, though you only have my word for this(!), a conscious life-project, imitation of a lifestyle, or immense investment of self-identity. What Bauman (1990b) calls the 'consumer attitude' – the conviction that every want can be satisfied through shopping – is ingrained in my orientations, but even then not all my practices are integrated into the circuit of commodity production. Acquisition appears to have entailed a variety of consumer orientations, including zweckrational, wertrational, traditional and affectual, to mention just four that came to mind. Yet I could be quite easily classified by my consumption pattern; a list of my monthly expenditure and an inventory of my possessions would make it very easy to identify most of the relevant socio-demographic attributes of my household. What I conclude is that models of the consumer help little in explaining my behaviour, but that my consumption practices could be read sociologically.

What my introspective interlude suggested to me was that the construction of ideal-typical models of the motives and orientations of all consumers is a hazardous exercise. The very notion of the individual consumer prevents us from appreciating the constraints people face in their consumption practices, as embodied persons rather than ghostly abstractions of economics. That which is sociologically interesting happens in the space between responsibility for one's own choices and the classification procedures of social groups. The social world is differentiated by the groups to which a person belongs and has on-going interaction. The use of the term 'the consumer' signifies an undersocialised actor; it exaggerates the scope and capacity for individual action.

FORDISM, POST-FORDISM AND CONSUMPTION

The second set of theoretical approaches that I want to consider arises from the analyses of economic restructuring since the mid-1970s which constitute 'the flexibility debate'. The common source of the term post-Fordism is the observation that capitalist firms, in response to heightened competition in worldwide recession, have developed new production strategies that deploy flexible new technologies and require a more flexible workforce. The conceptual frameworks portraying these new developments are confusingly diverse, but most owe intellectual debts either to French regulation theory (Aglietta, 1979) or to the flexible specialisation thesis of Piore and Sabel (1984). One of the great steps forward in early regulation school positions about the crisis of Fordism was the insistence that 'regimes of accumulation' comprised compatible modes of production and consumption. Thus, mass consumption was the 'norm of social consumption' associated with Fordist production arrangements. The temptation is then to speculate about new consumption practices that characterise post-Fordism. Many accounts of market-sector behaviour prophesy radical change in the guises of a new consumerism, niche markets and postmodern cultural dispositions. Given that theoretical approaches to consumption remain under-developed it would be a shame not to consider carefully this integral aspect of the general theory. Unfortunately, analyses of consumption practices are few, most concentrating on the new capacities for the manufacture of more differentiated products made possible by new flexible technology. Correspondence is assumed as a theoretical axiom and little attempt is made to specify how that is achieved.

Jessop (1991c) develops a position broadly consistent with the regulation approach with some affinities to that of Aglietta (1979). Though appropriately hesitant about the exercise, he offers one of the few sustained *positive* definitions of post-Fordism, trying to identify what positive features might be said to characterise such a social form. It is notable that he says relatively little about consumption in this context. He employs the contrast between mass and differentiated consumption. He makes particular use of the demise of the project of extending mass consumption norms to the whole population through generous welfare provision, which was associated with demand-led Keynesian economic strategies. He argues that it is being supplanted by strategies for a 'Schumpeterian workfare state', where welfare policy is directed primarily at regulating appropriate supplies of labour (Jessop, 1992d; this volume).

Flexible specialisation accounts of post-Fordism implicitly approach consumption in a manner different to regulation theory. Elam (1990) points out that the neo-Smithian flexible-specialisation thesis of Piore and Sabel gives much more causal power to the role of the market and particularly to consumer demand. As he summarises the position (Elam, 1990: 18–19), flexible specialisation responds to situations where there is demand for non-standardised items, where market demand is unstable, or where market demand is uncertain. The prime example considered is the fashion garment industry. However, the implication is that such circumstances are becoming widespread and that many other industries operate in similar environments. If so, the question arises, why has consumer demand changed so? Piore and Sabel are unable to explain. They maintain that 'an apparent shift in consumer taste in favour of diversity, even customisation' is best 'explained by changes in the production system' (Piore and Sabel, 1984: 189). They observe that 'the most sophisticated argument in favour of a long-term diversification of taste rests on the notion of a hierarchy of needs and wants' (ibid.), and they maintain that available evidence does not prove its key claim – that as incomes rise people can satisfy basic needs easily and therefore spend additional disposable income on more specialised and better-quality goods. Thus, they too effectively deduce consumption patterns from the logic of production. Subsequent writers likewise mostly deduce the nature of consumption from evidence of what is being produced.

It is hazardous to deduce consumer behaviour on the basis of evidence about the increased variety of products that firms are capable of producing. The potential logical error involved is obvious. Consumers' behaviour should not be construed as simply a response to the capacities of new production techniques, without eliciting what consumers actually do. Much of the literature assumes a simple and symbiotic relationship between producers and consumers, whereby new forms of production and new patterns of consumption fortuitously emerge together, without reference to considerations of what causes what, or to any problems of mutual adaptation (not to mention tensions and contradictions between) them.

In the absence of theoretical guidance, it is perhaps unsurprising that commentators often borrow from the cultural studies literature on consumer culture and postmodernism. There is a steady conflation of claims from the postmodernist debate about the nature of consumer culture with those from the discussion of changing political economy. There is a tendency to assume a relationship between flexible production and the cultural traits of postmodernism, and to make this suffice instead of an analysis of what consumers actually do. The description of postmodernism is made to bridge the gap, even though the theoretical derivations of each approach are not easily rendered compatible. Harvey (1989a), for instance, in *The Condition of Postmodernity*, asserts a correspondence between postmodern culture and post-Fordist production without any detailed specification of the linkages. He imputes a parallel or reciprocal relationship between production and consumption. Yet it requires much more than a claim of contemporaneity to establish the link. There seems to me to be a complicity between different economic and cultural accounts without sufficient reflection on their theoretical compatibility and their causal connection.

The most elaborate and explicit definition of the characteristics of post-Fordist consumption is offered by Urry. Presented as an ideal-typical contrast with mass consumption, he uses it in his investigation of changes in the nature of tourism. This too combines the deduction of consumption patterns from knowledge of new forms of production and some insights from the literature on postmodernism. In analysing 'the tourist gaze', he says,

> I shall now set out two ideal types of Fordist mass consumption and post-Fordist differentiated consumption.
>
> *Mass consumption*: purchase of commodities produced under conditions of mass production; a high and growing rate of expenditure on consumer products; individual producers tending to dominate particular industrial markets; producer rather than consumer as dominant; commodities little differentiated from each other by fashion, season, and specific market segments; relatively limited choice – what there is tends to reflect producer interests, either privately or publicly owned.
>
> *Post-Fordist consumption*: consumption rather than production dominant as consumer expenditure further increases as a proportion of

national income; new forms of credit permitting consumer expenditure to rise, so producing high levels of indebtedness; almost all aspects of social life become commodified, even charity; much greater differentiation of purchasing patterns by different market segments; greater volatility of consumer preferences; the growth of a consumers movement and the 'politicising' of consumption; reaction of consumers against being a part of a 'mass' and the need for producers to be much more consumer-driven, especially in the case of service industries and those publicly owned; the development of many more products each of which has a shorter life; the emergence of new kinds of commodity which are more specialised and based on raw materials that imply non-mass forms of production ('natural' products for example).

(Urry, 1990: 13–14)

This definition of post-Fordist consumption usefully identifies aspects of contemporary practice which do not depend on postulating a new type of individual consumer. As have other writers, Urry emphasises intensified commodification, the enhanced personal meaningfulness of consumption, the diversity of products arising from flexible production and sharper market segmentation among shoppers. Little is said about state provision, noting only briefly that there are tendencies to further commodification and pressures to reform the delivery of state services. No central mechanism gives this list of traits sociological coherence. Its plausibility arises from the contrast with a preceding period of producer-led, Fordist uniformity.

A NEW MODE OF CONSUMPTION?

The question that ensues is whether we might be justified in referring to 'a post-Fordist mode of consumption'. Inadequate information and conceptual imprecision make a conclusive answer impossible, but it is worth reflecting on whether there is a *prima facie* case for a historic shift in the mode of consumption. There are indeed more goods circulating, new marketing strategies, the technological capacity to produce more varied products and global distribution systems. On the other hand, product differentiation has a long history, it is doubtful if there ever was a period of 'mass consumption' and, even if there was, it did not suffuse the entire population. As to the conception of post-Fordist consumption, there are some real difficulties in demonstrating its emergence. I want first to pass some comments on the notion of 'Fordist consumption' and then look at some of the problems involved in empirically establishing that contemporary consumption has post-Fordist characteristics.

On mass consumption

The appropriateness of identifying a Fordist phase of production has quite often been questioned (Clarke, 1992). Whether a coeval period of mass consumption can be clearly identified is probably even more dubious. From the way that the term 'mass consumption' is used, one might be forgiven for thinking that for a period in modern history everybody had owned the same goods, that people could not be differentiated on the basis of their possessions, that individuals did not appreciate that goods could be made to act as social markers, that needs and desires were universal. In comparison with such a stereotype the present period – if characterised by concern with self-identity, lifestyle and distinction – would indeed be different! However, these are unlikely ways of characterising hundreds of millions of households in the mid-twentieth century.

If mass consumption means the very widespread possession of consumer durables and houses (Aglietta maintained that privately owned houses and automobiles were the key components of the social norm of working class consumption in this era) its incidence must be highly uneven, both between social groups inside different societies, and even more so between different countries. Mass consumption perhaps came to characterise the USA by the 1930s, but it would hardly fit the UK before the 1980s. Moreover, at least in Aglietta's formulation, the onset of mass consumption coincides with the proletarianisation of the labour force. Again this might fit the USA timing, but artisanal, peasant and petit-bourgeois alternative forms of existence were mostly eliminated much sooner in the UK, without any shift to a mass mode of consumption. Some of the evidence from Mingione (1991) about the persistence of extensive, non-commodified consumption practices in contemporary southern Europe also suggests that we hesitate before accepting that mass consumption was ever dominant. Periodisation of Fordism at a global level is potentially hard to square with the evidence about consumption.

Post-Fordist tendencies or consumption as usual?

In this section I want to raise questions about how we are to examine and interpret socially differentiated consumption in the 1990s. Two issues seem to me important. The first is whether consumption patterns have lost their grounding in the social categories that experienced unequal consumption through the market in industrial society (and its Fordist phase). Is consumption a free-floating activity, as is implied by the idea of being able choose to adopt and display a lifestyle regardless of one's biography and social position? Second, are patterns of consumption coherent or are they, because socially unanchored and a matter of personal taste and style, fundamentally disorderly? As we will see there are certain methodological difficulties in answering the second question, but initial systematic evidence on the first does not suggest vast change.

One instance of the belief that consumer behaviour is less grounded in socio-demographic position is the widespread claim that class is losing its importance in constraining consumption behaviour. In one of the most persuasive and most cited accounts of consumption practices, Bourdieu (1984) suggests the contrary. He uses the term lifestyle to indicate shared consumption practices across many domains and, without much explicit consideration but with considerable conviction, shows that they correspond to class positions in France in the 1970s. For Bourdieu, lifestyle represents or stands for something else. He maintains that habitus links a person's social and economic position with a corresponding position in 'the universe of life styles'. He marshalls evidence to show that French consumers' behaviours are not those of heroic consumers operating purely in terms of the shared-values criterion of taste. Perhaps, however, researching in the 1970s, he caught Fordist patterns and things have changed since? Certainly it has become *de rigeur* in British market research to lay aside demographic predictors of consumer behaviour and, instead, to construct lifestyle groups. The fact that many of these non-class groups are defined by demographic and occupational characteristics – for example, yuppies and woopies – might suggest that such formulations are not so very different from sociological categories. Moreover there is a suspicious lack of interest in considering the internal relationship between demographic variables and 'values', 'attitudes', or whatever style-projects properly speaking are.

Some of my recent research on changing British food habits examined expenditure on food and drink as recorded in the Family Expenditure Surveys of 1968 and 1988, looking for signs of change in the 1970s as would be anticipated by post-Fordist accounts. The evidence, subject to some reservations about the data, indicates almost no difference in the class structuring of taste. Using discriminant analysis, it is as easy to predict the class membership of a person or a household by their expenditures on food in 1988 as it was in 1968 (Tomlinson and Warde, 1993). Similarly, gendered and generational tastes are as differentiated now as then, though that is not true for regional variation. Despite some de-differentiation apparently occurring within the salariat, corroborating some of the arguments of Savage *et al.* (1992) about middle-class formation, overall little cultural de-differentiation is apparent in the field of food expenditure. Britons may be eating a wider range of foodstuffs and have become more competent with other ethnic cuisines, but class distances in food consumption have not narrowed.

A further question is whether consumption patterns are coherent. Much of the literature suggests that lifestyles are quite coherent, they are the properties of groups who express their social being in a distinctive and characteristic way. This is true of Bourdieu, for instance, who in defining taste identifies lifestyles as unitary:

the propensity and capacity to appropriate (materially or symbolically) a given class of classified, classifying objects or practices, is the generative formula of life-style, a unitary set of distinctive preferences which express the same expressive intention in the specific logic of each of the symbolic sub-spaces, furniture, clothing, language or body hexis.

(Bourdieu, 1984:173)

In his empirical research he attempts to demonstrate that coincidences and complementarities are observed – that many people do that, and their attempts are recognised by other insiders and outsiders.

An alternative account suggests that nowadays it is not incumbent on people to adopt a coherent style of life. Styles, indeed, are often very fluid, people changing from one mundane situation to the next. Featherstone points out that postmodernist culture to an important degree is disorderly:

The tendency within consumer culture is to present lifestyles as no longer requiring inner coherence. The new cultural intermediaries, an expanding faction of the new middle class, therefore, while well disposed to the lifestyle of artistic and cultural specialists, do not seek to promote a single lifestyle, but rather to cater for and expand the range of styles and lifestyles available to audiences and consumers.

(Featherstone, 1991: 26)

Indeed, people are even encouraged to have more than one style persona.

This exposes a further empirical problem, applicable to most postmodernist arguments, of how to tell the difference between disorderly lifestyles, niche consumption and the absence of pattern. How would we know if this condition was becoming more widespread? If norms, standards and criteria of taste become highly unregulated, then group differentiation gives way to individual atomisation. When each individual is adopting an eccentric melange of signs, style as an index of status, group-belonging or self-identity is rendered unreadable and unrecognisable. Too much individuality is just as destructive to meaningful reading of lifestyle symbols as is the imposition of uniformity. A rather bizarre but possible indication of the arrival of post-Fordism might be that distinct consumption patterns become undiscernible to statistical investigation because social differentiation has become too intricately detailed.

SOME CONCLUSIONS

This chapter has examined a diverse set of literature and issues. This is somewhat inevitable given the lack of precision in accounts of changing consumption practice from within the post-Fordism thesis. It has been shown that the way in which consumer behaviour in the market place is conceived has important implications for evaluation of the nature and effectiveness of welfare provision. Some of the dangers of operating with the model of 'the consumer' from neo-classical economics, or of embellishing it by attributing a narrow range of additional social motivations to all individuals, have been identified. Constructing any model of 'the consumer' is unhelpful. More promising is to examine consumption practices in general, providing they are not simply deduced from evidence about industrial production. Existing reliable empirical research that might demonstrate such a case is scant. Indeed, much contemporary sociological discussion of the issue is informed more by the language and strategies of market research and advertising than by knowledge of households and their everyday practices of consumption. Whether improved information would enhance the plausibility of a version of the post-Fordist thesis is anyone's guess.

References

Adam Smith Institute (1989) *Wiser Counsels: The Reform of Local Government* London: Adam Smith Institute.

Aglietta, M. (1979) *A Theory of Capitalist Regulation* London: New Left Books.

Alber, J. (1988) 'Is there a Crisis of the Welfare State?', *European Sociological Review*, vol. 4, pp. 181–207.

Albertsen, N. (1988) 'Postmodernism, Post-Fordism and Critical Social Theory', *Environment and Planning D: Society and Space*, vol. 6, pp. 339–65.

Alexander, A. (1991) 'Managing Fragmentation – Democracy, Accountability and the Future of Local Government', *Local Government Studies*, vol. 17, pp. 63–76.

Alford, K. (1975) *Health Care Politics: Ideological and Interest Group Barriers to Reform* Chicago: Chicago University Press.

Alibhai-Brown, Y. (1992) 'Race and the Single Nation', *The Guardian*, 29 Jan.

Allen, I. (ed.) (1991) *Health and Social Services: The New Relationship* London: Policy Studies Institute.

Altvater, A. (1991) *Die Zukunft des Marktes* Muenster: Westfaelisches Dampfboot Verlag.

Ambrose, P. (1985) *Whatever Happened to Planning?* London: Methuen.

Anthias, F. and Yuval-Davis, N. (1992) *Racialized Boundaries: Race, Nation, Gender, Colour and Class and the Anti-Racist Struggle* London: Routledge.

Ascher, K. (1987) *The Politics of Privatisation* Basingstoke: Macmillan.

Ashton, D. Green, F. and Hoskins, M. (1989) 'The Training System of British Capitalism: Change and Prospects' in F. Green (ed.) *The Restructuring of the UK Economy* Brighton: Harvester Wheatsheaf.

Atkinson, J. (1985) 'The Changing Corporation' in D. Clutterbuck (ed.) *New Patterns of Work* Aldershot: Gower.

Atkinson, J. and Meager, N. (1986) *Changing Working Patterns: How Companies Achieve Flexibility to Meet New Needs* London: NEDO.

Audit Commission (1988) *The Competitive Council* London: HMSO.

Audit Commission (1992) *The Community Revolution: Personal Social Services and Community Care* London: HMSO.

Audit Commission (1993) *Remote Control: The Administration of Housing Benefits* London: HMSO.

Bagguley, P. (1991a) 'Post-Fordism and Enterprise Culture: Flexibility, Autonomy and Changes in Economic Organisation' in R. Keat and N. Abercrombie (eds) *Enterprise Culture* London: Routledge.

Bagguley, P. (1991b) *From Protest to Acquiescence? Political Movements of the Unemployed* London: Macmillan.

Bagguley, P. (1992) 'Social Change, the Middle Class and the Emergence of "New Social Movements": a Critical Analysis', *Sociological Review*, vol. 40, pp. 26–48.

Bagguley, P. and Mann, K. (1992) 'Idle Thieving Bastards?: Scholarly Representations of the "Underclass" ', *Work, Employment and Society*, vol. 6, pp. 113–26.

Bagguley, P., Mark-Lawson, J., Shapiro, D., Urry, J., Walby, S. and Warde, A. (1990) *Restructuring: Place, Class and Gender* London: Sage.

Ball, M. (1983) *Housing Policy and Economic Power* London: Methuen.

Barnekov, T., Boyle, R. and Rich, D. (1989) *Privatism and Urban Policy in Britain and the United States* Oxford: Oxford University Press.

Barr, N. (1987) *The Economics of the Welfare State* London: Weidenfield and Nicolson.

Barr, N. and Coulter, F. (1990) 'Social Security: Solution or Problem?' in J. Hills (ed.) *The State of Welfare: The Welfare State in Britain Since 1974* Oxford: Clarendon Press.

Bauman, Z. (1987) *Legislators and Interpreters: On Modernity, Postmodernity and Intellectuals* Cambridge: Polity Press.

Bauman, Z. (1988) *Freedom* Buckingham: Open University Press.

Bauman, Z. (1990a) 'Philosophical Affinities of Postmodern Sociology', *Sociological Review*, vol. 86, pp. 411–44.

Bauman, Z. (1990b) *Thinking Sociologically* Oxford: Blackwell.

Beechey, V. (1988) 'Rethinking the Definition of Work: Gender and Work' in J. Jenson, E. Hagen and C. Reddy (eds) *Feminisation of the Labour Force* Cambridge: Polity Press.

Beechey, V. and Perkins, T. (1987) *A Matter of Hours* Cambridge: Polity Press.

Benington, J. (1986) 'Local Economic Strategies: Paradigms for a Planned Economy', *Local Economy*, vol. 1, pp. 7–33.

Bennett, R. (1991) *British Chambers of Commerce and Industry: Developing a National Network* London: Association of British Chambers of Commerce.

Bennett, R. and Business in the Community (1990) *Leadership in the Community. A Blueprint for Business Involvement in the 1990s* London: Business in the Cities.

Bennett, R.J. and Krebs, G. (1991) *Local Economic Development: Public–Private Partnership Initiation in Britain and Germany* London: Belhaven Press.

Bernstein, B. (1975) 'On the Classification and Framing of Educational Knowledge' in B. Bernstein *Class, Codes and Control, Vol. 3* London: Routledge.

Bertramsen, R.B., Thomsen, J.-P., and Torfing, J. (1990) *State, Economy and Society* London: Unwin Hyman.

Bligh, D. (ed.) (1982) *Professionalism and Flexibility in Learning* London: Society for Research in Higher Education.

Boddy, M. (1992) 'Training and Enterprise Councils and the Restructuring of Training Provision' in M. Campbell and K. Duffy (eds) *Local Labour Markets: Problems and Policies* London: Longman.

Borchorst, A. and Siim, B. (1987) 'Women and the Advanced Welfare State – a New Kind of Patriarchal Power' in A.S. Sassoon (ed.) *Women and the State* London: Hutchinson.

Bourdieu, P. (1984) *Distinction: A Social Critique of the Judgment of Taste* London: Routledge Kegan Paul.

Bovaird, T. (1992) 'Local Economic Development and the City', *Urban Studies*, vol. 29, pp. 343–68.

Bowles, S. and Gintis, H. (1982) 'The Crisis of Liberal Democratic Capitalism: The Case of the US', *Politics and Society*, vol. 11, pp. 51–93.

Boyer, R. (1990) *Regulation Theory: A Critical Introduction* New York: Columbia University Press.

Brake, M. and Hale, C. (1992) *Public Order and Private Lives: The Politics of Law and Order* London: Routledge.

Briggs, E. and Deacon, A. (1973) 'The Creation of the Unemployment Assistance Board', *Policy and Politics*, vol. 2, pp. 43–62.

Brooke, R. (1989) *Managing the Enabling Authority* London: Longman.

Brown, P. and Lauder, H. (eds) (1992) *Education for Economic Survival: From Fordism to Post-Fordism?* London: Routledge.

Brunskill, I. (1990) *The Regeneration Game: A Regional Approach to Regional Policy* London: Institute for Public Policy Research.

Bryan, B., Dadzie, S. and Scafe, S. (1985) *The Heart of the Race* London: Virago.

Bryson, A. and Jacobs, J. (1992) *Policing The Workshy* Aldershot: Avebury.

Bryson, L. (1992) *Welfare and the State: Who Benefits?* London: Macmillan.

Buckinghamshire Health Plan (1992) *Purchasing Better Health for Bucks People* Aylesbury: Buckinghamshire Purchasing Agency and Buckinghamshire Family Health Services Authority (Consultation Draft).

Burrows, R. and Marsh, C. (1992) 'Consumption, Class and Contemporary Sociology' in R. Burrows and C. Marsh (eds) *Consumption and Class: Divisions and Change* Basingstoke: Macmillan.

Burrows, R., Gilbert, N. and Pollert, A. (1992) 'Fordism, Post-Fordism and Economic Flexibility' in N. Gilbert, R. Burrows and A. Pollert (eds) *Fordism and Flexibility: Divisions and Change* Basingstoke: Macmillan.

Byrne, D. (1987) 'What is the Point of a UDC for Tyne and Wear?', *Northern Economic Review*, vol. 15, pp. 63–73.

Byrne, D. (1992) 'The City' in P. Cloke (ed.) *Policy and Change in Thatcher's Britain* Oxford: Pergammon.

Byrne, D. (1993) 'Property Development and Petty Markers vs. Maritime Industrialism: Past, Present and Future' in R. Imrie and H. Thomas (eds) *British Urban Policy and the Urban Development Corporations* London: Paul Chapman.

Calnan, M. and Cant, S. (1992) 'Principles and Practice: the Case of Private Health Insurance' in R. Burrows and C. Marsh (eds) *Consumption and Class: Divisions and Change* Basingstoke: Macmillan.

Campbell, C. (1987) *The Romantic Ethic and the Spirit of Modern Consumerism* Oxford: Blackwell.

Campbell, M. (ed.) (1990a) *Local Economic Policy* London: Cassell.

Campbell, M. (1990b) 'Towards a Local Labour Market Strategy', *Local Economy*, vol. 5, pp. 4–14.

Carney, J. and Townsend, A. (1977) *Social Consequences and Implications of the Teesside Structure Plan – Summary Report* NEAS, University of Durham.

Castells, M. (1983) 'Crisis, Planning and the Quality of Life: Managing the New Historical Relations Between Space and Society', *Society and Space: Environment & Planning D*, vol. 1, pp. 3–21.

Cave, M., Hanney, S., Kogan, M. and Trevett, G. (1988) *The Use of Performance Indicators in Higher Education* London: Jessica Kingsley.

Centre for Local Economic Strategies, (1990) 'Urban Regeneration: Local Authorities have the Key Role', *Local Work*, no. 15.

Chamberlayne, P. (1992) 'New Directions in Welfare? France, West Germany, Italy and Britain in the 1980s', *Critical Social Policy*, no. 33, pp. 5–21.

Chesnais, F. (1986) 'Science, Technology and Competitiveness', *STI Review*, vol. 1, pp. 86–129.

Christie, I., Carley, M. and Fogarty, M. with Legard, R. (1991) *Profitable Partnerships: A Report on Business Investment in the Community* London: Policy Studies Institute.

Clarke, J. and Langan, M. (1993) 'Restructuring Welfare: the British Welfare Regime in the 1980s' in A. Cochrane and J. Clarke (eds) *Comparing Welfare States: Britain in International Context* London: Sage.

Clarke, J. and Newman, J. (1993) 'Managing to Survive: Dilemmas of Changing Organisational Forms in the Public Sector' in N. Deakin and R. Page (eds) *The Costs of Welfare* Aldershot: Social Policy Association/Avebury.

Clarke, M. and Stewart, J. (1990) *Developing Effective Public Service Management* Luton: Local Government Training Board.

Clarke, S. (1988) 'Overaccumulation, Class Struggle and the Regulation Approach', *Capital and Class*, no. 36, pp. 59–92.

Clarke, S. (1992) 'What in the F---'s Name is Fordism?' in N. Gilbert, R. Burrows and A. Pollert (eds) *Fordism and Flexibility: Divisions and Change* Basingstoke: Macmillan.

Clegg, S. (1990) *Modern Organisations* London: Sage.

Cochrane, A. (1989) 'Britain's Political Crisis' in A. Cochrane and J. Anderson (eds) *Politics in Transition* London: Sage.

Cochrane, A. (1991) 'The Changing State of Local Government: Restructuring for the 1990s', *Public Administration*, vol. 69, pp. 281–302.

Cochrane, A. (1993) 'Challenges from the Centre' in J. Clarke (ed.) *A Crisis in Care? Challenges to Social Work* London: Sage.

Cockburn, C. (1977) *The Local State* London: Pluto.

Cohen, B. and Fraser, N. (1991) *Childcare in a Modern Welfare System: Towards a New National Policy* London: Institute for Public Policy Research.

Commission of the European Community (1991) *Memorandum on Higher Education in the European Community* Brussels: (COM) (91) 349 final.

Cooke, P. (1989) 'Locality, Economic Restructuring and World Development' in P. Cooke (ed.) *Localities: the Changing Face of Urban Britain* London: Unwin Hyman.

Cooke, P. (1990a) 'Manufacturing Miracles: the Changing Nature of the Local Economy' in M. Campbell (ed.) *Local Economic Policy* London: Cassell.

Cooke, P. (1990b) 'Globalization of Economic Organization and the Emergence of Regional Interstate Partnerships' (mimeo).

Cooke, P. and Imrie, R. (1989) 'Little Victories: Local Economic Development in European Regions', *Entrepreneurship and Regional Development* vol. 1, pp. 313–27.

Coombs, R. and Green, K. (1989) 'Work Organization and Product Change in the Service Sector: the Case of the UK National Health Service' in S. Wood (ed.) *The Transformation of Work*? London: Unwin Hyman.

Cooper, R. (1992) 'Formal Organization as Representation: Remote Control, Displacement and Abbreviation' in M. Reed and M. Hughes (eds) *Rethinking Organization* London: Sage.

Costello, N., Michie, J. and S. Milne (1989) *Beyond the Casino Economy* London: Verso.

Council of Mortgage Lenders (1991) *Housing Finance*, 12 (November).

Cousins, C. (1987) *Controlling Social Welfare* Brighton: Wheatsheaf.

Cousins, C. (1988) 'The Restructuring of Welfare Work: the Introduction of General Management and the Contracting Out of Ancillary Services in the NHS', *Work, Employment and Society*, vol. 2, pp. 210–28.

Cox, C. and Mair, A. (1989) 'Levels of Abstraction in Locality Studies', *Antipode*, vol. 21, pp. 21–32.

Coyle, A. (1985) 'Going Private: the Implications of Privatisation for Women's Work', *Feminist Review*, no. 21, pp. 5–22.

CSO (Central Statistical Office) (1991) *Social Trends* 21, London: HMSO.

Davenport, E., Geddes, M. and Benington, J. (1990) 'The Future of Motor Industry Regions: New Local Authority Responses to Industrial Restructuring', *Local Economy*, vol. 5, pp. 129–46.

Davis, M. (1990) *City of Quartz* London: Verso.

Dawson, J. (1992) 'European City Networks: Experiments in Transnational Urban Collaboration', *The Planner*, 10, January, 7–9.

Dearlove, J. (1979) *The Reorganisation of British Local Government* Cambridge: Cambridge University Press.

Department of Health (1992) *Health of the Nation* London: HMSO.

Docklands Consultative Committee (1990) *The Docklands Experiment* London: Docklands Consultative Committee.

Doyal, L., Hunt, G. and Mellor, J. (1981) 'Your Life in Their Hands: Migrant Workers in the National Health Service', *Critical Social Policy*, no. 1.

Duffy, K. (1992) 'Disadvantage and Exclusion: the Case of Peripheral Estates' in M. Campbell and K. Duffy (eds) *Local Labour Markets: Problems and Policies* London: Longman.

Duffy, K. and Geddes, M. (1990) *Women and Work in Harlow* Local Government Centre, Warwick University for Harlow District Council.

Duke of Edinburgh (1991) *Inquiry into British Housing* (Second Report) York: Joseph Rowntree Foundation.

Duncan, S. and Goodwin, M. (1988) *The Local State and Uneven Development* Cambridge: Polity Press.

Dunford, M. (1990) 'Theories of Regulation', *Society and Space: Environment & Planning D*, vol. 8, pp. 297–321.

Dunleavy, P. (1980a) 'The Political Implications of Sectoral Cleavages and the Growth of State Employment', *Political Studies*, vol. 28, pp. 364–84 and 527–49.

Dunleavy, P. (1980b) *Urban Political Analysis* London: Macmillan.

Dunleavy, P. (1981) *The Politics of Mass Housing in Britain* Oxford: Clarendon Press.

Dyson, K. (ed.) (1989) *Local Authorities and New Technologies: The European Dimension* London: Croom Helm.

Economist (1992), 5 September.

Edgell, S. and Duke, V. (1991) *A Measure of Thatcherism: A Sociology of Britain* London: Harper Collins.

Elam, M. J. (1990) 'Puzzling Out the Post-Fordist Debate: Technology, Markets and Institutions', *Economic and Industrial Democracy*, vol. 11, pp.9–38.

Elbaum, B. and Lazonick, W.J. (eds) (1986) *The Decline of the British Economy* Oxford: Clarendon Press.

Esping-Andersen, G. (1990) *The Three Worlds of Welfare Capitalism* Cambridge: Polity Press.

Esser, J. and Hirsch, J. (1989) 'The Crisis of Fordism and Dimensions of a "Post-Fordist" Urban and Regional Structure', *International Journal of Urban and Regional Research*, vol. 13, pp. 417–37.

Fairbrother, P. (1987) 'Restructuring Production, Models of Flexibility and Union Renewal: Japanization in Progress', Paper Presented at Cardiff Business School, September.

Featherstone, M. (1991) *Consumer Culture and Postmodernism* London: Sage.

Flynn, N. (1990) *Public Sector Management* Brighton: Harvester Wheatsheaf.

Fogarty, M. and Christie, I. (1990) *Companies and Communities: Promoting Business Involvement in the City* London: Policy Studies Institute.

Foucault, M. (1977) *Discipline and Punish* London: Penguin.

Frampton, K. (1992) *Modern Architecture: A Critical History* (3rd edn) London: Thames and Hudson.

Fulton, O. (1989) *Access and Institutional Change* Buckingham: Open University Press.

Friend, J. and Jessop, W. (1969) *Local Government and Strategic Choice: An Operational Research Approach to the Process of Public Planning* London: Tavistock.

Gallie, D. (1991) 'Patterns of Skill Change: Upskilling, Deskilling or the Polarization of Skills?', *Work, Employment and Society*, vol. 5, pp. 319–51.

Gamble, A. (1985) *Britain in Decline: Economic Policy, Political Strategy and the British State* (2nd edn) London: Macmillan.

Garrahan, P. and Stewart, P. (1992) *The Nissan Enigma* London: Mansell.

Geddes, M. (1988) 'The Capitalist State and the Local Economy: "Restructuring for Labour" and Beyond', *Capital and Class*, no.35, pp. 85–120.

Geddes, M. (1991) 'The Social Audit Movement' in D. Owen (ed.) *Green Reporting: Accountancy and the Challenge of the Nineties* London: Chapman and Hall.

Geddes, M. (1993) *Sustainable Development and Local Public Services*, Working Paper 15, Local Government Centre, University of Warwick.

Geddes, M., Field, P., Dickinson, P., Mizen, P. and Benington, J. (1992) *Local Government and the Motor Industry* Report to the Motor Industry Local Authority Network (MILAN).

Giddens, A. (1979) *Central Problems of Social Theory* Basingstoke: Macmillan.

Giddens, A. (1981) *A Contemporary Critique of Historical Materialism* Basingstoke: Macmillan.

Giddens, A. (1991) *Modernity and Self–Identity* Cambridge: Polity Press.

Gilbert, N., Burrows, R. and Pollert, A. (eds) (1992) *Fordism and Flexibility: Divisions and Change* Basingstoke: Macmillan.

Ginsburg, N. (1989) 'The Housing Act, 1988 and its Policy Context: a Critical Commentary', *Critical Social Policy*, pp. 56–81.

Ginsburg, N. (1992) *Divisions of Welfare* London, Sage.

Glasson, J. (1992) 'The Fall and Rise of Regional Planning in the Economically Advanced Nations', *Urban Studies*, vol. 29, pp. 505–31.

Glendinning, C. (1992) 'Residualism Versus Rights: Social Policy and Disabled People' in N. Manning and R. Page (eds) *Social Policy Review 4* Canterbury: Social Policy Association.

Glennerster, H., Power, A. and Travers, T. (1991) 'A New Era for Social Policy: A

New Enlightenment or a New Leviathan?', *Journal of Social Policy*, vol. 20, pp. 389–414.

Glyn, A. (1992) 'The Costs of Stability: the Advanced Capitalist Countries in the 1980s', *New Left Review*, no. 195, pp. 71–96.

Gorz, A. (1982) *Farewell to the Working Class* London: Pluto Press.

Gott, M. and Warren, G. (1990) *A Report on the North Staffordshire Initiative to Increase Democracy by the Introduction of Neighbourhood Forums* Stoke: North Staffordshire Health Authority.

Gough, I. (1979) *The Political Economy of the Welfare State* London: Macmillan.

Gould, A. (1993) *Capitalist Welfare Systems: A Comparison of Japan, Britain and Sweden* London: Longman.

Graham, S. (1991) 'Telecommunications and the Local Economy: Some Emerging Issues', *Local Economy*, vol. 6, pp. 116–36.

Granovetter, M. (1985) 'Economic Action and Social Structure: the Problem of Embeddedness', *American Journal of Sociology*, vol. 91, pp. 481–510.

Griffiths, R. (1988) *Community Care: Agenda for Action* London: HMSO.

Hadley, R. and Young, K. (1990) *Creating a Responsive Public Service* Brighton: Harvester Wheatsheaf.

Hakim, C. (1990) 'Core and Peripheries in Employers' Workforce Strategies: Evidence from the 1987 ELUS Survey', *Work, Employment and Society*, vol. 4, pp. 157–88.

Halifax Building Society (1992) *House Price Index*, 48, Halifax.

Hall, P. (1988) *Cities of Tomorrow* Oxford: Blackwell.

Hall, S. (1989) 'The Meaning of New Times' in S. Hall and M. Jacques (eds) *New Times* London: Lawrence and Wishart.

Hall, T. and Hall, P. (1980) *Part–time Social Work* London: Heinemann.

Hallett, C. and Birchall, E. (1992) *Co-Ordination and Child Protection: A Review of the Literature* Edinburgh: HMSO.

Hambleton, R. and Hoggett, P. (1990) *Beyond Excellence: Quality Local Government in the 1990s* Working Paper 85, Bristol: School for Advanced Urban Studies.

Hambleton, R., Hoggett, P. and Tolan, F. (1989) 'The Decentralization of Public Services', *Local Government Studies*, vol. 15, pp. 39–56.

Harding, A. (1990) 'Public–Private Partnerships in Urban Regeneration' in M. Campbell (ed.) *Local Economic Policy* London: Cassell.

Harloe, M., Pickvance, C. and Urry, J. (eds) (1989) *Place, Policy and Politics: Do Localities Matter?* London: Unwin Hyman.

Harvey, D. (1987) 'Flexible Accumulation Through Urbanisation – Reflections on "Postmodernism" in the American City', *Antipode*, vol. 19, pp. 260–86.

Harvey, D. (1989a) *The Condition of Postmodernity: An Enquiry into the Origins of Cultural Change* Oxford: Basil Blackwell.

Harvey, D. (1989b) 'From Managerialism to Entrepreneurialism: the Transformation in Urban Governance in Late Capitalism', *Geografiska Annaler*, vol. 71B, pp. 3–17.

Healey, P. (1991) 'Urban Regeneration and the Development Industry', *Regional Studies*, vol. 25, pp. 97–110.

Health Services Journal (1992a) 27 August.

Health Services Journal (1992b) 10 September.

Heath, A., Curtice, J., and Jowell, R. (1991) *Understanding Political Change* Oxford: Pergamon.

Hepworth, M. (1992) 'The Municipal Information Economy', *Local Government Studies*, vol. 18, pp. 148–57.

Heydebrand, W. (1977) 'Organizational Contradictions in Public Bureaucracies', *Sociological Quarterly*, vol. 18, pp. 83–107.

Hills, J. (ed.) (1990) *The State of Welfare: The Welfare State in Britain since 1974*. Oxford: Clarendon Press.

Hills, J. and Mullings, B. (1990) 'Housing: A Decent Home for All at a Price Within Their Means?' in J. Hills (ed.) *The State of Welfare: The Welfare State in Britain Since 1974* Oxford: Clarendon.

Hindess, B. and Hirst, P.Q. (1975) *Pre-Capitalist Modes of Production* London: Routledge and Kegan Paul.

Hirsch, J. (1991) 'From the Fordist to the Post-Fordist State' in B. Jessop, H. Kastendiek, K. Nielsen and O. Pedersen (eds) *The Politics of Flexibility* London: Edward Elgar.

Hirsch, J. and Roth, R. (1986) *Das neue Gesicht des Kapitalismus* Hamburg: VSA.

Hirst, P. and Zeitlin, J. (1991) 'Flexible Specialisation Versus Post-Fordism: Theory, Evidence and Policy Implications' *Economy and Society*, vol. 20, pp. 1–56.

HM Treasury (1979) *The Government's Expenditure Plans 1980–1* Cmnd. 7746, London: HMSO.

HM Treasury (1991) *Public Expenditure Analyses to 1993–4* Cmnd. 1520, London: HMSO.

Hoggett, P. (1979) 'Conceptualising Long Waves', *Intervention: Contributions to Marxist Studies*, vol. 3, pp. 27–42.

Hoggett, P. (1987) 'A Farewell to Mass Production? Decentralisation as an Emergent Private and Public Sector Paradigm' in P. Hoggett and R. Hambleton (eds) *Decentralisation and Democracy*. Occasional Paper 28, School for Advanced Urban Studies, University of Bristol.

Hoggett, P. (1990) 'Modernisation, Political Strategy and the Welfare State' *Studies in Decentralisation and Quasi-Markets* no. 2, School for Advanced Urban Studies, University of Bristol.

Hoggett, P. (1991a) 'Long Waves and Forms of Capitalism', *New Interventions*, vol. 2, pp. 3–17.

Hoggett, P. (1991b) 'A New Management in the Public Sector?', *Policy and Politics*, vol. 19, pp. 243–56.

Hoggett, P. (1992) 'Reversing the Tide', *Chartist*, no. 137, pp. 33–4.

Hoggett, P. and McGill, I. (1988) 'Labourism: Ends and Means', *Critical Social Policy*, no. 13.

Home Office and Department of Health (1992) *Memorandum of Good Practice on Video Recorded Interviews with Child Witnesses in Criminal Proceedings* London: HMSO.

House of Commons (1987–8) *The Employment Effects of UDCs I and II* London: HMSO.

Hudson, B. (1990) 'Social Policy and the New Right – the Strange Case of the Community Care White Paper', *Local Government Studies*, vol. 16, pp. 15–34.

Hudson, R. (1989) *Wrecking a Region* London: Pion.

Humphries, J. and Rubery, J. (1992) 'The Legacy for Women's Employment' in J. Michie (ed.) *The Economic Legacy 1979–1992* London: Academic Press.

Institute of Manpower Studies (IMS) (1986) *New Forms of Work Organisation*, IMS Report no. 121, Falmer, University of Sussex.

Jacobs, B. (1992) *Fractured Cities: Capitalism, Community and Empowerment in Britain and America* London: Routledge.

Jenson, J., Hagen, E. and Reddy, C. (eds) (1988) *Feminisation of the Labour Force* Cambridge: Polity Press.

Jessop, B. (1982) *The Capitalist State* Oxford: Martin Robertson.

Jessop, B. (1988) *Conservative Regimes and the Transition to Post-Fordism: The Cases of Britain and West Germany* Essex Papers in Politics and Government, Colchester: University of Essex.

Jessop, B. (1989a) *Thatcherism: The British Road to Post-Fordism?* Essex Papers in Politics and Government, Colchester: University of Essex.

Jessop, B. (1989b) 'Conservative Regimes and the Transition to Post-Fordism' in M. Gottdiener and N. Kominos (eds) *Capitalist Development and Crisis Theory: Accumulation, Regulation and Spatial Restructuring* London: Macmillan.

Jessop, B. (1990a) 'Regulation Theories in Retrospect and Prospect', *Economy and Society*, vol. 19, pp. 153–216.

Jessop, B. (1990b) *State Theory: Putting Capitalist States in Their Place* Cambridge: Polity Press.

Jessop, B. (1991a) 'The Welfare State in the Transition from Fordism to Post-Fordism' in B. Jessop, H. Kastendiek, K. Nielsen and O.K. Pedersen *The Politics of Flexibility: Restructuring State and Industry in Britain, Germany and Scandinavia* London: Edward Elgar.

Jessop, B. (1991b) 'Thatcherism and Flexibility: the White Heat of a Post-Fordist Revolution' in B. Jessop, H. Kastendiek, K. Nielsen and O.K. Pedersen *The Politics of Flexibility: Restructuring State and Industry in Britain, Germany and Scandinavia* London: Edward Elgar.

Jessop, B. (1991c) *Fordism and Post-Fordism: A Critical Reformulation* Lancaster Regionalism Group Working Paper No.41, University of Lancaster.

Jessop, B. (1992a) 'Fordism and Post-Fordism: A Critical Reformulation' in A.J. Scott and M. Stormper (eds) *Pathways to Industrialization and Regional Development* London: Routledge.

Jessop, B. (1992b) 'Regulation und Politik: Integrale Ökonomie und Integraler Staat' in A. Demirovic *et al.* (eds) *Akkumulation, Hegemonie und Staat* Münster: Westfälisches Dampfboot.

Jessop, B. (1992c) 'From Social Democracy to Thatcherism' in N. Abercrombie and A. Warde (eds) *Social Change in Contemporary Britain* Cambridge: Polity Press.

Jessop, B. (1992d) *From the Keynesian Welfare State to the Schumpeterian Workfare State* Lancaster Regionalism Group Working Paper No.45, University of Lancaster.

Jessop, B. (1993a) 'Towards the Schumpeterian Workfare State', *Studies in Political Economy* (in press).

Jessop, B. (1993b) 'Politics in the Thatcher Era: The Flawed Economy and the Weak State' in D. Grimm (ed.) *Staatsaufgaben* Baden: Nomos.

Jessop, B., Bonnett, K., Bromley, S. and Ling, T. (1988) *Thatcherism: A Tale of Two Nations* Cambridge: Polity Press.

Jessop, B., Kastendiek, H., Nielsen, K. and Pedersen, O. (1991) *The Politics of Flexibility: Restructuring State and Industry in Britain, Germany and Scandinavia* London: Edward Elgar.

Johnes, J. and Taylor, J. (1990) *Performance Indicators in Higher Education* Milton Keynes: Society for Research in Higher Education/Open University.

Johnson, N. (1987) *The Welfare State in Transition: The Theory and Practice of Welfare Pluralism* Brighton: Wheatsheaf.

Johnson, N. (1990) *Reconstructing the Welfare State: A Decade of Change 1980–1990* Hemel Hempstead: Harvester Wheatsheaf.

Johnson, T. (1972) *Professions and Power* London: Macmillan.

Jones, G. and Stewart, J. (1983) *The Case for Local Government* London: Allen and Unwin.

Karan, T. (1984) 'The Local Government Workforce – Public Sector Paragon or Private Sector Parasite?', *Local Government Studies*, vol. 10, pp. 39–58.

Kavanagh, D. (1987) *Thatcherism and British Politics: The End of Consensus?* Oxford: Oxford University Press.

Keat, R. and Abercrombie, N. (eds) (1991) *Enterprise Culture* London: Routledge.

Kelly, A. (1991) 'The Enterprise Culture and the Welfare State: Restructuring the Management of the Health and Personal Social Services' in R. Burrows (ed.) *Deciphering the Enterprise Culture: Entrepreneurship, Petty Capitalism and the Restructuring of Britain* London: Routledge.

Keman, H., Paloheimo, H. and Whitely, P. (eds) (1987) *Coping with the Economic Crisis: Alternative Responses to Economic Recession in Advanced Industrial Societies* London: Sage.

Kennedy, R. (1991) *London: World City Moving into the 21st Century* London: HMSO.

King, D. (1989) 'Economic Crisis and Welfare State Recommodification' in M. Gottdiener and N. Kominos (eds) *Capitalist Development and Crisis Theory: Accumulation, Regulation and Spatial Restructuring* London: Macmillan.

Knott, J. (1986) *Popular Opposition to the 1834 Poor Law* London: Croom Helm.

Kosonen, P. (1991) 'Flexibilization and the Alternatives of the Nordic Welfare States' in B. Jessop, H. Kastendiek, K. Nielsen and O. Pedersen (eds) *The Politics of Flexibility: Restructuring, State and Industry in Britain, Germany and Scandinavia* London: Edward Elgar.

Lane, C. (1988) 'Industrial Change in Europe: the Pursuit of Flexible Specialisation in Britain and West Germany', *Work, Employment and Society*, vol. 2, pp. 141–68.

Langan, M. and Ostner, I. (1991) 'Gender and Welfare' in G. Room (ed.) *Towards a European Welfare State?* Bristol: School for Advanced Urban Studies.

Lash, S. and Urry, J. (1987) *The End of Organised Capitalism* Cambridge: Polity Press.

Le Grand, J. (1990) 'The State of Welfare' in J. Hills (ed.) *The State of Welfare: the Welfare State in Britain Since 1974* Oxford: Clarendon.

Le Grand, J. (1992) 'Paying for or Providing Welfare?', *Studies in Decentralisation and Quasi-Markets*, no. 15, School for Advanced Urban Studies SAUS: University of Bristol.

Lee, F. (1992) 'The Undeveloping Society', *Chartist*, no. 139, pp. 17–19.

Lever, E. F. (1991) 'Deindustrialization and the Reality of the Post-Industrial City', *Urban Studies*, vol. 28, pp 983–99.

Lewis, J. (1992) 'Gender and the Development of Welfare Regimes', *Journal of European Social Policy*, vol. 2, pp. 159–73.

Lewis, N. (1992) *Inner City Regeneration* Buckingham: Open University Press.

Leys, C. (1989) *Politics in Britain* London: Verso.

Lipietz, A. (1987) *Miracles and Mirages: The Crises of Global Fordism* London: Verso.

Lipietz, A. (1988) 'Accumulation, Crises and the Ways Out: Some Methodological

Reflections on the Concept of "Regulation" ', *International Journal of Political Economy*, vol. 18, pp. 10–43.

Local Government Information Unit (LGIU) (1991) *Powers to Act: The Case for Local Government* London: LGIU.

Local Government Training Board (LGTB) (1987) *Getting Closer to the Public* Luton: LGTB.

Luck, M. (1991) 'Gender and Library Work: the Implications of Dual Labour Market Theory' in N. Redclift and S. Thea (eds) *Working Women* London: Routledge.

McGregor, A. and Sproull, A. (1992) 'Employers and the Flexible Workforce', *Employment Gazette*, May, pp. 225–34.

McInnes, J. (1987) *Thatcherism at Work* Buckingham: Open University Press.

MacShane, D. (1990) 'Why the Tories Need a Rentier Economy', *Chartist*, no. 132, pp. 24–6.

Mandel, E. (1975) *Late Capitalism* London: New Left Books.

Mann, K. (1992) *The Making of an English 'Underclass'* Buckingham: Open University Press.

Marquand, D. (1988) *The Unprincipled Society* London: Jonathan Cape.

Marsh, D. (1991) 'Privatization Under Mrs Thatcher: a Review of the Literature', *Public Administration*, vol. 69, pp. 459–80.

Marsh, D. and Rhodes, R. (1992) *Implementing Thatcherite Policies: Audit of an Era* Buckingham: Open University Press.

Marvin, S. (1992) 'Urban Policy and Infrastructure Networks', *Local Economy*, vol. 7, pp. 225–47.

Marx, K. (1977) *Capital* (vol I) London: Lawrence and Wishart.

Massey, D. (1984) *Spatial Divisions of Labour* London: Macmillan.

Meegan, R. (1988) 'A Crisis of Mass Production?' In J. Allen and D. Massey (eds) *The Economy in Question* London: Sage.

Meiksins-Wood, S. (1984) 'Marxism and the Course of History', *New Left Review*, no. 147, pp. 95–107.

Mingione, E. (1991) *Fragmented Societies: A Sociology of Economic Life Beyond the Market Paradigm* Oxford: Blackwell.

Mishra, R. (1990) *The Welfare State in Capitalist Society* Brighton: Harvester Wheatsheaf.

Mohan, J. (1988) 'Restructuring, Privatisation and the Geography of Health Care Provision in England, 1983–1987', *Transactions of the Institute of British Geographers*, vol. 13, pp. 449–65.

Montgomery, J. and Thornley, A. (eds) (1990) *Radical Planning Initiatives* Aldershot: Gower.

Moran, M. (1988) 'Crises of the Welfare State', *British Journal of Political Science*, vol. 18, pp. 397–414.

Morris, J. (1991) *Pride Against Prejudice* London: The Women's Press.

Moss Kanter, R. (1989) *When Giants Learn to Dance: Mastering the Challenges of Strategy, Management, and Careers in the 1990s* London: Unwin Hyman.

Moulaert, F., Swyngedouw, E., and Wilson, P. (1988) 'Spatial Responses to Fordist and Post-Fordist Accumulation and Regulation', *Papers of the Regional Science Association*, vol. 64, pp. 11–23.

Munro, M. and Smith, S. J. (1989) 'Gender and Housing: Broadening the Debate', *Housing Studies*, vol. 4, pp. 3–17.

Murray, R. (1987) *Breaking with Bureaucracy: Ownership, Control and Nationalisation* Manchester: Centre for Local Economic Strategy.

Murray, R. (1991a) *Local Space: Europe and the New Regionalism* Manchester: Centre for Local Economic Strategies.

Murray, R. (1991b) 'The State After Henry' in *Marxism Today*, May, pp. 22–27.

Newman, J. and Clarke, J. (1994) 'Going about our Business? The Managerialisation of Public Services' in J. Clarke, A. Cochrane and E. McLaughlin (eds) *Managing Social Policy* London: Sage.

Newton, S. and Porter, D. (1988) *Modernization Frustrated: the Politics of Industrial Decline in Britain Since 1900* London: Unwin Hyman.

Nielsen, K. (1991) 'Towards a Flexible Future – Theories and Politics' in B. Jessop, H. Kastendiek, K. Nielsen and O. Pedersen (eds) *The Politics of Flexibility: Restructuring, State and Industry in Britain, Germany and Scandinavia* London: Edward Elgar.

O'Connell Davidson, J. (1990) 'The Commercialisation of Employment Relations: the Case of the Water Industry', *Work, Employment and Society*, vol. 4, pp. 531–49.

O'Connor, J. (1973) *The Fiscal Crisis of the State* New York: St Martin's Press.

OECD (1985) *Social Expenditure 1960–1990: Problems of Growth and Control* Paris: OECD.

OECD (1988) *The Future of Social Protection* Paris: OECD.

Offe, C. (1984) *Contradictions of the Welfare State* London: Hutchinson.

Offe, C. (1985) *Disorganized Capitalism* Cambridge: Polity Press.

Offe, C. (1987) 'Democracy Against the Welfare State?', *Political Theory*, vol. 15, pp. 501–37.

Oliver, M. (1990) *The Politics of Disablement* Basingstoke: Macmillan.

Oliver, N. and Williams, B. (1988) *The Japanization of British Industry* Oxford: Basil Blackwell.

Orloff, A. (1992) 'Gender and the Social Rights of Citizenship: State Policies and Gender Relations in Comparative Perspective' paper presented to the Conference on Comparative Studies of Welfare State Development, University of Bremen, Germany, September.

Overbeek, H. (1990) *Global Capitalism and National Decline* London: Unwin Hyman.

Painter, J. (1991a) 'Compulsory Competitive Tendering in Local Government: the First Round', *Public Administration* vol. 69, pp. 191–210.

Painter, J. (1991b) 'Regulation Theory and Local Government', *Local Government Studies*, Nov/Dec, pp. 23–44.

Papadakis, E. and Taylor–Gooby, P. (1987) *The Private Provision of Public Welfare* Brighton: Wheatsheaf.

Penn, R. (1992) 'Flexibility in Britain During the 1980s: Recent Empirical Evidence' in N. Gilbert, R. Burrows and A. Pollert (eds) *Fordism and Flexibility: Divisions and Change* Basingstoke: Macmillan.

Penna, S. (1990) 'Thatcherism, Ideology and State Practice: an Analysis of the 1984 Reviews of Social Security' unpublished Ph.D. Thesis, Department of Sociology, Lancaster University.

Peters, T. and Waterman, R. (1982) *In Search of Excellence: Lessons from America's Best Run Companies* New York: Harper and Row.

Pfaller, A., Gough, I. and Therborn, G. (eds) (1991) *Can the Welfare State Compete?* London: Macmillan.

Pickvance, C. (1991) 'The Difficulty of Control and the Ease of Structural Reform: British Local Government in the 1980s' in C. Pickvance and E. Prétèceille (eds)

State Restructuring and Local Power: A Comparative Perspective Oxford: Blackwell.

Pickvance, C. and Prétèceille, E. (1991) 'Conclusions', in C. Pickvance and E. Prétèceille (eds) *State Restructuring and Local Power: A Comparative Perspective* Oxford: Blackwell.

Pierson, C. (1990) 'The "Exceptional" United States: First New Nation or Last Welfare State?', *Social Policy and Administration*, vol. 24, pp. 186–98.

Pierson, C. (1991) *Beyond the Welfare State?* Cambridge: Polity Press.

Pietroni, M. (ed.) (1991) *Right or Privilege? – Post-Qualifying Training with Special Reference to Child Care* London: Central Council for Education and Training in Social Work.

Pinch, S. and Storey, A. (1992a) 'Labour-Market Dualism: Evidence from a Survey of Households in the Southampton City-Region' *Environment and Planning A*, vol. 24, pp. 571–89.

Pinch, S. and Storey, A. (1992b) 'Flexibility, Gender and Part-Time Work: Evidence from a Survey of the Economically Active' *Transactions of the Institute of British Geographers*, vol. 17, pp. 198–214.

Pinch, S., Mason, C. and Witt, S. (1991) 'Flexible Employment Strategies in British Industry: Evidence from the UK Sunbelt' *Regional Studies*, vol. 25, pp. 207–18.

Piore, M. and Sabel, C. (1984) *The Second Industrial Divide* New York: Basic Books.

Piven, F. and Cloward, R. (1977) *Poor Peoples' Movements* New York: Pantheon Books.

Pollert, A. (1988) 'Dismantling Flexibility', *Capital and Class*, no. 34, pp. 42–75.

Pollert, A. (1989) 'The "Flexible Firm": Fixation or Fact?', *Work, Employment and Society*, vol. 2, pp. 281–316.

Pollert, A. (ed.) (1991) *Farewell to Flexibility?* Oxford: Blackwell.

Pollitt, C. (1990) *Managerialism and the Public Services: The Anglo-American Experience* Oxford: Blackwell.

Poulantzas, N. (1978) *Political Power and Social Classes* London: Verso.

Pratt, J. and Burgess, T. (1974) *The Polytechnics: A Report* London: Pitman.

Pratt, J. and Silverman, S. (1989) *Responding to Constraint: Policy and Management in Higher Education* Milton Keynes: Society for Research in Higher Education/Open University.

Prosser, Y. (1981) 'The Politics of Discretion' in M. Adler and S. Asquith (eds) *Discretion and Welfare* London: Heinemann.

Pulkingham, J. (1992) 'Employment Restructuring in the Health Service: Efficiency Initiatives, Working Practices and Workforce Composition', *Work, Employment and Society*, vol. 6, pp. 397–421.

Radical Statistics Group (1987) *Facing the Figures: What is Really Happening to the NHS?* London: Pluto.

Rhodes, R. (1988) *Beyond Westminster and Whitehall: Sub-Central Governments of Britain* London: Unwin Hyman.

Roberts, R. (1992) 'Religion and the "Enterprise Culture": the British Experience in the Thatcher Era (1979–1990)', *Social Compass*, vol. 39, pp. 15–33.

Robson, B.T. (1969) *Urban Analysis* Cambridge: Cambridge University Press.

Roobeek, A.J.M. (1987) 'The Crisis in Fordism and the Rise of a New Technological Paradigm', *Futures*, vol. 19, pp. 129–54.

Rubery, J. (1989) 'Labour Market Flexibility in Britain' in F. Green (ed.) *The Restructuring of the UK Economy* Brighton: Harvester Wheatsheaf.

Rustin, M.J. (1986) 'The Idea of the Popular University: a Historical Perspective' in

J. Finch and M. Rustin (eds) *A Degree of Choice: Education After 18* Harmondsworth: Penguin.

Rustin, M.J. (1989) 'The Politics of Post-Fordism: Or, the Trouble with "New Times" ', *New Left Review*, no. 175, pp. 54–77.

Salzberger-Wittenberg, I., Henry, G. and Osbourne, E. (1983) *The Emotional Experience of Learning and Teaching* London: Routledge.

Saunders, P. (1979) *Urban Politics: A Sociological Interpretation* Harmondsworth: Penguin.

Saunders, P. (1986) *Social Theory and the Urban Question* (2nd edn) London: Hutchinson.

Saunders, P. (1990) *A Nation of Homeowners* London: Unwin Hyman.

Savage, M., Barlow, J., Dickens, P. and Fielding, T. (1992) *Property, Bureaucracy and Culture: Middle-Class Formation in Contemporary Britain* London Routledge.

Sayer, A. (1989) 'Post-Fordism in Question', *International Journal of Urban and Regional Research*, vol. 13, pp. 666–95.

Scharpf, F. (1987) *Sozialdemokratische Krisenpolitik in Europa: Das 'Modell Deutschland' im Vergleich* Frankfurt: Campus.

Schmitter-Heisler, B. and Hoffman, J. (1989) ' "Threats to Homes" as Grievance: Targets and Constituencies' in L. Kriesberg (ed.) *Research in Social Movements, Conflicts and Change* Greenwich, CT: JAI Press.

SERC (n.d.) *Sheffield 2000* Sheffield: Sheffield Economic Regeneration Committee.

Shaver, S. (1990) 'Gender, Social Policy Regimes and the Welfare State', *Social Policy Research Centre Discussion Paper*, No. 26, University of New South Wales, Australia.

Sloan, P.J. (1989) 'Flexible Manpower Resourcing: a Local Labour Market Survey', *Journal of Management Studies*, vol. 26, pp. 129–50.

Smith, D. (1989) 'Customer Care and Housing Services – a Practitioner's View' paper presented to Seventh Urban Change and Conflict Conference, Bristol.

Smith, D. (1992) *Understanding the Underclass* London: Policy Studies Institute.

Smith, D. and Saunders, M.R. (1991) *Other Routes: Part-Time Higher Education Policy* Milton Keynes: Society for Research in Higher Education/Open University.

Stewart, J. (1989) 'The Changing Organisation and Management of Local Authorities' in J. Stewart and G. Stoker (eds) *The Future of Local Government* London: Macmillan.

Stewart, J. and Stoker, G. (1988) *From Local Administration to Community Government* Fabian Research Series 351, London: Fabian Society.

Stewart, J. and Walsh, K. (1989) *The Search for Quality* Luton: Local Government Training Board.

Stoker, G. (1989a) *The Politics of Local Government* London: Macmillan.

Stoker, G. (1989b) 'Creating a Local Government for a Post-Fordist Society: the Thatcherite Project?' in J. Stewart and G. Stoker (eds) *The Future of Local Government* Basingstoke: Macmillan.

Stoker, G. (1990) 'Regulation Theory, Local Government and the Transition from Fordism' in D. King and J. Pierre (eds) *Challenges to Local Government* London: Sage.

Stone, C. (1989) *Regime Politics: Governing Atlanta 1946–1988* Lawrence, KS: University of Kansas Press.

Tarbuck, K. (1991) 'Monopoly Capital Revisited', *Critique*, no. 23, pp. 101–25.

Taylor-Gooby, P. (1985) *Public Opinion, Ideology and State Welfare* London: Routledge and Kegan Paul.

Taylor-Gooby, P. (1988) 'The Future of the British Welfare State', *European Sociological Review*, vol. 4, pp. 1–19.

Taylor-Gooby, P. (1990) 'Social Welfare: The Unkindest Cuts' in R. Jowell, S. Witherspoon and L. Brook (eds) *British Social Attitudes: The Seventh Report*, Aldershot: Gower.

Tickell, A. and Peck, J. (1992) 'Accumulation Regimes and the Geographies of Post-Fordism: Missing Links in Regulationist Theory', *Progress in Human Geography*, vol. 16, pp. 190–218.

Tight, M. (1991) *Higher Education: a Part-Time Perspective* Milton Keynes: Society for Research in Higher Education/Open University.

Tomlinson, M. and Warde, A. (1993) 'Social Class and Change in Eating Habits', *British Food Journal*, vol. 95, pp. 3–10.

Totterdill, P. (1989) 'Local Economic Strategies as Industrial Policy: a Critical Review of British Developments in the 1980s', *Economy and Society*, vol. 18, pp. 478–526.

Totterdill, P. (1992) 'The Textiles and Clothing Industry: a Laboratory of Industrial Policy' in M. Geddes and J. Benington (eds) *Restructuring the Local Economy* London: Longman.

Turner, R.H. (1961) 'Modes of Social Ascent through Education' in C. Anderson, J. Floud and A.H. Halsey (eds) *Education, Economy and Society* Glencoe: Free Press.

Turok, I. (1990) 'Public Investment and Privatisation in the New Towns: a Financial Assessment of Bracknell', *Environment and Planning A*, vol. 22, pp. 1323–36.

Tyne and Wear County Council (1978) *Choosing the Strategy* Newcastle: Tyne and Wear County Council.

Tyne and Wear County Council (1979) *The Report of Survey* Newcastle: Tyne and Wear County Council.

Urry, J. (1990) *The Tourist Gaze* London: Sage.

Valocchi, S. (1990) 'The Unemployed Workers Movement of the 1930s: a Re-examination of the Pivan and Cloward Thesis', *Social Problems*, vol. 37, pp. 191–205.

Walker, D. (1992) *Getting on with it (Vol. 2): Managing Local Authorities* Luton: Local Government Management Board.

Walker, J. and Moore, R. (1987) 'The Impact of Privatization on the United Kingdom Local Government Labour Market' in R. Tarling (ed.) *Flexibility in Labour Markets* London: Academic Press.

Walsh, K. (1991) *Competitive Tendering for Local Authority Services* London: HMSO.

Warde, A. (1985) 'Spatial Change, Politics and the Division of Labour' in D. Gregory and J. Urry (eds) *Social Relations and Spatial Structures* London: Macmillan.

Warde, A. (1992) 'Notes on the Relationship Between Production and Consumption' in R. Burrows and C. Marsh (eds) *Consumption and Class: Divisions and Change* Basingstoke: Macmillan.

Watson, D. (1989) *Managing the Modular Course: Perspectives from Oxford Polytechnic* Milton Keynes: Society for Research in Higher Education/Open University.

Watson, S. (1988) *Accommodating Inequality: Gender and Housing* Sydney: Allen and Unwin.

Webster, B. (1985) 'A Woman's Issue: the Impact of Local Authority Cuts', *Local Government Studies*, vol. 11, pp. 19–46.

Whiteley, P. and Winyard, S. 1987 *Pressure for the Poor* London: Methuen.

Widdicombe Report (1986) *The Conduct of Local Authority Business* Committee of Inquiry into the Conduct of Local Authority Business. Cmnd 9797–9801. London: HMSO.

Williams, F. (1989) *Social Policy: A Critical Introduction* Cambridge: Polity Press.

Williams, F. (1992) 'Somewhere over the Rainbow: Universality and Diversity in Social Policy' in N. Manning and R. Page (eds) *Social Policy Review 4* Canterbury: Social Policy Association.

Williams, F. (1993) 'Gender, Race and Class in British Welfare Policy' in A. Cochrane and J. Clarke (eds) *Comparing Welfare States: Britain in International Context* London: Sage.

Wood, S. (1989) 'Introduction' in S. Wood (ed.) *The Transformation of Work?* London: Unwin Hyman.

Young, G. (1976) 'The Fundamental Contradiction of Capitalist Production', *Philosophy and Public Affairs*, vol. 5, pp. 196–234.

Young, K. (1986) 'Attitudes to Local Government' in *Widdicombe Report*, Research vol. III, The Local Government Elector.

Name index

Subject index